Cor Blimey, Where 'ave you come from?

by Winifred Tovey with sections by Frank Tovey

When the London cabby asked the Tovey family, 'Where on earth 'ave you come from?' it was not the first, nor the last time that they had to cause to ask themselves the same question.

Winnie and Frank started their married life in China just after World War II, and, following the birth of their first child, they had to flee from Mao's Red Army; an experience that they have written about in their book 'Strangers in Chaotung'. After a brief stay in England, undaunted by their earlier experience, they got back on a passenger ship, this time bound for India with two-year-old Rosemary and a new small baby in tow.

When they arrived in the recently independent India of 1951, the 'old mission hands' took them aside to instruct them in the protocol inherited from the Raj, and strictly remind them that they were there 'to listen, learn, and on no account express an opinion'.

But in no time at all Winnie and Frank were involved in work that extended beyond Frank's role as a surgeon at the Holdsworth Memorial Hospital, with projects to alleviate sickness and famine in the areas outside of Mysore City.

Their children, likewise, mixed with both the very rich and very poor, on one day attending nursery school in the Maharaja's Palace, and, on the next, visiting remote villages, where the last few miles could only be travelled on foot.

With the advent of 'Dapsone' (in 1950) as an effective treatment for leprosy Winnie and Frank helped establish village clinics, providing reconstructive surgery and rehabilitation for leprosy sufferers, as well as practically eradicating new cases from local districts. With help at home from an ayah, cook and mali, Winnie took on other projects as well, bringing bore wells and cottage industry to drought-stricken villages that had previously suffered regular famines, and assisting in the resettlement of Tibetan refugees in nearby Bylakuppe.

Now, both in their nineties, Winnie and Frank have written their story. It is an exceptional tale about some of the events and people that have shaped the India of today.

Cor Blimey!
Where 'ave you come from?

by Winifred Tovey, with sections by Frank Tovey

Editing assistance by
Jenny Knowles (nee Tovey)

Published by
Little Knoll Press
Second imprint – January 2012

ISBN No. 978-0-9565359-3-1

Copies of this book can be obtained from
mail@LittleKnollPress.co.uk
Tel: 023 8084 2190

Printed in Great Britain by
Think Ink
Ipswich

Cor Blimey!
Where 'ave you come from?

Acknowledgements by Winnie

I would like to convey my thanks to the people mentioned in the book, without whom there would be no tale to tell. Many have been most generous in letting me include parts of their own personal stories.

A special thank you goes to Frank, who has contributed two chapters and several inserts within the book, as well as looking out many of the photographs from our collection and helping with revisions. He also has been my mainstay throughout the time of writing, getting most of our meals and most of our shopping, because I can no longer manage long periods of standing.

Frank and I are very grateful to the Dalai Lama for his generosity in permitting, through his agent, the reproduction of some sections from his book, *Freedom in Exile*, and to Victoria Hislop, for her encouraging words and for allowing us to refer to her award-winning novel, *The Island*.

We have been most fortunate to have access to facts and details from old Holdsworth Hospital reports and from the letters that were kept by our relatives at home in England.

In writing this account we have had continuous editorial support from our daughter, Jenny, and the indispensable help of our son, David and our dear friend, Helen Rolton, who proof-read our manuscript.

Our other children, Rosemary and John, and the extended family, have been wholeheartedly behind us in the long task of compiling the book and its illustrations. It has been an enjoyable journey for us and we hope you will have pleasure in reading the result.

Winnie & Frank

Cor Blimey!
Where 'ave you come from?

INDIA

with place names as they were in 1951 to 1967

A more detailed map of the Mysore City area can be seen on page 131

Chapter One
From Chaotung to Mysore

In 1955 on the 19th of December, London was drably wrapped in the grey, chilly cloak of a short winter's day. Cloud drifted across the sky and the sun intermittently showed as a white orb, washing the streets and buildings with its watery light. Our three little children, Rosemary, then six years old, Jenny, aged four, and John, a wide-eyed two and a half year old, peered through the dull glass of the taxi window. John had been born in India, and neither Rosemary nor Jenny could remember anything of England, our family unit having left for India when Rosemary was two years old and Jenny a baby of just two months. They were agape at their first views of the country that we had always referred to as 'home'. They looked out for any familiar landmarks that they had seen in the black and white pictures of the book on the Coronation of the Queen that had been sent to us by airmail by kind relatives.

John was always especially inquisitive and he turned from the misty taxi window to look at us in bafflement. 'Why is the moon shining in the middle of the day?' he piped in his high voice. The girls laughed. 'Don't be silly John, that's not the moon, it's the sun.' John looked puzzled for a moment, and then said, 'Why is it that funny colour then?'

We could see the cabby stifling a guffaw as he wagged his head from side to side. A few minutes later John called out again, 'Oh look! There's Big Ben!' This was just too much for the cabby. He turned his head around to look at us in disbelief. 'Cor blimey! Where on earth 'ave you come from?' he exclaimed. Frank and I tried to ignore his remark to spare the children's blushes. We had actually just driven past a small clock tower that stood in front of a flight of steps that led down from the pavement to a public convenience!

This experience brought home to Frank and me how very different our life in India was, and how, although the children had already seen and done many things that probably could not be imagined by our cabby, their thoughts and concepts were already shaped differently and would always be so.

The 1950s and 60s, the time when we worked in India, were years when the country was emerging from the days of the rule of the British Empire and, as a young and vibrant democracy, was taking over the reigns of its own destiny. We were privileged to be there and to be part of so much friendship and growth, and we would like to share this with you in the story to come.

Frank and I started our married life in China, or rather on 'the slow boat to China', in the winter of 1947. This was the 'TSS Empire Brent' that had been carrying troops and at that time was newly refurbished for the Australian passenger route. The ship carried 680 passengers, of which 200 were children. Men were accommodated sixteen to a cabin on the lower deck, and the women and children in similar size cabins on the upper deck, single ladies being mixed in with mothers, young children and babies. All of the passengers used communal bathrooms and toilets. There was no air conditioning throughout the ship.

Frank had just qualified as a surgeon and on qualification had been assigned by the Methodist Missionary Society to work in China. He was given only three weeks from notice of his appointment to the time of his departure for China, and was told that he either went for five years as a bachelor or, if he had any plans to marry, he should do so immediately before he left England. We borrowed wedding clothes and married by special licence, at the same time rushing around to get our health checks and inoculations and accumulate all the household and personal items that we would need for a five-year stint abroad.

Five days after our wedding day we climbed the gangway onto Empire Brent. We, alongside our other British passengers, had come from the austere conditions of wartime Britain. Frank and I found the plentiful food on board ship almost too much, and alongside the close living conditions of the airless sixteen bunk male and female cabins, the journey itself made a more dramatic change to our lives than the fact that we were newly wed.

We knew very little of what we were steaming towards. While on board ship we learnt a little about China from the 'Old China Hands' who were travelling with us, but nothing that could have prepared us for the reality of inland China in 1948.

When we arrived in China we spent some time in Hankow, where we started our Chinese language (Mandarin) studies and Frank got experience in the Methodist General Hospital and the Union Hospital. I spent time learning the rudiments of physiotherapy at 'The Union', experience that was destined to become very useful later on when we lived in India.

At the time, in 1948, we really thought our lives would be bound to China for many years. It was true that the country was teaming with troops, especially noticeable when we had to travel, but we did not feel particularly threatened, perhaps because our adult years had been spent in wartime England. At the end of September 1948 we took up our post in a small mission hospital just outside the walls of the ancient city of Chaotung (Zhaotung) in the Province of Yunnan. We were high in the mountains, in an area still dominated by feudal rule, where bandits plagued every road and the indigenous Miao tribal people were downtrodden by the warlords and Han people alike.

Frank and I relished the newness of every experience and we became quickly absorbed into the work of Chaotung Hospital and into the running of a household within the hospital compound. It was only six months later, around the time of the birth of our first daughter, Rosemary, that the tumult of the start of the Communist Revolution overtook the country, reaching even remote Yunnan. We have written about this time in our book 'Strangers in Chaotung'.

We had a telegram from Mission House in England instructing us to stay put, but we knew that the longer we stayed we were placing both ourselves and anyone associated with us in increasing danger. On June 1st 1949 I left Chaotung, along with four and a half week old Rosemary and a group of other missionary men, women and children. We flew out on a small twin propeller plane that we had locally chartered for our evacuation. Frank was anxious to hand over the hospital in a state where it could continue to function with local staffing, and he did not leave

Chaotung until August 27th. He escaped only just in time, as four days later the Yunnan revolution was reported.

It was not easy to adjust back to life in Britain. Even in such a short time away we had seen and done many things that had a deep influence on us and could not be related to our family and friends. We still felt the pull to work overseas and Frank had only completed two years of his five-year contract with the Methodist Missionary Society (MMS), so he looked for employment in England until such time as MMS called him to further work overseas.

Fortunately, within a very short time, he obtained a post as Surgical Registrar in Southmead Hospital, Bristol. He was very happy to accept as, having spent a large part of his medical training in Bristol, he was already familiar with the hospitals and had many friends amongst the medical fraternity.

After working in Chaotung, as the only surgeon for hundreds of miles around and where Chinese doctors hung upon his every word, Frank realised that this opportunity to gain actual operative hands on experience could not have come at a better time. It meant that in his future work overseas he would be able to undertake almost any type of operation with confidence. In addition, now that he knew some of the problems and shortages with which he would be confronted when abroad, Frank was able to prepare his professional skills much more objectively.

Thus began his eighteen months as Surgical Registrar in General Surgery at Southmead Hospital working with Mr W. Capper, a renowned Gastric surgeon, from whom he gained invaluable knowledge in the field of gastroenterology.

During the spring of 1951 a call came from Mission House saying that there was an opening for Frank in the Holdsworth Memorial Hospital, Mysore City, South India and this would be for a five-year term. At the time I was pregnant again, and our second daughter, Jennifer, was born in Bristol on the 20th of June 1951.

Jenny was christened in Bath in August 1951

By the time Jenny arrived the arrangements for our journey to India were already underway. All our goods and chattels were packed and towards the end of August, Frank, Rosemary, Jenny and I set sail from Southampton on the P & O liner 'Chusan' for the two-week voyage to Bombay (now called Mumbai).

I can still remember the thrill of walking up the steep gangway and stepping onto the deck of the passenger ship SS Chusan. She was a 24,215-ton vessel, huge compared to the 11,000 ton TSS Empire Brent that took us to China in 1947. SS Chusan's capacity was 474 First Class passengers and 514 Tourist Class passengers. Only a few cabins were as large as six berths. At that time (1951) Chusan was the largest P & O passenger liner for the Far East run.

She was also the first ocean going passenger ship fitted with anti-roll stabilizers. The stabilizers were a novel attraction to the gentlemen passengers in particular. The first time they were put to use everybody (men, women and children alike) rushed to the railings to see what would happen. Alas, the blades were not visible, being too far below the turbulence of the sea. The stabilizers were used for two days and were quite effective in reducing the roll of the ship, but when in use it was found that the blades reduced the speed of the ship so they only used them when conditions were really bad.

We had been allotted a four-berth cabin with a porthole and an en-suite bathroom. There was no air conditioning throughout the ship (this was added in the 1960s). We were travelling Tourist Class and this meant that access to deck space was restricted by locked doors and barriers, but there was sufficient deck area available for deck games and there were plenty of deck chairs to laze in.

The times when we could grab some relaxation in the deck chairs were very rare though. Travelling with two-month-old Jenny and two and a half year old Rosemary proved to be rather a marathon. This was because there were no facilities where young children could be left under supervision during parents' meal times. Every day Rosemary, as an under five year old, had to be accompanied by an adult for each meal, then Frank and I found that we each were obliged to take our meals separately in order that one of us was free to watch over the children. In addition there was Jenny to be fed every four hours. She was being part bottle fed by then and in order to manage this on board we had procured a pressure cooker with a special rack that held five prepared bottles of milk. Each day, after we had prepared the daily supply of milk, the ship's galley staff, intrigued by this new invention, gladly dealt with the cooker for us. This kept us supplied with baby milk ready to hand in the cabin. After the two week long voyage we were tired of the sight of food, even though it was excellent fare and much better than the ration diet that was still imposed in England.

The voyage itself was very pleasant. Because the ship was not air conditioned, on reaching the Mediterranean Sea the crew changed into their white uniforms. This done we, the passengers, were called in alphabetical order to go down into the luggage hold, open our trunks and change our 'wardrobe' from winter to summer wear. This was quite an exciting event for we were leaving the cold chilly weather behind and looking forward to basking in warm sunshine.

Travelling tourist class was no hardship really, food was good and plentiful and the cabins and public places on board were comfortable. Although we did not have full access to the deck, it was possible to take exercise by walking around half the deck and back again.

We reached Bombay in mid September, Frank and I then parted company for a day while I took Rosemary and baby Jenny on the air flight from Bombay to Bangalore and Frank travelled by train with the luggage. We met up again in Bangalore and took the night train to our new home, Mysore City, South India.

Our first impression of Mysore was unforgettable. On the very day we arrived, Frank and I, with two and a half year old Rosemary, stood in the warm evening twilight beneath a magnificent stone gateway. We were surrounded by a tremendous cacophony of sound, drums beating and trumpets playing. The smell of roasting peanuts, coconut oil and roasting coffee beans hung in the air, mingling with the drifting scent of jasmine flowers worn in the hair of the Indian women. Thousands of people were gathered together dressed in their best and chattering excitedly in a tongue foreign to our ears as they jostled for the most advantageous position in the crowd. The excitement was tangible and the noise grew in volume.

As we waited, darkness descended, then a low murmur rippled through the crowd and suddenly the whole scene was illuminated by thousands of tiny electric light bulbs. It was magical! There, before our eyes, appeared a magnificent palace silhouetted by countless tiny lights, shining brilliantly against the darkening sky. A huge cheer rent the air.

The Mysore Palace lights

Little Rosemary was enchanted and her eyes shone with wonder and delight as she whispered, 'Fairies. It's a fairy palace.' Many months were to go by before we managed to convince her that a real live Maharaja actually lived in the palace, along with his wife and family.

Earlier that day when our train drew up in Mysore railway station we were met by a number of colleagues-to-be and very quickly taken across the city to Government House Road, where we were to live in one of the bungalows owned by the Church of South India and kept for missionary personnel.

A senior lady colleague, Lillian Stone, who was due to retire soon after many years of service in Mysore, had kindly agreed that we could share her part of the bungalow for the remainder of her stay. The bungalow was within five minutes walk of the palace, and when evening approached on that first day, although we were very weary, Lillian, anxious that we should get our first glimpse of Mysore in all its glory, insisted that we leave Jenny for a short time in the care of Rukmani, the ayah whom she had engaged as nursemaid for us, and take Rosemary for a short walk along the road. 'When you reach the palace gate,' she said, 'just stand around and see what happens'.

Mysore city was renowned for its magnificent palace, its wide, tree-lined streets, and its parks and gardens. When India gained independence from British rule in 1947, the Maharaja Jayachamarajendra Narasimharaja Wodeyar, having become Governor of Mysore State, remained in residence at the Palace.

Our arrival in Mysore coincided with the annual Dasara Festival, when for ten days various ceremonies took place in the palace during the daytime. In addition a nightly Durbar was held, during which the palace was illuminated for four hours and the Maharaja sat in splendour upon a jewel-encrusted throne to receive homage from hundreds of loyal citizens. The palace grounds were opened to the public and people came from far and wide to witness the whole event.

In readiness for the spectacular procession on the tenth day, rows and rows of tiered, wooden seats were erected along the roadside outside the palace grounds. These were for specially invited guests.

Lillian had obtained tickets in the VIP stand for us, and, as the weather was quite warm, Frank, following our previous practice in China, dressed in a pair of neatly pressed white shorts and an open neck, white shirt. He walked out onto the veranda ready to go.

Lillian took one horrified look at him and exclaimed, 'You cannot go dressed like that. Go and put a suit on this minute!' Poor Frank scuttled away and hurriedly changed. Only when dressed to Lillian's approval did we set off, this time leaving both Rosemary and Jenny at home in the care of Rukmani, the ayah.

This was our first lesson in protocol, and over the coming weeks we had much more to learn.

When we saw the Dasara procession we realised what an extremely important occasion it was. The crowd of spectators swelled by the minute, people crammed together eight, nine, ten deep, behind a rope barrier that stretched the length of the road. Many climbed trees in order to obtain a better view. Everyone was chattering animatedly, and an atmosphere of excited anticipation hung in the air.

On a twenty-one gun salute the procession began to move, led first by the Palace infantry, then by the artillery and cavalry forces with their immaculately groomed horses. Next in line were gun carriages drawn by bullocks, and decorated elephants, their trunks and forelegs painted in colour and their toenails in gold, and carrying on their backs precarious-looking, gilded wooden howdahs. Behind the elephants loped two camels and several horses with their manes and tails dyed in rainbow colours.

The people taking part in the procession wore distinctive coloured uniforms. Behind them came a carriage that could have come straight from the pages of 'Cinderella', drawn by an elephant and filled with a group of eminent dignitaries, and behind this a silver carriage drawn by horses. Next came the State bullock, State horse and State elephant, dressed in silk and gold woven cloths, their coats and hides glowing with grooming.

Finally, soldiers carrying the symbols, titles, banners and flags of the Royal State of Mysore escorted the Maharaja, who sat high up in a huge golden howdah atop the most magnificently caparisoned elephant. The Maharaja looked remote and grand, dressed in clothes of gold, with a gold turban upon his head.

Maharaja Jayachamarajendra Wodeyar in the State howdah

It took a good two hours for the parade to make its way from the palace, through the city, beyond the Holdsworth Hospital where Frank worked and out to the parade ground at Bannimantap. Here the Maharaja took the salute from his subjects and did puja (worship) to the sacred Banni Tree. As dusk fell pitch torches were lit, and, after a time of rest and refreshment, the Maharaja, followed by his escort, made his final spectacular torchlight procession through the city and back to the illuminated palace.

Throughout the ten days of Dasara the city was alive with tens of thousands of people. Very little serious work was done, everybody being fully occupied caring for visitors. For us it was a wonderful introduction to our new life in Mysore.

When Dasara was over we began to settle down to what was to become normal daily life for us, and with welcome guidance from Lillian, we addressed ourselves to the protocol of introducing ourselves to the city.

As newcomers our first job was to go 'on the street' and obtain some printed visiting cards. In 1951 India was emerging from decades of British rule and there was still a certain amount of the Raj etiquette to be observed. As soon as we had the visiting cards, one had to be delivered to the palace to inform the Maharaja that we had taken up residence in the city. Then it was expected that we would deliver a card to each of the missionary households. Only when these formalities were completed, could invitations to coffee, tea or dinner be exchanged.

In this way we began to meet our colleagues, but as newly appointed missionaries, we were instructed by our more experienced seniors that we should not express opinions of our own on any aspect of the work during our first year, but were there 'to listen and to learn'.

Winnie, Frank, Rosemary and baby Jenny
outside Government House Road bungalow in late September 1951

Frank had been sent to work at Holdsworth Memorial Hospital in Mysore at the request of the Church of South India (CSI). The Methodist Missionary Society had established the hospital in 1906 and Frank's salary was paid by MMS in England, although his remit was to work with and for the CSI. This was a time of transition when, following the formation of the CSI in 1948, the church in India was gradually taking over full responsibility for staffing and financing every aspect of the church's work, whether in schools, churches or hospitals.

The Holdsworth Memorial Hospital main building in the early 1950s

We quickly realised that there was indeed a huge amount to be absorbed regarding the cultures and customs of the various groups within the Mysore population. Hindus, Muslims, Christians, Dalits (outcasts) and beggars all attended the hospital for treatment. We learnt to always use the right hand when eating or giving a gift, and to be considerate regarding differences in diet. Religious customs were to be strictly respected, and this was just the beginning.

Before their departure for work overseas most of our missionary colleagues had spent one or two years at Selly Oak, a training college in Birmingham, where they were given valuable information on the country to which they were being sent, as well as instruction regarding religious customs and way of life of its inhabitants. Four years earlier we had been asked to leave England for China with only ten days to prepare, which left very little time to find out anything about the country before our departure. Likewise, when called to Mysore, there had not been sufficient time for us to do much research about India. So at the beginning of our time in Mysore we felt somewhat isolated from our fellow missionaries because of the lack of shared experience in Selly Oak.

Mysore State, now called Karnataka, was historically a Princely State of some importance, and in the 1950s and 60s the city of Mysore was still dominated by the Palace of the Maharaja. The City itself lies in the centre of South India, positioned on the spine of India, the Deccan Plateau, which at two thousand feet above sea level has a delightful climate that does not reach the very high temperatures or humidity of cities like Madras (now Chennai) or Bombay (now Mumbai).

Towards the end of the 19th century the Wesleyan Methodist Mission was well
established in Mysore City and in the village area of Chamrajanagar about thirty
miles away. The Superintendent Minister at that time was the Reverend William
Holdsworth, whose wife was Mary Calvert Holdsworth.

Mary Holdsworth

In the late 1800s there were regular outbreaks of bubonic plague, typhoid, smallpox
and cholera, plus periods of monsoon failure and famine. Mary Holdsworth was
very concerned for the women and children who suffered badly during these
epidemics. At that time the only hospital in Mysore city was a small government
hospital and, because it was staffed only by male doctors, neither Hindu nor Moslem
women could go to it. Likewise children could not go because their mothers would
have to be with them.

Mary Holdsworth, determined to do something about the situation, drew up plans
and started to look for a suitable site for a hospital for women and children. In 1901
Mary and her husband returned to the UK for furlough and sadly Mary became ill.
and died in 1902.

The Reverend George Sawday, who had come to India with the Wesleyan
Mission in 1876, moved to Mysore in 1901 to fill the Superintendent Minister post
when the Holdsworths left for furlough.

George Sawday, who had already set up a Boys' Orphanage in Tumkur, took up
Mary Holdsworth's project with the energy and determination that he gave to
everything he believed in. In his diary he noted, 'when I wrote to Mr and Mrs
Holdsworth I found them full of interest and enthusiasm. Mrs Holdsworth was then
struggling with the illness which soon after proved fatal.'

The Reverend George Sawday
Superintendent of Holdsworth Memorial Hospital for twenty-six years

Rev. Sawday put the proposal to build a hospital for women and children in memory of Mary Holdsworth before the Church Synod of the Mysore District, and they agreed. The original cost estimate was £3,000 and he took the responsibility of raising this sum upon himself. As the fundraising got underway, the cost estimate rose to £7,500.

Mrs James Calvert

Rev. Sawday's sister, Mrs James Calvert, worked tirelessly back in England and, along with a gift of £2,500 from Mrs Lisle Williams, Mary Holdsworth's mother, they raised sufficient funds to start the hospital building.

The next concern was a suitable site. Rev. Sawday agreed with Mary Holdsworth's idea that the hospital should be close to the poorest and most densely populated area of the city, and midway between the Hindu and Muslim communities. This land was not going to be easy to obtain or afford, but the project attracted the sympathy of Maharaja Krishnaraja Wodeyar IV (the uncle of Maharaja Jayachamarajendra, whom we knew), and he acquired the seven and a half acres of land and gave it for the Wesleyan Mission to build the hospital.

In June 1904 Mrs Calvert, sister of George Sawday, laid the foundation stone for the hospital where it stands today.

The hospital building was completed in 1906 at the final cost of Rs 120,000 (£10,000) of which Rs 95,000 had been raised by the efforts of the Sawday and Holdsworth families and Rs 25,000 donated by the Mysore Government.

Early in 1906 the first doctors, Dr Elsie Watts and her sister Dr Edith Watts, had arrived in Mysore to prepare all that was needed to start the work of the hospital.

His Highness Sir Sri Krishnaraja Wodeyar IV

On August 21st 1906 Maharaja Krishnaraja Wodeyar IV officially opened the hospital. The name originally chosen by George Sawday for the hospital was

'Karuna Shala', meaning the 'Home of Compassion', a place where God's love could be shown to all in need regardless of caste, creed or ability to pay, but in memory of Mary Holdsworth it was called 'The Mary Calvert Holdsworth Memorial Hospital'. The Reverend George Sawday was Superintendent of the hospital for twenty-six years.

Dr. Elsie Watts and Sister Campbell, a nursing sister, were both employed by the Methodist Missionary Society. Dr Edith Watts joined the team, offering her work as a volunteer. In its first year the Holdsworth Memorial Hospital treated one thousand nine hundred and ninety seven patients.

Dr Elsie Watts and Dr Edith Watts at a patient's home

At that time there was no established nursing in India and nursing was not an approved occupation for respectable girls. The early recruits were illiterate village girls who had to be first taught simple hygiene, such as scrubbing, and then the practice of very basic nursing care. Over the years the Nursing School became established and the Hospital grew in size. There were periods of shortage of doctors and nursing staff, but by 1951 the hospital had 200 inpatient beds and a widespread reputation for its high standard of medicine, surgery and midwifery. In 1951 the hospital staff comprised two English doctors, three English Nursing Sisters and around forty Indian medical and nursing staff. The high standard of Nurse Training was recognised throughout India, but the training was still confined to the care of women and children. New Indian 'Standards of Training for Nurses' required the care of men patients to be included. The decision was therefore made for it to become a general hospital and Frank was invited to join the staff and open up a Men's Department and develop the surgery.

The year we arrived in India, 1951, was an interesting time. It was just four years after India had achieved its Independence and also after the inauguration of the Church of South India. Following thirty years of deliberations the Anglicans, Methodists, Congregationalists and the Reformed Churches had decided to unite to form one church, the 'Church of South India' (CSI). Within Mysore city there were five CSI churches where Kanarese was spoken and one, St. Bartholomew's, where English was spoken. In addition, there was the Catholic Cathedral, St. Philomena's.

13

St. Bartholomew's Church had been built in 1830 for the use of churchgoers among the British residents of Mysore - mostly civil and military officers attached to the Residency staff. On our arrival in 1951 the congregation was made up of local English-speaking Indian residents and members of the Holdsworth Hospital staff, including many of the nurses whose homes were in the neighbouring State of Kerala and whose mother tongue was Malayali.

St Bart's Church, Mysore

You can see from this that not only did we need to understand the many religions and customs of the population of Mysore, but we also needed a better understanding of the most common languages spoken. This was particularly important for Frank who daily consulted with patients who spoke little (if any) English. The local dialect was Kanarese (these days called 'Kannada'). The main language of government was still English; a legacy of British rule, but many people also understood Hindi, the most widespread language of India.

When we arrived in Mysore Frank was eager to begin work but we needed a few days in which to settle down in our new surroundings. First of all we arranged for one hour of language study each morning. This would leave Frank free to go to the hospital for the rest of the day whilst I attended to the more domestic side of life.

The entrance porch of Government House Road bungalow

14

The Government House Road bungalow, where we first lived in 1951, was typical of the British colonial houses built during the 1800s. It stood in a large walled compound with a latched gate and short driveway leading from the main road to an imposing whitewashed front porch. A flight of shallow steps led up to a shady veranda that ran right along the front of the bungalow, behind which were the living rooms. The house provided three separate living areas and ours was the nearest to the road and all at ground floor level. The rooms were wide and lofty and the floors throughout the whole building were covered with red, unglazed ceramic tiles, beautifully cool to the feet. The walls, inside and outside, were whitewashed, and the windows had no glass, but instead metal bars for security and louvered wooden shutters for shade. The dining room and lounge were divided by half doors, which allowed air to pass freely between the rooms, ideal in a hot climate.

The furniture stayed with the Mission houses (and it is still there at Government House Road as I write). It was heavy colonial style, mostly made of rosewood. In the centre of the dining room of our new home was a handsome, highly polished dining table surrounded by a set of twelve chairs. On one side of the dining room stood a massive sideboard and opposite, the 'dumb waiter' stretched across the whitewashed inner wall, securely anchored by stacks of crockery that provided a whole dinner and tea service with sets of twelve plates, cups and saucers, along with numerous serving dishes of every type, all ready for immediate use. The lounge contained easy chairs, some made of rosewood and others of cane, a number of occasional tables and two glass-fronted bookcases.

There were three bedrooms, each furnished with two large bedsteads with posts at each corner supporting the mosquito nets. The beds had woven rattan bases on which were placed kapok filled mattresses.

Beds with kapok mattresses and mosquito nets

Also in each bedroom were bedside tables, a huge almirah (wardrobe), a chest of drawers and a couple of chairs. Next to each bedroom were a dressing room and a separate bathroom with an old-fashioned washstand, enamel washbasin, large enamel water jug, soap dish, towel rack and zinc bathtub. On the floor were two

15

large padded baskets, each holding a lidded zinc drum, one for hot water and one for cold water. Also provided was a metal dipper, rather like a very large mug with handle, used for ladling water from the drums into the bath.

It was the daily task of the mali, (gardener/water carrier) to draw sufficient water from the compound well to fill one drum in each bathroom with fresh cold water. He then drew a further supply of water from the well, which he heated in the kitchen and transferred to the second drum ready for bath time. The mali worked so hard, for it was also his job to water and tend the garden.

A zinc bathtub (just like the one we had used in my grandfather's house when I lived in Bedford as a child) stood within a sunken area in the bathroom floor and, after bathing, we tipped the bathtub and emptied the dirty water out into the sunken floor to drain through a hole in the wall and into a soakage area just outside the bungalow. Banana and papaya trees were planted here and flourished with the regular watering. The bathrooms also gave accommodation to the humble 'thunder boxes', our nickname for commodes. These were vital items of furniture as there was no main sewer. Each individual adult member of the household had their own commode, an enamel container suspended within an iron four-legged stool with a wooden seat and lid. Twice daily a 'sweeper' lady collected the containers by entering the bathrooms discreetly through a back door. She would empty their contents into the cesspit situated in the farthest corner of the compound. Sweepers were from the lowest Hindu caste, the so-called 'untouchables', and they were paid a very small amount of money for their services. Shortly after our arrival new cesspits were dug outside each bathroom and the commodes were replaced by more 'modern', hand-flushed toilets. However, the water for flushing still had to be carried to the bathrooms by the mali. This new situation meant that the sweeper had less work to do, but the servants' latrines remained to be dealt with and we continued to pay her a small amount for her services.

The bungalow compound area was about two acres, and it was enclosed by a four foot high, brick and cement rendered wall that, like the house, needed regular whitewashing. A fairly large area of the compound was rough grassland, yellow for most of the year, but brightly green during the rainy season. Jacaranda, peepal and sandalwood trees provided welcome shade, and poinsettia and hibiscus shrubs added bright splashes of colour. There were a few flowerbeds, which the mali planted out with zinnias, marigolds and salvias in season, although for much of the year the ground remained very dry and dusty.

The Government House Road garden was home to a number of birds, including raucous black crows and hoopoes with their colourful plumage and distinctive call. Other wildlife thrived in the garden and while in this bungalow one day Frank found it impossible to start the car. After trying every means he could think of to get the car going, Frank opened the bonnet and there inside he found a bandicoot, peacefully sleeping.

There were also many different types of ants and insects, the most common and by far the most troublesome being the mosquitoes. We used a mixture of paraffin and DDT, which we sprayed with a flit gun into the corners of rooms, especially in damp places in the bathrooms. (We did not know then how dangerous DDT was).

16

Even so, every evening at sunset the mosquitoes became very active, and it was impossible to escape from their attention. If we sat in the living room or on the veranda after dark, we put Mylol on our legs. It did smell strongly, but it was better than getting bitten. At night we let down the mosquito nets, draping them into a tent around our beds, and after making absolutely sure that no mosquitoes were trapped inside, tucked the net edges securely under the mattress.

At the far end of the bungalow compound was the Church of South India (CSI) Calvert Girls' Home, where about fifty girls aged between seven to fourteen years, and from Christian families in the outlying villages, came to live during the school term time. They attended Victoria Girls' School in the city. The Home's compound was separately walled and contained a large garden. Here, after their schoolwork, the girls learnt how to grow their own vegetables, and under the motherly eye of the matron, 'Anandamma', they kept their dormitories clean and tidy and took turns in washing their linen and clothing. I often walked across the compound with Rosemary and Jenny to visit them and the girls would proudly show us their latest vegetable patches. Some girls paid a small fee according to their family means, while others were accommodated free.

Anandamma's Girls' Home in 1966

Anandamma frequently called on us at the bungalow for a chat and always refused coffee in favour of a glass of boiling hot water. She would use the visit to offload the anxieties of her job and sometimes some tears as well. The Home was always desperately short of funds and Anandamma felt a truly motherly concern for every one of her girls.

When later we were moved to another bungalow on the other side of the city close to the hospital, we continued to keep in touch, and with visits both from Anandamma to us and from us to the Girls' Home our relationship continued until we left Mysore in 1966.

Chapter Two
A Memsahib in the City

We gradually became acquainted with the other missionary personnel, doctors, nurses, teachers and ministers, working within Mysore city and surrounding countryside. Amongst them there were a few families with young children and we regularly organised days when the children could meet. This was a good idea as they quickly learnt to mix with each other and play. We found that working abroad within a small community of our own nationality it was important to maintain a certain amount of give and take between individuals and families. We were, after all, destined to work together for five years, Frank having agreed before we embarked to India to a renewed five-year term of service with the Methodist Missionary Society. I am happy to say now that the friendships we made then have stood the test of time and as a result we still keep in touch with one another.

When we arrived in Government House Road bungalow my first task was to learn how to run a household with Rukmani, our ayah, Dayakka (Lillian's cook), and Perumal the mali (gardener). Each servant had his or her own allotted tasks and on no account was I allowed to cook or clean. Under the excellent guidance of Lillian, our senior colleague, I met with Dayakka each morning, we decided upon the menu for the day, I gave him some money and away he went to market.

All perishables were purchased fresh daily. Fish and chicken were bought live, then killed and cleaned at home when needed, because we had no refrigerator. The ayah took care of the children's clothes and nappy washing and watched over the children in my absence. All household linen and adult clothing was collected by the dhobi to be returned washed and neatly pressed a few days later, leaving me free to concentrate on language study and attend meetings and social functions arranged by senior colleagues.

To begin with I found it very difficult to leave my young children in somebody else's care, although I always made a point of putting the children to bed and reading a bedtime story. I felt a bit lost with no housework, shopping or cooking to do, but plenty of other activities came my way very quickly, along with opportunities to do things that I could not have imagined doing back in England.

Each morning after an early breakfast Frank and I began our one-hour language session, often sitting on the veranda, with our Kanarese speaking language teacher. After this Frank rode off on his bicycle to spend the rest of the day at the hospital. Rosemary and Jenny gradually settled down to a completely different routine from the one they had been used to in England and they thoroughly enjoyed the freedom of playing out of doors every day. Frank and I had taken our bicycles out to India with us and I regularly cycled around the city with Rosemary perched on a little seat attached to the handlebars.

Winnie with Rosemary perched on her bicycle

The cook, Dayakka, prepared and cooked our meals over a wood and/or charcoal fire in a small kitchen building situated about a hundred feet away from the rear of the bungalow. Before the meal was ready Dayakka would bring hot charcoal and put it on the lower shelf of the large zinc-lined cupboard that stood on the back veranda. On the top shelf he placed the serving dishes and plates required for the next meal. Later he brought the hot food across from the kitchen and put it on the middle shelf; thus, everything was ready to hand when 'Memsahib' asked for dinner to be served.

Our meals were usually a simple curry (either vegetable or meat and sometimes fish) and boiled rice for lunch, with a larger menu for the evening meal, that could be a light soup, followed by main meat or fish course with potatoes or vegetables and a dessert of jelly, blancmange or fruit, of which there was a huge variety in season. Afternoon tea was always available, together with homemade biscuits or Victoria sponge cake. We also had home-baked bread. Having come from my mother's household in Bedford where we all helped with the shopping, cooking and washing up, I felt rather lost to start with in Mysore, having nothing to do with the preparation, cooking or serving of the meals. After time I adjusted and became quite happy to sit at table while Dayakka, the cook, dressed in immaculate white jacket and trousers, served our meal.

The back veranda was also the place where Dayakka and the mali washed all the crockery and cutlery after a meal and before returning it to the 'dumb-waiter' in the dining room. This arrangement led to one of many funny episodes that occurred during our early days in the Government House Road bungalow.

One day some of the household teaspoons were found to be missing. In those times almost everyone used silver plate cutlery and this was quite a loss. Lillian thought that one of the servants must have stolen them but when she tackled the cook about it he replied, 'No Missy, I not take it, crow took it!' Lillian did not believe him until one day, when the washing-up was being done on the back veranda, she actually saw a crow fly down and make off with a spoon. After this she got the back veranda fenced in with strong wire mesh.

Another time the rather Victorian custom of keeping all the crockery at hand in the dining room brought about a calamity which I think must have made poor Lillian Stone rue the day she agreed to having a young family to stay with her, albeit temporarily. The 'dumb waiter' that took pride of place along one wall of the dining room had three highly polished, wooden shelves to carry the crockery set for the household. Under the crockery were laid three white linen runners with lace borders that overhung the edges of the shelves.

The living rooms were divided by half-doors, which were ideal, not only for allowing air to circulate freely, but also for a small child to pass under from one room to another. Rosemary had a small chair on wheels and she spent many happy hours propelling the chair from room to room across the tiled floors. One morning, when the servants were all about their daily tasks and I was giving Jenny a bath, the peace was shattered by a loud crashing and clattering, and above the noise Rosemary was calling, 'Mummy! Mummy!' We all rushed to see what had happened and found Rosemary sitting in her chair surrounded by shattered crockery. She had obviously been attracted by the lace cloth on the bottom shelf, given it a tug and brought down a stack of dinner plates. I cannot remember how much it cost to replace the broken pieces but fortunately it was not too difficult because the service was plain white. Even so it was quite an ordeal for us to confess to Lillian what had happened.

The servants and their families lived rent free in brick and tiled roof rooms (go-downs) situated behind the kitchen. As I mentioned before we mostly ate curry and rice for lunch and there was always enough to feed the servants and their families as well. Their working hours were from 6am to 1pm and 4pm to 8pm for six days a week and, where possible, they had one other half-day free each week.

After a few weeks of adjustment to 'memsahib' duties and the language study hour, I decided to acquaint myself better with this new city that was to be our home for the following five years. First I walked out on my own, following a path that led past a small park into a narrow, dusty street. As I approached the street I would catch the wonderful smell of freshly roasted coffee coming from a small roadside coffee shop. It was tempting to stop and buy a drink but other sights and sounds and the pungent aroma of herbs and spices drew me further on into the heart of the shopping area. In one street most of the shops sold cooking vessels - anything from a small tiffin carrier to hold a meal for one person, to huge, round pans with diameters over fifteen inches and at least twelve inches deep, suitable for cooking large quantities of rice or curry for wedding parties. The wares were brightly arranged along the shop frontage, with lovely shining vessels glistening in the sunlight. Beyond the narrow street I found the main shopping area, with its wide tree-lined road and shops on both sides.

A tiffin carrier shop in Mysore

The city at that time was very clean and pleasant and the trees along the main streets gave welcome shade during the hottest part of the day. There was very little motor traffic. The most popular means of transport were the hired tongas, small horse-drawn carriages. Cycle rickshaws were also available although I was not keen on the idea of allowing another fellow human being working so hard to pull me along the road. Bicycles were used everywhere. Frank and I were glad that we had decided to bring our bicycles from England and with Rosemary perched on the handlebars of my cycle I investigated further. I discovered a large post office and a bank within easy walking distance from the bungalow. Nearby numerous small shops opened directly onto the street. They put up their shutters from mid morning and traded until late at night. Small stalls littered the pavements, selling colourful bangles, ribbons, combs, hair extensions, plastic baskets, cigarettes and a variety of knick-knacks. In another area more modern shops with glazed windows displayed gorgeously coloured silk saris and lengths of material for making salwar kameez and scarves. Nearby jewellers tempted those with wedding plans to purchase beautiful gold bangles, necklaces and jewelled earrings.

Behind the shops a large market could be entered through archways on each of its four sides. Here fresh produce was abundant. Pyramids of fruit and vegetables were laid out in a glorious display of red tomatoes, green beans, yellow/red chillies, purple aubergines and sweet potatoes, all very fresh and almost crying out to be bought. Alongside were fruits: guava, mangoes, grapes, melons, oranges, limes, grapefruit and many others in their season, not forgetting the ever-present plantains. Next to the fruit there was a wonderful area full of perfumed flowers and a veritable hive of activity. Women sat on the ground surrounded by piles of creamy coloured jasmine flowers. Using fine cotton string they deftly and swiftly created flower garlands of all sizes, from a small single string of flower head for decorating the hair to really weighty garlands used to mark special occasions such as weddings, birthdays, or the birth of a baby.

21

A market stall selling coloured powders for puja

But when you looked beyond the colour it was not as idyllic as it might seem. Many vendors had their little children with them and were not concerned that they spent much of their time crawling around on the ground, picking up and eating morsels of the fruit or vegetables that lay in the dirt. This was the accepted fabric of daily living. There were two or three Municipal Water stand taps at intervals within the market place and overnight the whole paved area was swilled down. Nevertheless, as each day wore on, plenty of debris and dirt accumulated on the paving, alongside the pieces of fruit and vegetable, that were very tempting to small children looking for something to eat.

Almost hidden away in the far corner of the market were the live chickens and fish, and alongside were stalls that sold mutton and goat meat. In Mysore State, as in most of India, the cow is a holy animal so never slaughtered. Pork was also not available as it is prohibited to Muslims and is also not safe meat to eat in India. In the hot climate this area of the market smelt unpleasant and swarmed with flies and hungry pye-dogs.

In the city at this time, in every street there were men walking along the curb side each with a large cylinder slung over the shoulder and an equally large spray gun in hand. They were liberally spraying some substance in every nook and cranny. Later I discovered they were spraying DDT into the gutters and drains all over the city in an effort to control mosquitoes. This treatment proved to be excellent in killing off the mosquitoes but unfortunately it was very soon discovered that DDT itself was quite harmful to the environment, consequently the spraying was discontinued and the mosquitoes returned with a vengeance.

I was delighted to find that nobody turned to stare as I walked alone in the crowded market place. In contrast to China, where we were frequently referred to as 'red devils', largely I think because during the hottest weather our faces became red and flushed, in striking contrast to the beautiful, smooth, delicately tanned complexion of the Chinese people. As time went by we were to learn how important Mysore was and that, because of its long history of contact with the British since the 1700s, many people in the city spoke English.

22

In the early days I did not attempt to shop in the open market on my own because it was customary to bargain for everything. The vendor would state a price that was usually far in excess of an item's real value. In response you needed to offer half the asking price. This good-natured bartering would go on for some time, until eventually a sum somewhere between the two starting points would be agreed. Once my knowledge of Kanarese improved, I could cope with this situation and I very much enjoyed a shopping trip to market.

The city radiated from the Palace, like spokes from a hub. The wide streets were lined with shade trees, giving Mysore its reputation as 'The Garden City' of India. The Palace building that stood then (and still stands) in the centre of the city, was opened in 1912 after taking twelve years to build from 'fire proof' cast iron. The previous wooden palace, which had burned down, had been built in 1803 following the reinstatement of the Wodeyar family as the Maharajas of Mysore State, the British having defeated the infamous Tipu Sultan in the 1799 siege on the fort of Srirangapatna.

In 1610 the Wodeyar rulers had moved their capital from Mysore to the fort of Srirangapatna, situated about nine miles away, on an island surrounded by the sacred Cauvery River. From that time onward the Wodeyar family was beset with a so-called 'curse' that foretold that the Maharaja would never again produce a male heir to the throne. Through 1673 to 1704 Mysore enjoyed a time of great progress under the rule of the forward thinking Maharaja Chikka Devaraja Wodeyar, but three following Maharajas made no notable impact on the Kingdom. Then, during the reign of Krishnaraja Wodeyar II (1734-1766), the kingdom of Mysore became dominated by powerful military command and this paved the way for the humble foot soldier, Hyder Ali Khan, to become the ruler. Hyder Ali deferred the power he had gained to his son, Tipu Sultan, who ruled with ambitious cruelty, killing many thousands of Hindus and Christians, and laying waste the countryside.

At this time France and Britain were fighting for domination in India, and in 1798 Napoleon Bonaparte made plans 'to send 15,000 men to India to join the forces of Tipu-Sahib and drive away the English'. Tipu was holding many British subjects in captivity, soldiers and civilian men, who were shackled and held in wretched dungeons or, if young, were subjected to cruelty and humiliation. There were many reasons why the British wished for Tipu's downfall, not least their ambition to open access to Mysore and its wealth of sandalwood and silk, so desired by the East India Trading Company, and to the large resources of gold that at that time were believed to exist in the Kolar Hills.

After several unsuccessful battles to overcome Tipu, the British troops, under the command of Colonel Wellesley (later to become the Duke of Wellington) and others, planned a final assault on his stronghold in Srirangapatna. In the small hours of May 4th 1799, under cover of darkness a mixed force of 2,494 British and 1,882 Indian troops hid in trenches some distance from Srirangapatna fort. The soldiers waited while the sun moved across the sky and it was not until 1.30 in the afternoon that the order was given to advance across the river. It was reasoned that during the hottest part of the day the defenders of the fort would be taking rest and least expecting the enemy.

Accounts from Colonel Beatson detail the siege, vividly describing blasting the breach in the fort wall, the ensuing hand-to-hand battle, the death of Tipu and subsequent release of British prisoners.

Having lived myself in Mysore and visited Srirangapatna many times, I can just imagine the soldiers in full uniform, sweating in the midday heat of May, and the dangers they faced in crossing the river, scrambling over slippery rocks and into channels of fast moving water, trying to hold their muskets above their heads in a vain attempt to keep the gunpowder dry, while all the time cannon, musket and rocket fire rained down upon them. Those who survived the crossing made for the breaches in the fortress walls and did battle with their bayonets. Tipu Sultan, true to his reputation as 'The Tiger of Mysore', took part himself in combat and was fatally wounded. This was the signal for the British to claim their victory.

After the death of Tipu, five-year-old Prince Krishnaraja Wodeyar III was installed on the throne and the capital was shifted back to Mysore. A new wooden palace was built and the annual Dasara celebrations were reinstated on a grand scale, but Mysore remained under British administration until 1881. This perhaps explains the establishment of one of the first 'Free English' schools in the city of Mysore in 1833.

In 1865, having no natural male heir, Krishnaraja Wodeyar III adopted Chamaraja Wodeyar X as his legal heir. Krishnaraja Wodeyar III was determined to restore Mysore to Indian rule and he took his campaign beyond the colonial powers to the British Parliament. Here his supporters brought pressure to bear on the British Government, who eventually agreed to restore the Kingdom to Chamaraja Wodeyar X on his coming of age. So it was that in 1881 Mysore returned to the rule of the Maharajas. In the 1880s, among other changes, the Maharani's Women's College was established in Mysore City.

Following Chamaraja Wodeyar X, in 1895 Krishnaraja Wodeyar IV became the 24th ruler of Mysore. Krishnaraja Wodeyar IV continued to develop Mysore along modern lines. It was he who in 1904 built an underground water drainage system in the city and who gave the land for the building of the Holdsworth Memorial Hospital.

Mary Holdsworth as mentioned earlier had determined to build a hospital for women and children after experiencing the amount of sickness that beset them, particularly those living in the poor housing that crowded the marshy area surrounding the palace. Here she had visited families afflicted by bubonic plague, typhoid, cholera and smallpox.

It may not have been a total disaster that in 1897, during the wedding of Princess Jayalakshmanni, the wooden palace was accidentally burnt down. This presented the necessity to build a new palace and the opportunity for the Maharaja to set about further improvements to the planning and development of the city. Under Maharaja Krishnaraja Wodeyar IV the slums were cleared and many wide boulevards, green spaces, the main shopping district and grand institutions of Mysore were built.

After the wooden palace burnt down, Maharaja Krishnaraja Wodeyar IV also commissioned the present palace, designed by the British architect Henry Irwin. It is a three-storey building with several state and durbar halls that are supported by tall, decorated, cast iron pillars, which were brought by sailing ship from England. It was the first time in India that cast iron columns and roof frames were used. One hall has a stained glass ceiling, also imported from England, while another has a wall of windows in English cut and ground glass, depicting pastoral and forest scenes. The building of the palace was completed in 1912.

The grand Durbar Hall was added to the front of the building in 1940. It is a lofty space, thirty or forty feet high, with a central arch flanked by six large and two smaller arches. The hall is open along one side so that the audience within can look out over the large courtyard cum parade ground in which there are twelve Hindu temples.

The Durbar Hall in the 1960s during the Dasara festival

The exterior of the palace was fitted with 97,000 electric light bulbs that outline its shape at night, transforming it into the 'fairy palace' that Rosemary discovered on our first night in Mysore. To deter theft, the Maharaja had instructed that the bulbs and holders were designed to a unique size so that they would fit no other electrical system. When we were in Mysore the Palace lights were switched on at weekends and on all state occasions.

In addition to the Palace, Mysore contained many other interesting buildings, most of which had been built during the British Raj. There was a large mosque at the end of Sawday Road (the road that led from the Holdsworth Hospital main entrance through the Muslim quarter), and quite near this was the Catholic Church, St. Philomena's. Poor St Philomena's, it had been designed on a grand and well proportioned scale, but unfortunately its twin spires had to be modified because no building was allowed to be taller than the palace dome. The shortened spires of the church always looked a little odd.

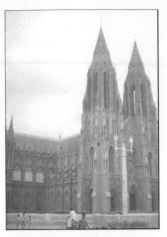

St Philomena's Church, Mysore

On the main road that formed part of the route for the Dasara parade, there was the large Government Hospital, named the 'Krishna Rajendra Hospital', and opposite stood a grand Arts and Crafts Emporium where you could, and still can, purchase rosewood tables delicately inlaid with ivory (now white plastic or bone) and woods of different colours. Mysore is famous for its carved elephants of all sizes, made of rosewood or precious sandalwood. Fifty years ago you could buy hand carved ivory necklaces and ornaments, wrought and soldered silverware, traditional hand woven carpets, fabric and leather bags and belts, ceramics, hand painted pottery and wooden ornaments and toys. It was (and still is) possible to spend a whole afternoon walking around the Emporium admiring the wonderful display.

On those first exploratory walks into the city I did not have time to wander away from the shopping area, but later on we discovered many beautiful houses connected with the royal family, some of which were open to the public. Also, scattered about the city were numerous Hindu temples, mosques and quite a number of churches attended by the thriving and longstanding Christian community of Mysore.

We had been sent from England to live and work alongside our fellow Christians within the Church of South India. At St. Bartholomew's the services were conducted in the English language, and many of the hospital staff, including nurses from the Indian State of Kerala whose mother tongue was Malayali, attended Sunday worship there regularly.

Shortly after we arrived I was asked if I would become organist for St. Bart's. I willingly accepted and continued in this office until I left India in 1966. It was a task that I thoroughly enjoyed even though it meant attending an eight o'clock service every Sunday morning. For special occasions such as Christmas and Easter some of the nurses formed a small choir. We sang festive hymns and occasionally I would sing a solo, accompanying myself on the organ.

The same organ was in St Bart's when we visited in 1995

Whenever there was a wedding I would be invited to play. Sheet music was virtually unobtainable, but I had brought most of mine with me from home including quite a collection of special voluntaries ready for such occasions. Often the bride would arrive late, so I would play away filling in the time. The violin was quite a popular instrument among the Indian gentlemen and frequently one or two of the guests assembled in the church would bring their violin to the service. With no prior arrangement they would leave their seats, come and stand behind me and quietly pick up the tune that I was playing, gradually joining in to create a joyful noise. It was a unique and heart-lifting sound, especially when one or two violins were not quite in tune. As soon as the bride arrived at the church door I would switch to a triumphant wedding march and the multi-tonal violins would follow with enthusiasm. We really enjoyed our unrehearsed performance!

The view of Chamundi Hill from Holdsworth Hospital roof

Dominating, or perhaps I should say overshadowing the city, is Chamundi Hill. Its shape when you look up from the city of Mysore resembles a huge giant laid flat on his back. Myth has it that it is the body of the demon Mahishasura, who was defeated and killed by the Hindu Goddess Chamundeshwari in a battle that lasted ten days. The goddess was aided by her accompanying beast, a tiger, whose job it was to lap up each drop of the demon's blood before it fell to the ground, where it would have sprung up as an additional demon.

A statue of Mahishura stands on Chamundi Hill

One way to reach the summit of Chamundi Hill was to walk up the 1,000 steps, a great challenge which we enjoyed when younger. Alternatively, it was possible to drive a car up to the summit. I learnt to drive in Mysore and it was on a steep section of the Chamundi Hill road that Frank taught me to make a hill-start successfully. The children were not too impressed with my initial attempts! The Hindu temple on Chamundi Hill is dedicated to Charmundeshwari, and outside, where now the taxis gather, stands a statue of the wicked demon Mahishura.

At the foot of Chamundi Hill stood Lalitha Mahal, a magnificent palace building where the Maharaja sometimes entertained important guests.

On one occasion our friend Sydney Watsa, advisor to the Maharaja, showed us around the interior of Lalitha Mahal. Inside the entrance we stood agape at the splendour of the marble floors, the huge windows furnished with rich damask curtains, the fine carpets, glittering chandeliers and luxurious furniture, and at the magnificent dance hall with its minstrels' gallery and sprung floor. Upstairs the bedrooms were lofty and grand, with imported wallpaper and furnishings. The bathrooms alone were palatial, with gold taps and absolutely huge baths.

At the time, coming from England not long after World War II, and from a modest working class background, such opulence, and the Palace seemed absolutely out of this world. Later we realised just how many thousands of citizens relied upon the Maharaja for their livelihood. Nowadays Lalitha Mahal is a luxury hotel where you can stay as a tourist.

Lalitha Mahal Hotel in 2006

Between the city of Mysore and Lalitha Mahal there was a racecourse with a large stable block where the palace horse guards had their quarters. The Maharaja's horses and elephants were also stabled nearby. Adjacent to the stables was a building where the Maharaja's fleet of cars was kept. He had quite a collection, including a number of vintage models, mostly Rolls Royces. From time to time I took the children out to the stables to watch the horses being exercised.

Another building nearby was 'The Club' that prior to 1951 had admitted only expatriates through its doors. During our early years in Mysore a dinner and dance was occasionally held in the Club, giving me a wonderful opportunity to wear an evening dress, and all of us the chance to set work aside for a few hours and enjoy the company of the wider local community, including those not closely connected to the hospital or church. Frank did not like to dance and many times our great friend, Hugh Warren, would come to my rescue and valiantly whirl me around the dance floor at breakneck speed.

Hugh Warren ('Uncle Hugh' to the children)

Hugh worked in the Wesley Press, a printing house dedicated to the publication of educational and Christian literature, and he lived in a bungalow on the press compound, which was situated just across the road from St. Bartholomew's Church. (The Club, the racecourse and one or two other areas within the city were used in the filming of 'The Jewel in the Crown').

A few weeks after our arrival in Mysore we began to receive invitations for dinner, part of the order of introduction to some of our fellow missionaries and Indian colleagues. On one memorable occasion we were entertained to dinner by a very senior couple, with about ten guests present. The dinner parties were quite formal occasions with servants waiting upon the table, and here much of the Raj protocol, with its great deference to more senior colleagues, persisted. After a really excellent soup and main course our hostess served ice cream for dessert. This was a first ever for Mysore and a great luxury at the time. Naturally, we waited until everybody had been served before commencing to eat. So when our host and hostess picked up their spoons, we picked up ours and took one mouthful. It was unbelievably salty. We held it in our mouths and quickly glanced around, not quite sure what to do. We looked towards our hostess who was making subtle signals to her husband who was seated at the opposite end of the table. In silence they raised their eyebrows while he, waiting for guidance, paused with his spoon in mid-air. His wife took up her spoon once again and proceeded to eat the ice cream without even blinking her eyes. Our host nobly followed her lead and so of course did we, all without comment or the slightest grimace. The evening carried on happily and smoothly with coffee after dinner and relaxed, if formal, conversation continued.

On returning home later, Frank and I could only imagine what took place between our hostess and her cook after we left. At that time ice cream was made with the aid of an 'ice bucket' and to obtain such an item of equipment in Mysore was a great achievement. It consisted of a zinc-lined wooden bucket with a lid and a stainless steel cylinder with a handle attached. The prepared ice cream mixture would be poured into the cylinder and lowered into the wooden bucket. Then into the bucket and around the cylinder, small blocks of ice were packed with some salt and the whole left to stand. The salt melted the ice into a freezing cold sludge that very effectively chilled the mixture until the ice cream had set. On this occasion it looked likely that the cook had misunderstood the instructions and put salt into the ice cream mixture instead of into the ice bucket that surrounded the ice cream container. I leave you to imagine the actual flavour of the ice cream.

Throughout 1952 life continued on an even keel with me at home with Rosemary and Jenny. Frank and I persevered with daily language study and Frank acquired enough Kanarese to ask questions of his patients, although he often found it difficult to understand their replies and had to ask the nurses to interpret. As time went on, Frank's hospital workload increased, which unfortunately greatly hampered his linguistic progress.

For myself, when the initial spate of social functions had passed, with no housework to do and an ayah to attend to the washing of nappies and the ironing, I found plenty of time to spend with Rosemary and Jenny in the small park opposite Government Road House bungalow. It was an ideal place for Rosemary to play with her ball and ride on her small tricycle, while I walked around pushing Jenny in her pram. Little did I know how much life would change for me over the next few years.

Rosemary and Jenny playing on Government House Road

Chapter Three
The Holdsworth Memorial Hospital

Frank has written this chapter describing the development of surgical and other work in the Holdsworth Memorial Hospital. To set the scene I thought it would be of interest to include a section about staffing from the 1950 edition of the Annual Hospital Report.

Bed capacity   200

Medical staff   2 Medical Missionary Doctors
4 Indian Doctors
8 Nursing Sisters (two of whom were missionaries),
2 Staff Nurses
26 Student Nurses (1st, 2nd, 3rd & 4th year)
4 Trained Midwives
4 Student Midwives
9 Nurse Aids

Servants

2 Chaperons	2 Sewing women
2 Carpenters	2 Dhobis
13 Scrubbers	7 Peons
4 Malis	1 Plasterer
1 Whitewasher	2 Cooks
7 Sweepers	

Some of the job titles are quaintly outdated now and some are Indian names for the job. I have therefore briefly described their roles below.

2 Chaperons The hospital authorities were responsible for the safety of the Student Nurses who were not allowed to go outside the hospital compound on their own.
Sewing Women It was their job to make small items such as cot sheets, face masks, slings and draw sheets. They also repaired linen and uniforms as necessary.
Dhobis The Dhobis provided laundry services and collected all the hospital laundry daily. Later a proper Laundry was built within the hospital compound.
Scrubbers They were responsible for keeping all the floors throughout the hospital washed and cleaned daily.
Peons From the time we arrived until 1965 there was only one telephone for the hospital and that was in the Medical Superintendent's house. All messages between wards and staff were carried by the peons.
Cooks One of the cooks worked for the Nurses' Hostel, and the other prepared food for those patients who had no relatives or were too poor to buy food from outside. Because of different religious diet requirements and the need to keep the running costs of the hospital low, patients would be brought their own food by relatives,

rather than have it provided by the hospital. Behind the hospital wards there stood a row of small rooms, which could be hired by relatives and used to prepare food.

The Malis They kept the whole compound swept and tidy and tended the garden areas.

Plasterer and Whitewashers Each year the whole inside of the hospital was whitewashed and the walls were kept repaired inside. Every other year the whole of the outside received the same treatment. (It was rather like the Severn Bridge maintenance!)

Sweepers They were responsible for cleaning all toilets and washrooms. This was all very labour intensive and needed a good deal of careful supervision by the Nursing Sisters.

The hospital dhobi

Fortunately, water was not too big a problem. In the compound there was a huge underground water tank that was filled with water from the Municipal supply. This water was pumped up into tanks on the hospital roof to ensure a steady supply throughout the hospital at all times. There were occasions when the Municipal water would be turned off without notice.

During our time in Mysore the mains electricity was generated, at least in part, by the Hydroelectric Power Project at Pykara Dam, situated not far from Ooty and about 100 miles from Mysore City. This enlightened renewable energy plant was commissioned in 1932 and since then many hydroelectric dams have been built in the Nilgiris. The electricity supply was quite reliable in Mysore, but there were still times when it failed unexpectedly, especially during the hot, dry season, or when the monsoon failed.

In 1951 there were three private European-style rooms set aside for use by planters from the Coorg coffee estates. About eight years later more private rooms were built greatly helped by gifts from the Planters' Association. These rooms were always full, there being no such facilities available elsewhere in the city. (These days there are many private hospitals in the city of Mysore.)

Continued by Frank

When Winnie and I arrived, the Hospital was still a female stronghold, leaving Mr Obed, the radiographer, and me as the only male members of the medical and paramedical staff. We seemed none the worse for that however. It was not long before a small, twenty bedded ward, for male patients was opened by the Bishop, Norman Sargent, who knocked on a closed door with his Bishop's crook only to find that it was the wrong door! Despite this the ward was officially opened and blessed and, with the help of Sister Matthew, the work rapidly grew. Initially, my work was both medical and surgical. In fact, I was treating medical patients as well as surgical for almost eight years.

Sister Hannah David presided in the theatre in those days, to be followed later by Sister C K Aley. It was a tribute to the vision of the original builders that the theatre suite built by them in 1906 was still proving to be a very efficient design. It had a simple operating table and an overhead shop light with reflecting mirrors. It was modernised in 1956 with the installation of a modern Hanulux theatre lamp, an up-to-date operating table, a new sterilizer and air conditioning. My Aunt Irene sent a spark-gap diathermy machine from England, which revolutionised a lot of surgery.

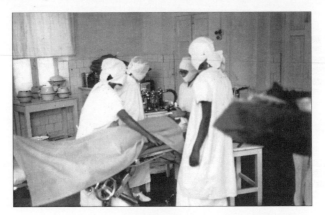

Holdsworth Hospital's operating theatre in the late 1950s

Mr. Obed was a genius for improvising equipment. He made a suction machine by reversing a vacuum cleaner. The electricity supply was intermittent and would often fail during the night. Torches were kept ready in the theatre for emergency use, until Mr. Obed came to the rescue and made a very efficient operating light out of a car sealed beam headlamp and a car battery. Later on, one of the Coorg coffee planters donated a small diesel generator for emergency lighting in the theatre. There were occasions when I had to 'de-scrub' during an operation, go outside and start the generator, then return and 'scrub-up' once again. Another planter friend made a wooden frame to put on the operating table to position patients with a fractured neck of femur for insertion of a Smith Petersen Pin under X Ray control.

To make surgery safe, one of my first tasks was to establish the manufacture of pyrogen free intravenous fluids. Prior to this it had been accepted that all patients receiving intravenous fluids were liable to get rigors due to pyrogens. (Pyrogens are the products of dead bacteria.) It meant the installation of a special still in the Pharmacy for manufacturing pyrogen free distilled water. A large quantity of pyrogen free fluid was required, not only for the intravenous fluids but also to make the giving sets and storage bottles pyrogen free. The intravenous fluids once made also needed to go through a special filter to remove any pyrogens that might be present in the electrolytes that were added to the distilled water.

The organisation of a Blood Bank marked a major achievement. When working in hospitals in England I had often been responsible for finding blood donors, cross matching and the giving of blood transfusions, so I knew how to organise the preparation of taking sets and bottles, the storing and the cross matching of blood. Initially we used European friends and colleagues as voluntary donors, but blood transfusion services in the underdeveloped countries were very dependent upon paid donors. We made advertising slides, which were shown in the local cinemas and recruited mostly coolie donors. This was quite successful and we ended up with a goodly number of donors, many of whom were workers at the railway station. They were given five rupees a time, the equivalent of a week's wage. Our greatest difficulty was to prevent the donors from giving blood too frequently. They were up to all the tricks of changing their appearance, wearing a moustache one day and no moustache the next, putting on a different turban and so on. Even photographing donors was not a complete safeguard. For several years the blood was stored in the paraffin-burning refrigerator in Dr Grace Gillespie, the Medical Superintendent's dining room.

Many patients coming to the hospital were severely anaemic due to hookworm infection. Most villagers walked barefoot and the soil was often contaminated with faeces containing hookworms. The hookworms would penetrate the skin of the foot, enter the bloodstream and infect the wall of the duodenum where they fed on the subject's blood. Examination of a stool specimen would reveal the presence of hookworm ova. The treatment at that time was with carbon tetrachloride, which killed the hookworms, followed three hours later by a large dose of magnesium sulphate to eradicate the dead worms. The patient would then be given a supply of iron tablets to correct the anaemia.

The cost of x-ray films made it necessary to do much more x-ray screening (with the patient behind or below a fluorescent screen) than would have been needed when in England. In the exclusion of TB (tuberculosis) and management of chest cases, a large number of patients required chest screening. In addition, the high incidence of duodenal ulcer required doing a large number of Barium Meal x-rays. I was carrying out about 450 to 500 Barium Studies of the stomach and intestines a year. When doing Barium Meals, we took spot films when required with a homemade wooden cassette holder.

It is amazing how much was done with the rudimentary x-ray equipment that we had, an '80KV 30 MA. Plant', a gift from Mrs Whittaker, a planter from Coorg

State. In 1960 a larger x-ray plant was installed, but with the initial small ex-Army machine there was very little that could not be done. It was true, that fat people were a source of trouble, and we could not do aortograms or biligrafin studies well. Despite the difficulties our technicians obtained excellent intravenous pyelograms, cholecystograms, bronchograms, myelograms and splenic venograms.

Having to do so much screening, it was necessary to keep a close check on radiation exposure. The Indian Atomic Energy Commission helped us to do this, by surveying our plant and providing us with individual film exposure badges to record our weekly exposure to x-rays. For use on the wards we had the ex-Army portable x-ray machine as well as a smaller machine, which could be taken apart and packed into the boot of a car for use in patients' homes.

It is surprising what can be done in surgery with relatively unskilled anaesthetic help, but it is of inestimable value to have good anaesthesia. During the later years from 1956 we had all the help that modern anaesthesia could give, with relaxants and other techniques, and we were able to do quite an amount of thoracic surgery. Even so, the surgeon often had to take much of the responsibility for the anaesthetic as well as the operation. Before relaxants were available I used to be very keen on a light ether, or if available, nitrous oxide, oxygen ether anaesthetic, supplemented by an intercostal or other suitable local anaesthetic block with Xylocaine or Nupercaine to provide relaxation for abdominal operations, although many surgeons preferred to use spinal or epidural anaesthesia. We owed a great debt to Dr Norman Cockett, an anaesthetist from the leprosy hospital in Dichpalli, who from 1956 became a regular visitor and developed our anaesthetic service with the introduction of relaxants and modern anaesthetic drugs. He introduced the use of a lytic cocktail, which we used for many hundreds of head and neck operations and for leprosy surgery.

With Norman Cockett's help we were also able to undertake chest surgery. We had regular operating sessions at the local Tuberculosis Sanatorium removing parts of diseased lungs. There was a trained chest surgeon at the Sanatorium, but there was no equipment for chest surgery in the operating theatre, so on the Sanatorium operating days at 7.30am we would load our anaesthetic apparatus, together with all the necessary surgical instruments, plus theatre staff and bottles of blood, into the Holdsworth Hospital ambulance and drive over to the Sanatorium for a morning's operating.

The years following 1951 were years of steady growth for the Holdsworth Hospital. The men's medical and surgical work increased in size and there was a chain of building development. The scope of Nurse Training and the number of nurses increased. A separate Nursing School was built with a three-stage extension of the Nurses' Home.

In 1956 and '57 a new Medical Superintendent's bungalow was built behind the Hospital house and the old Medical Superintendent's bungalow was incorporated into what was now called the 'New Block' for private patients. New Block provided single bed wards for people (such as planters) with the ability to pay a little more, many of whom lived a considerable distance away from Mysore City. The number of Indian doctors grew, and more accommodation was built for doctors and paramedical staff. Later on a separate Senior Nurses' Home was built.

The nurses' graduation day 1958

On November 12th 1955, a separate Children's Hospital building was opened by His Highness the Maharaja Jayachamaraja Wodeyar of Mysore and his young daughter, Princess Gayathri. The Children's Hospital had 50 in-patient beds, its own Out-patient Department and Pharmacy. Dr Margaret Pierce (now Collins) took on the paediatric work and later Dr Stanley Bell became the first physician, starting a separate Medical Department.

Rajkumari (Princess) Sri Gayathri Devi opening the Children's Hospital

Each day work in the Hospital began with the doctors and nurses gathering for prayers in the Hospital Chapel at 7.15am. On operating days this was followed by a quick ward round and operating sessions began at 8.00am. Women's outpatients were held in the mornings, and Men's outpatients three times a week in the afternoons from 4.00pm onwards.

The work on the wards was always interesting. On the medical side typhoid was a common problem. The accepted treatment was with chloramphenicol in large doses, which was expensive, and relapses were common. We tried smaller doses with the addition of another antibiotic, Achromycin, with favourable results, and published a paper. Some cases developed a perforation of the small intestine and required emergency surgery.

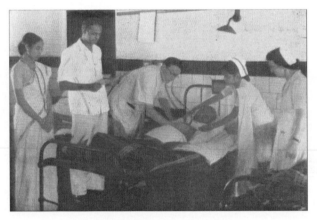

Frank and his team on a ward round

Malaria at that time was not a problem because of the widespread use of the insecticide, DDT. As a result, mosquitoes were rarely seen. Tetanus was an ever-present problem. It was not possible to treat Tetanus with relaxants and artificial ventilation, but for the majority of cases chlorpromazine combined with barbiturates controlled the spasms. An early tracheotomy was often required to facilitate breathing, together with intragastric tube feeding (because of difficulty in swallowing) and regular turning to prevent pressure sores. The cost of antitoxin was very high and often one had to be content to give very small doses.

Type 2 Diabetes was common, as were patients with heart problems. In 1956, Dr. Gillespie brought from England an Electrocardiograph machine, which used the vibrations of a fine hair of gold fibre to make a tracing of the heart beats upon a photographic plate. This was later replaced with a more modern machine.

On the surgical side a good deal of the surgical work was orthopaedic. With the help of Mr. Obed we improvised Balkan beams, which could be erected over a bed for fractured femurs. Using pictures from an invaluable book, published in 1939 by Mr. Eric L. Farquharson, on 'Orthopaedic Appliances', Mr. Obed went out 'on the street' to small workshops with the pictures from the book and got local carpenters and craftsmen to make Thomas splints, Bohler frames, callipers and other appliances for the treatment of different fractures and of polio victims with leg paralysis. (Many years later, when I was working in Basingstoke, Mr. Farquharson's daughter worked as my Registrar and later became a Consultant Surgeon.)

Frequent orthopaedic problems were tuberculosis of bones and joints, osteomyelitis, poliomyelitis and the correction of congenital or acquired deformities. A continual problem was the making of Plaster of Paris bandages. The quality of Plaster of Paris was very variable, even when it was bought from the same reliable firm, and much time was wasted with a bad batch of plaster. This needed constant checking. After much experimenting a suitable make of gauze was found. Large rolls were bought, stripped into lengths for plaster bandages and then starched. Being in a rice-eating country, it was an easy matter to starch the gauze. It was just dipped into rice water left over after cooking the rice for the patients or nurses. A special inclined plane with rubber bands was used to rub the Plaster of Paris powder into the bandages.

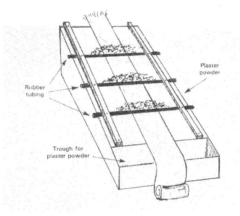

Inclined plane for making Plaster or Paris bandages

The making of plaster beds for patients with TB spines was a source of continual trouble because after a week the patients often would not use them and went home or, within a month, the plaster bed might be ruined by water or other misuse by the patient. After a period of using plaster beds, we followed the method of 'Rollier of Leysin', treating the patients by nursing them in the prone position with regular hyperextension exercises. This prevented the diseased vertebrae from collapsing and they did even better than those treated in plaster beds. We published a paper comparing these patients with the results of those previously treated with the conventional plaster beds. Later the situation was further improved by surgical anterior spinal fusion and removal of the diseased bone, followed by Rollier's method of minimal immobilisation.

One of the most difficult deformities to treat was clubfoot. When children came from villages it was unrealistic to expect the parents to leave their baby far from home in hospital for a year or more, but it was also difficult to find successful treatment because any strapping method was ruled out by the hot climate, which caused maceration of the skin under the strapping. Plaster treatment was the most suitable, but the plasters very quickly got ruined by water or by wear and tear, and many patients lived too far away for frequent changes. Often all one could do was an early wedge tarsectomy, removing a wedge of deformed bone, before the child began to walk, and then a triple arthrodesis to fuse the bones later on in life.

In the East it is a great disability for people who habitually squat to have a stiff knee or hip and one had to do all one could to avoid this. For this reason, a synovectomy, removing diseased synovial membrane, and minimal bone excision was frequently done for tuberculous knees, often with gratifying results. An arthrodesis to fuse the bones could be done later if this failed.

In the realm of abdominal surgery the most frequent operation for male patients was for duodenal ulcer. Very few could manage or even afford medical treatment, and the treatment of choice in a large number of cases was surgery. Where people's food habits are such that they depend on having a large sized meal once a day, the effect of an operation on the patient's nutrition is of a very great importance. In the 1950s in the West a partial gastrectomy, removing a large part of the acid secreting area of the stomach, was the accepted operation, but this was not suitable for many Indian patients, as with one large rice meal a day they could not eat enough. A new procedure at that time, a vagotomy operation, dividing the acid secreting nerves to the stomach, plus a stomach drainage operation, leaving a normal sized stomach, proved much more satisfactory, enabling the patients to have normal sized meals. We were concerned however about the nutritional effects of this operation and did a long study comparing different methods of doing a vagotomy together with different types of drainage procedures. These results were published.

Another interesting development was the realization that the duodenal ulcer patients were coming from the irrigated rice growing areas around Mysore and not from the dry millet growing areas. This led to a long-term, world wide, research study into the relationship between staple diets and duodenal ulcer prevalence, which extended over the next 50 years.

Tuberculosis of the abdomen in all its forms was met with very frequently, a little hard to explain in India where bovine TB is almost unknown because all milk is boiled before use. It was due to human transmission from infected subjects. Amongst women a right hemicolectomy operation (removal of the right colon) for hypertrophic tuberculosis of the caecum was very common. Tuberculous peritonitis was often a difficult diagnostic problem.

Ascariasis, or roundworm, caused a variety of conditions, from obstruction or spontaneous perforation of the gut to a peculiar acute abdomen, which resolved itself spontaneously. Suspicion of this latter condition was aroused where we found a patient who looked like a case of generalised peritonitis, but whose abdomen was not as hard as it should be and who had frequent bowel sounds. The condition usually cleared up after a few hours with suction and intravenous therapy and the patient would then pass a lot of worms.

A common surgical emergency was acute obstruction from various causes, and, as these cases frequently came to hospital late, they often had gross distension of the intestines. Initial decompression of the intestines through an opening high up in the small bowel, using a rectal tube to suck out the contents and collapse the bowel, was very helpful, and then the cause of the obstruction could be dealt with. The abdominal closure and post-operative progress was wonderfully helped by this procedure.

Acute appendicitis occurred, but not nearly so frequently as in England. Most cases came in with an appendix mass or abscess or recurrent subacute attacks. In India at that time doctors in general practice were not paid for their advice but for the treatment they gave, and this policy led to most cases being treated conservatively at home, first of all with antibiotics, and they were sent to hospital only if they did not improve.

In the realm of plastic surgery there was always much to be done, with harelips and cleft palates to be repaired, and burns to be skin grafted. Many extensive burns were caused by the saris worn by women and girls catching fire when they were preparing meals over an open fire in the home. The treatment of acute extensive burns was a big problem as infection was common after both the closed and exposure methods of treatment and grafting had often to be delayed.

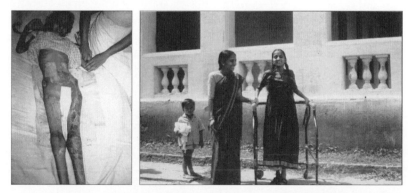

This poor girl was badly burnt but made a good recovery.
We met her, with her husband and son, when we visited Mysore in 1995

There were always acute and chronic empyemas in the chest and these needed draining. Management of the residual chest cavity and the site of the drainage tube with repeated x-ray sinograms was very important. Ear infections were also common and mastoid abscesses required drainage operations.

When people climb coconut palm trees to pick the fruit, head injuries are common and it was necessary to be prepared to do burr holes for intracranial haemorrhage. It was not possible to undertake any more advanced neurosurgery. Burr holes, too, for aspiration of a cerebral abscess or ventricular aspiration in TB meningitis patients with raised intracranial pressure were life-saving at times.

For those interested a more detailed account of surgical problems and surgical cases is included in the Appendix at the end of this book.

In later years I was appointed as Medical Adviser to several coffee estates in Coorg State and tea estates in the Nilgiris Hills, which are eighty to one hundred miles distant from Mysore. These estates had their own Medical Officers and small hospitals and I paid them six-monthly visits to inspect the medical services and to see any problem patients. There were also occasional calls for emergencies. One such call was for a possible fractured spine. The hospital's small portable x-ray machine was packed into the car, along with containers of developing and fixer fluid, plus processing trays. After examining the patient I decided that an X ray of the spine was necessary. In order to process the films in the dark I crawled under a horse blanket in the open air, under the hot sun. I have never been so hot in my life. Luckily, there was no evidence of a fracture. These visits were a welcome change from the usual hospital routine.

Apart from the medical, surgical, gynaecological and maternity work, over the years the other departments of the hospital also grew. The laboratory played an important part in the hospital work. In the beginning, from 1906 and onwards, the laboratory tests, apart from urine testing, had to be done by the doctors. Later, unqualified technicians took over routine tests and the doctors only helped with special tests.

In 1938 the first qualified laboratory technician was appointed and routine testing of blood, urine and faeces of all patients began. By the year 1944 there were four trained staff and a Technicians' Training Diploma Course under the Christian Medical Association of India (CMAI) was started with two pupils from Mysore. The examinations were conducted in Vellore or Madnapalle. In 1955 the number of pupils increased to four and the examinations were held in the hospital. The teaching and supervision of the laboratory was one of the responsibilities of a hospital doctor (for many years Dr Angeline Stephen) until the appointment of Mr Nandy in 1958.

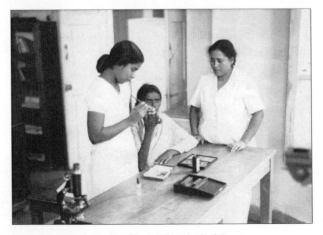

Dr Angie Stephen teaching in the laboratory

From 1962 to 1965 the appointment of the Revd Barton, who had been working in Arogyavaram, led to great advances in bacteriology and biochemistry. At last we were able to test our own cultures for bacteria sensitivity to antibiotics. There was then a temporary break in the training until a successor to Mr Barton was appointed.

The pharmacy has already been mentioned in conjunction with the production of pyrogen free intravenous fluids. In 1907 Menorrhamma, a former pupil of the Bangalore Girls' Boarding School, who had been trained as 'dispenser' by Dr Watts, dispensed the medicines. She was joined in 1909 by a trained compounder. The compounders not only dispensed medicines but were also trained to give the anaesthetics until 1915. The hospital was recognised for a one-year course for the training of compounders by the Government of Madras in 1922, and this was increased to a two-year course in 1937. As there was no registered trained Pharmacist on the staff, a doctor (for many years Dr Pierce) was responsible for teaching, keeping the stock and dispensing dangerous drugs. At that time most prescriptions had to be made up, some in liquid medicine form and some as powders. It was fascinating to watch a compounder first carefully spread a quantity of medicine powder on to a grid, which was marked out in squares, then fastidiously divide the powder into minute portions using a spatula. Each 'dose' was separated off the grid and folded into a small square of paper, to be given to the patient as prescribed.

The compounding room in the 1950s

This method of dispensing continued until 1957 when the new Drugs Act required the appointment of a trained pharmacist. At that time Margaret Smith (later Benfield) was appointed, followed by Miss Denny and in 1966 by Alan Cranmer.

The hospital was able to play an increasing role in the training of doctors. We built up a small medical library for the use of the medical staff. The shelves required dusting with the insecticide DDT to prevent the primitive 'silver fish' insects from devouring the books.

In 1952 the hospital was recognised by the Indian Medical Council for the training of house surgeons and physicians, and in 1962 the Royal College of Surgeons (Eng) recognised surgical training for the Primary Fellowship examination. Students were also sent to Holdsworth Hospital from Vellore for clinical postings and from the Ayurvedic College for work experience.

The extension of medical work into the villages increased. A special feature of the period following 1954 was the involvement in reconstructive surgery on cured leprosy patients, made possible by the advent of Dapsone therapy. This led to leprosy control and the extension of the existing medical outreach in several village areas. This is described in detail in a later chapter of this book.

Over the years from 1931 to 1956 a great debt was owed to Dr Grace Gillespie, who joined the hospital staff in 1931, for her great organisational skill and vision. In addition to her administrative work, she built up a wide reputation for the medical and surgical work for women and children.

It was in 1937, during Grace Gillespie's time as Superintendent, that Dr Angeline Stephen joined the hospital staff, to play an important part, especially in the development of the obstetrics department, building an unrivalled reputation in the city of Mysore for the care of mothers and babies. It was very much due to her, that the Sawday Maternity Ward, built in 1939 above the Outpatients' Department, was constantly occupied by new mothers and their babies.

Sawday Maternity Ward built in 1939 above the Outpatient's Department

The hospital grew and thrived, fostered by the constant interest of previous staff and supporters. The Sawday family continue today to raise money and make possible projects, such as upgrading of the Special Baby Care Unit (correct to the name given to the unit), that otherwise would not happen. In records of the 1950s and of later decades, there is much evidence of the close connections kept between the people involved in the hospital's earlier development.

Dr Angie Stephen with Drs Elsie and Edith Watts in England in 1955

Dr Grace Gillespie was the Superintendent at the time that I arrived and the hospital started to take male patients. In 1949 her work and dedication was recognised when she was appointed M.B.E., a well-deserved honour.

In 1956 Grace retired home to England and Dr Angie Stephen became the first Indian Medical Superintendent, ably taking up the administration of the hospital.

Ten years later, in 1966, Angie Stephen retired from her position in Holdsworth Hospital and established a private maternity home nearby. This coincided with the time that Winnie and the children travelled back to England so that Rosemary could start her A level studies, which she needed to pursue her career in medicine. I remained in Mysore to complete my five year term with M.M.S. and, from Angie's retirement in 1966 until September 1967, I acted as Superintendent.

It was in 1966 that I received the appointment OBE, which we felt was an honour to be shared by the hospital. I moved to the U.K. in 1967, when Dr John Iswariah, a surgeon, returned to India from further surgical training in the USA and took on the post of Superintendent.

In order for the Holdsworth Hospital to provide care for poorer patients, who were either treated free or paid modest fees according to their means, sufficient income had to be made through charges for treatment of patients who could afford to pay. Despite all this, the Holdsworth Hospital was a place to which patients of all means could come to find treatment and a spirit of loving care and concern, in keeping with its original name, 'Karuna Shala' (Home of Compassion). This remains the situation to this day.

Chapter Four
Hill Station Holidays and Family Life

The State of Mysore lies on the Deccan Plateau, 2,000 to 2,400 feet above sea level, making the climate more temperate in comparison to places nearer sea level. Even so the months before the monsoon in April and May can be very hot and humid. During the hot season it was the custom, when possible, for British families to go to the cooler climate of the Nilgiri Hills, about a hundred miles from Mysore City. The hills are at a height of 6,000 to 7,000 feet, rising from the Mysore Plain on one side and from Metapalayam in Madras State (now called 'Tamil Nadu') on the other. The highest area covers about forty square miles, the highest point being Doddabetta at 8,800 feet.

The word Nilgiri comes from two Sanskrit words, Nilam and Giri, meaning blue and hill. The Nilgiris were called 'The Blue Mountains' for three reasons, partly because they looked blue when viewed from the plains, because a semi-precious blue stone, Amazonite, was found there, and also because every six to twelve years a tall bushy shrub, called Strobilanthes Kunthianus, came into bloom covering the hillsides with its light blue flower. The principal town is Ootacamund (called 'Ooty' for short) at 7,200 feet, and slightly lower are the small towns of Coonoor and Kotagiri. The children's schools, Hebron and Lushington, mentioned later, were situated in Coonoor and Ootacamund.

Our very first holiday in the Nilgiris took place in April and May 1952, seven months after our arrival in Mysore. Rosemary was just three years of age, and Jenny ten months. Colleagues had given us advice on the preparations necessary for this annual trek away from the heat and dust of Mysore and we duly assembled clothing, bed linen, towels, clothes line and pegs, cooking utensils - all the paraphernalia essential for running our semi-European kind of household with two small children. Our destination was 'Burton Cottage', a bungalow set amongst some trees on the hillside overlooking the lake in Ootacamund.

My stay with the children in the hills was to last two months and Frank was to stay with us for the first month. We were granted the use of the hospital car for the first month of our holiday, and very early in the morning on the day of our departure, we loaded all the goods and chattels into the car. We then took our cook, with his wife and family, to the bus station. They travelled by bus to Ooty on the same day and would stay with us throughout the holiday period. We were responsible for providing them with warm clothing and bedding; consequently they also were travelling with a fair amount of luggage that was tied, along with other passengers' baggage, to the roof of the bus. Finally, we piled a picnic and lots of drinks, plus the two girls and their toys, into the car and set off on our adventure.

All went well for about eight miles, then suddenly the engine stopped. Frank got out of the car, opened the bonnet and tried this and that to get it started, but to no avail. Just as we were discussing what would be the best plan of action, along came a lorry and the driver clambered down from his cab and came over to help. Within moments he found the fault and to our amazement produced a matchstick with which he proceeded to fix a wire, which had become detached from the coil, firmly back into its socket. Wonder of wonders, the engine started immediately and we drove away happily, having been reassured by the driver that his repair would last the whole journey. It did. It is said that ignorance is bliss and, had we known what an endurance test the road would pose, I guess we should have turned back to the hospital there and then. However, off we went with great confidence with most of the hundred miles journey yet to come!

In 1952 the main road from Mysore city across the plateau to the Nilgiri Hills was largely made of granite chippings bedded down into a hard corrugated surface. This was full of large potholes and deep ruts worn by the hundreds of bullock carts, which traversed the road daily. Being unaccustomed to this rough terrain, and mindful of the car's suspension and the matchstick, Frank drove very carefully and our progress was painfully slow. After about thirty miles we came to a stretch of newly laid concrete road and thought, 'Ah, now we can really get going.' Alas, the concrete surface lasted for only a few miles, and then we were back onto the corrugated road. The car juddered along, severely shaking us passengers, the car repair tools and our luggage. Thankfully, this did not seem to bother Rosemary or Jenny. The sun rose high in the heavens and the temperature soared to over 100°F. At intervals, we stopped for drinks and to attend to the girls. This endurance test lasted right across the open countryside area of the plain. As we entered the jungle, the road improved slightly and there were more trees. We continued driving on the level for a further twenty-five miles or so, after which we gradually began to climb. It was wonderful to pass gently from hot, dusty countryside into a cool, green, shady world. The air freshened as the rough and rutted tarmac road wound upwards between grassy banks, woodlands, with coffee estates on the lower slopes changing to tea plantations at the higher level. We negotiated seven hairpin bends en route before eventually reaching the top of the mountain range and then travelled onwards across rolling hills to the town of Ootacamund.

This first journey took about eight hours to complete and we seriously wondered whether it really was worth the effort just to get away from the heat. Later, Frank was to learn that the easiest way to tackle the corrugated road surface was to drive at a speed of between thirty and forty miles an hour. Later still, the length of the road across the plain was covered with concrete, providing a better surface that considerably reduced the journey time.

When we eventually reached 'Burton Cottage' the servants had already arrived and opened up the bungalow. It was furnished with the basic necessities and we searched in the drawers and cupboards for pillows and extra blankets, and found where the cutlery, crockery, and cooking vessels were stored. Frank and I then explored the bungalow in order to decide which rooms we would occupy, as another family would be joining us in a couple of weeks' time. This accommodation was very similar to the holiday bungalows in Kuling in China, where two or more households would share the rooms and catering for their holidays.

We had arrived in the Nilgiris about a week in advance of the general exodus from the plains and this enabled us to settle down on our own in 'Burton Cottage'. We found opening up the bungalow eight months after its closure at the end of the previous year's holiday season was a major operation. Everything felt damp, the rooms smelt musty, and with the drop in temperature we were quite cold. One great discovery was a good supply of wood, already chopped and dry, which we used to light a fire quickly. The warm, glowing fire quickly restored our flagging spirits. Our initial food supplies were hastily assembled and we, together with the servants, were able to prepare some supper and settle down for the night.

Burton Cottage was surrounded by potato fields inhabited by plenty of well-fed rats, which for eight months of each year used the bungalow as a safe, cosy haven for their families. This was not an entirely new situation to us as we had been continually invaded by rats in our first home in Chaotung, China. There was little we could do about it. The rats had become used to their freedom in the empty bungalow and during the first few days of our arrival they would scamper across the living rooms in the evening. Eventually they accepted our invasion and made do with chasing around in the roof space.

Ootacamund, situated at about 7,500 feet above sea level, is the highest town on the Nilgiri range of mountains. At this height, the climate was most pleasant for those who, like us, were not yet used to the heat of the plains. Ooty had much to offer: it boasted a cinema, a racecourse, a golf course, a library, a small hospital, some reasonably stocked shops and a very large fruit, vegetable and meat market. After India gained its Independence in 1947 many expatriates, who had spent all their working lives in India, decided to remain in the country and settle down in the Nilgiris.

Nestling in the town of Ooty was a large lake, where it was possible to hire a boat by the hour, and there were numerous easy walks around the nearby area. I must also mention Ooty Club, reputedly the place where the game of snooker was invented. Membership to 'The Club' was regarded as an important necessity in the lives of the British residents. The bar was grandly hung with trophy heads of wild bison, sambar deer and cheetahs. For many years after Independence the club retained its tradition of grandly turbaned bearers, and only in the 1970s were the first Indian citizens allowed to become members.

The whole tempo of life in the Nilgiris was gentle and leisurely compared to the life experienced by us in Mysore. Most of Ooty's British residents lived in comfortable houses with large gardens. All households employed servants whose day-to-day tasks included housework, shopping, cooking and gardening. The planters from the outlying tea and coffee estates would come into the town for shopping and business, and 'The Club' was the focal point of their social life. Ooty had its own hunt with the huntsmen and women dressing in red coats and riding out with the beagles to chase jackals. It also had a grand racecourse, and during the 'hill station season', horse racing took place and Ooty buzzed with activity and excitement. Numerous other social events ranged from a visiting circus to a dog show. There was also the annual garden party given by His Royal Highness the Maharajah of Mysore at his summer residence, and of course, there was the round of private dinner parties one was expected to attend. The whole 'season' ended with the excitement of a ball at the Club.

After breakfast on our first morning in Ooty, we put the girls into the pushchair and set off to explore the town and our immediate surroundings. A footpath led us through the garden of 'Burton Cottage' and down the hillside, which was covered with bushes and young trees, to the main road that ran through the centre of Ooty town. In all, it was a distance of about one mile. We found the market and shops well stocked with fresh vegetables fruit, and all household necessities. The most noticeable difference from the Mysore market was the extremely wide range of fruit and vegetables, which included most English varieties. Houses and hotels nestled all over the hillside, always full to overflowing during the 'season' when everyone flocked up to the hills to escape from the heat below.

All around were miles of open countryside, covered by grass and scrub, and it was possible to walk long distances without encountering another human being. There were many areas of natural woodland that contained, among other species, indigenous rhododendron trees. The wildflowers were prolific. A hillside covered with Strobilanthes in bloom was an unforgettable sight. We were told that this occurred only once in seven years. Imagine the joy of walking across a hillside covered by acres and acres of vibrant blue-mauve blossom!

In addition to the untouched countryside, huge areas were given over to tea plantation and the occasional coffee estate on the lower slopes. Nearer the town most of the land had been taken over by the potato industry, whole hillsides being denuded of trees to make way for this. Although the steep slopes had been very well terraced, this measure by no means prevented vast quantities of precious topsoil being washed away during the torrential monsoon rains. Mimosa, also known as 'silver wattle', and eucalyptus trees had been planted extensively as an additional means of preventing further erosion. Both trees provided cash crops; the wattle bark was used for tanning leather, and the eucalyptus leaves were crushed and heated to produce eucalyptus oil.

Rosemary loved to climb the apple tree

Rosemary loved the 'Burton Cottage' garden and spent many hours sitting amongst the branches of the apple tree that commanded a good view of Ooty Lake.

Almost every day she rode on one of the local ponies that regularly took children for rides alongside the lake. I lost my confidence in ponies when one bit my shoulder quite hard as I walked along beside her. The pony was annoyed with one of the other ponies and unfortunately I just happened to be in the way.

Rosemary on a pony by Ooty Lake

After two weeks with Burton Cottage to ourselves, we were joined by the Pitts family, Bertha, Hubert, and their children, Howard and Susan, along with their Ayah and houseboy. All of our meals were taken together, the wives being expected to take turns, usually fortnightly, attending to the servants' duties and working out the daily 'menus' and shopping to be done for the whole household. Catering could be a bit tricky because each family would have their own way of managing servants and finance. As a newcomer I was told that it was absolutely essential to keep the food stocks locked away at all times to prevent pilfering. This practice meant keeping a bunch of keys permanently pinned to one's dress or skirt waist. Unfortunately, I was not aware of the situation at first and was severely reprimanded when items of food went missing from the pantry.

Within the bungalow there was a large room where we would gather together in the evening for recreation. During the daytime we usually amused ourselves out-of-doors. There being no radio or television we made our own pastimes, reading, writing, drawing, knitting, sewing, playing card games and so on. Frank stayed with us in 'Burton Cottage' for about a month, then returned to Mysore on his own in order to free Grace Gillespie to take her holiday. I moved with Rosemary, Jenny and the Pitts family, over to another holiday bungalow, 'Mount Pleasant' in Kotagiri, where we remained for a further month.

For a considerable time Jenny found it difficult to sleep. I have been reminded by comments made in correspondence written at that time that I was losing a lot of sleep and becoming very tired. Our house colleagues were of course aware of the problem, it being quite impossible to share a house and not hear a baby crying in the night. Everyone was very understanding and concerned for my well being, and one day Hubert weighed us all. I quote from a letter written at the time, 'Jenny 13lbs, Susan 18lbs, Howard 34lbs, Rosemary 30lbs, and Winnie 7st.13lbs'.

Hubert was a great help in educating me into the ways of dealing with servants. Frequently they would ask for an advance of salary for one reason or another. Their wages were very low, therefore it was difficult for the uninitiated to judge whether the need was genuine or not. The wise thing was never to give in to such requests, but rather say a definite no, and then, if within the course of time it became obvious that there was a difficulty, give the money outright with no strings attached.

Returning to the 'plains' after the hot season hill station break, we found life took on again its usual demands. Frank was extremely preoccupied because he was working at the hospital for six days of the week from 7am to 5pm. On top of this we both were required to set aside time for language study. I was able to leave the girls with the ayah for a while each day, and although it took some time before I felt happy with this arrangement, as time went by I found it an absolute necessity. A missionary's wife was expected to take on quite a number of responsibilities outside the home and actually this was a good thing for me because with Frank away from home so much I needed the company of other adults.

Looking back on this period in our lives and browsing through some of our letters home, I realise what a huge adjustment this meant for us as a family. I now regret that at that time we had little chance to take in a lot about the Indian way of life, its culture and customs. My time was taken up with the pre-occupations of our young family, and Frank was absorbed in hospital work, learning about new diseases, teaching nurses and young doctors.

After the Ooty break I can remember Jenny starting to walk and talk and Rosemary spending time with me reading, learning to write the letters of the alphabet and to do simple addition.

Lillian, the single lady missionary who had shared the bungalow with us for the first period of our time in Mysore, moved out of the other end of the Government House Road bungalow and the Nelson family moved in. Billy, their son, was about Rosemary's age and made a good companion for her, as did Gillian Mason who lived in the Wesley Press compound situated a short distance away. It was easy to walk with the children across Government House Road into the small park where they could play ball games or ride their tricycles. The bungalow garden was large but we did not allow the children to play in there unsupervised because of the risk of encountering a cobra. Living in this bungalow we did see snakes. In fact, during our very first week there, a huge cobra was caught by the mali and on another occasion a krait, a small, very dangerous snake, found its way into a bathroom through the drainage hole.

As mentioned earlier, I regularly used my sit-up-and-beg bicycle to take Rosemary out. She liked nothing better than riding through the city with me, waving gaily to the traffic policemen as we passed. The roads were quite safe because there were very few motorcars in Mysore during the 1950's.

Towards the end of 1952 All India Radio asked a few of us 'Mysoreans' to record a programme for Christmas, including the Christmas story and a few carols. The recording was to happen in the small recording studio belonging to All India Radio just outside Mysore city. We duly set about practising for this and an extract from one of our letters to an Aunt mentions the fact that, 'Frank took the part of Joseph and a Wiseman and I, Mary and an angel'. I also sang, as a solo, one verse of 'Sleep Holy Babe'. For the broadcast we were paid a small fee, which went straight into the hospital funds. Over the course of time we took part in a number of Christmas programmes and also, on request, formed a team for a series of 'Twenty Questions'.

At that same time, in November or December 1952, to our great consternation Rosemary awoke one morning with a squint. Her eyes were most definitely crossed. At first we were so surprised by this sudden phenomenon that we wondered whether she was playing. (It is not unknown for a child to produce a squint for the fun of it). However, we soon realised that this was not the case. We consulted with our medical colleagues as to where we should go for advice and treatment, and Dr Gillespie recommended a small mission hospital situated in Kotagiri in the Nilgiri Hills. Two lady doctors ran the hospital, Dr. Jeffrey, who in addition to general medicine had specialised in Ophthalmology, and Dr. Herlufsen, who had specialised in midwifery. We contacted Dr. Jeffery and hastened to Kotagiri where she examined Rosemary and prescribed spectacles and eye exercises. Frank's father was a qualified Optician and the prescription was immediately sent to him in England asking for his help. What a blessing! He made up a pair of spectacles as quickly as possible and dispatched them to Mysore. In the meantime, Auntie Irene, also an Optician, sent a Stereoscope and Frank, myself and Rosemary all proceeded to go through the exercises together. Frank and I found the exercises quite difficult to do, but Rosemary managed very well indeed.

Christmas Eve 1952 found us in the hospital helping with the decorations while Rosemary and Jenny occupied themselves walking around the ward chatting to 'the mens in bed'. After this Rosemary helped with the distribution of presents, handing them to each of the patients. When we got home in the evening a rather concerned Rosemary asked, 'Mummy, how will Father Christmas be able to bring our presents tonight? We don't have a chimney'. A vital point! After a little thought I suggested, 'Would you be happy if we left one of the doors unlocked and placed a glass of milk on a table nearby? You can help me get it ready for him before you go to bed'. 'Oh, yes please Mummy, that's a lovely idea. Do you think he would like a biscuit as well?' This arrangement was continued for many years. That evening when everything was duly organised, two rather tired but contented little girls went happily to sleep with a pillowcase draped across the foot of each bed. We made a small Christmas tree using a branch from a thorn bush and decorating it with silver paper and candles. It really looked quite pretty.

On Christmas Day the usual programme would be 8am service at St. Bartholomew's Church then home for breakfast and opening of presents. Whilst we were at church our cook would prepare a wonderful curry for lunch, which we shared with the house servants and their families, all of us sitting together on the lounge floor in a large circle. After the meal we presented the servants with their gifts, two sets of uniform each, clothing for their children and some sweetmeats. Following this we went to the hospital and took part in a charade type of entertainment for the nurses followed by the distribution of their gifts. The final event of the day was the Christmas Dinner, a traditional meal with turkey, Christmas pudding, mince pies and fruit, attended by all adult expatriate residents living in the city as well as the missionary personnel. The Queen's Speech, broadcast worldwide over the radio, coincided with our dinnertime and we all listened with great respect. Frank and I were quite bemused to discover that it was the tradition to stand during the playing of the National Anthem no matter at what point during the meal this occurred. Each subsequent year the meal was held in a different bungalow. Crockery, pots and pans, cutlery and servants were transported from their various houses to the chosen venue and everyone had a wonderful time. We always made sure that the servants were given some time off to attend church and be with their families over the Christmas period.

By the time New Year 1953 came we really had begun to feel quite at home. Our Indian friends and colleagues within the hospital and church were so helpful, and they adored the girls. When Lillian left to retire to England we had a change of cook and Kantaraj started with us. The servants had become part of the family and Frank's work in the hospital increased as more and more people came to know that men were being treated as well as women.

In February 1953 Rosemary's spectacles arrived. I deliberately took to wearing my distance pair all day long and Rosemary followed suit, happily wearing her new spectacles in order to be 'grown-up' like Daddy and Mummy. Fortunately, she was quite proud of them and told her friends, 'Grandpa sent them 'specially from England'.

Rosemary happily wore her new spectacles sent 'specially from England'

One thing I missed terribly was not having a piano in the house. To compensate for this I would sail around the house singing at the top of my voice - much to the amusement of the servants, although they often asked for more. Mostly my repertoire consisted of songs popular at the time. I would burst through a doorway with arms outstretched, singing, 'Come into the garden Maude' and bump into Kantaraj our cook or the mali in the process. In quieter mood, 'Have you not seen my Lady, Go down the garden singing' was another favourite.

During February and March of 1953 the weather was exceptionally hot due to the failure of the monsoon. I was pregnant again, therefore, it was decided that I, together with the girls, should go to the Nilgiris and stay in Kotagiri. Frank would follow on later just before baby was due and we would stay there for baby's first few weeks before returning to the heat of the plains.

Early in April I travelled up to Kotagiri, with Rosemary, Jenny and the servants. We went to Kotagiri because there was a small hospital near 'Mount Pleasant', where Dr. Herlufsen and Dr. Geffrey worked. The baby was not due until mid-May and, as a friend was driving us up to Kotagiri and space in his car was limited, we took the minimum of luggage. Frank planned to join us on the 1st May, driving up in the borrowed hospital car, which would be loaded with more clothing and, most important of all, clothes, nappies and other items essential for the arrival of the new baby.

Kotagiri was much smaller than Ooty and I must admit to feeling quite isolated, alone with two small children in 'Mount Pleasant' bungalow at night. The bungalow nestled on a hillside surrounded by huge eucalyptus trees, and the creaking of the bending trees was most unnerving during the violent thunderstorms that frequently blew up in the middle of the night. Often we had to clear up water from leaks in the roof and once our roof almost blew off. The girls will remember a later occasion when they were at school in Coonoor and a tree blew down and damaged one of the dormitories.

As we were fairly isolated in Kotagiri and without transport, on the 26th of April, when a friend very kindly offered to take us out for the day to visit some mutual friends in Ketti about twenty miles away, I gladly accepted. The road was pretty rough and we were driven at such a fast speed that those of us in the back of the car were thrown around. During the following night, my tummy began to churn a little and this continued throughout the next day. I felt sure that the baby was going to make an early entry into the world. 'What shall I do?' I thought, 'I have absolutely no clothes here suitable for a newborn baby'.

Dr Herlufsen came to see me during the afternoon and after saying, 'Oh, no need to worry, I think things will settle down,' she went straight out again. However, I was not so easily reassured and immediately she had gone I sent Kantaraj, our cook, to the village to buy an ounce of white wool and a pair of knitting needles, with the idea of making a small vest. I think I could have won a medal for the speed with which I knitted that one small vest. The garment completed, I gave a sigh of satisfaction, went to bed and tried to settle down to sleep.

The baby, however, was most anxious to escape the confines of my body and after an hour or two I gave up trying to sleep, being afraid that if I relaxed baby would pop out. I called Kantaraj, who was an absolute treasure, and he immediately understood my predicament. He rushed over to a neighbour who came with his car and delivered me to the hospital. Within half an hour our new son, John, arrived with no medication and no medical assistance. Actually, the doctor had left the room in order to fetch some enema equipment. I was shocked by the suddenness of it all, and the resulting trembling took quite a while to settle.

We were thrilled with our new addition to the family, especially Rosemary, who had longed for a brother and looked upon John as her birthday present because, after all, he was born on her fourth birthday. Messages were hastily sent to Frank, who immediately packed the car and drove up to join us for a month. John did not have to spend many hours with just one knitted vest!

The 'English summer' type weather and quiet countryside of the Nilgiris were so refreshing after the noise, heat and busyness of Mysore life that we contentedly spent our holiday in the immediate vicinity of our accommodation. The Nilgiri 'Hill Station', Ooty, being 1,000ft higher than either Kotagiri or Coonoor (where the children later went to boarding school), was much cooler and often misty. Coonoor had a population roughly between that of Ooty and Kotagiri, and standing at about 6,000ft it boasted a wonderfully temperate climate that made it a gardener's paradise, with flowers and vegetables of every description growing profusely. In particular, I remember the cyclamens, begonias, zinnias and bougainvillaea.

In the holiday bungalows cooking was done over a charcoal or wood burning fire in a separate room adjacent to the servants' quarters. Cold water was collected from a single tap situated at the back of the compound and distributed into the various bathrooms in buckets. Hot water was heated in the kitchen and carried to the bathrooms when needed. We did have electricity for lighting but the supply was subject to frequent failures. We had to keep an oil lamp readily available as well as a good stock of candles and matches. One great blessing was the stock of firewood logs. On a rainy day the temperature would drop dramatically in the evening and it was always possible to light a huge fire in the hearth of the main sitting room. The servants also kept warm beside the fire in the kitchen of their living quarters. We, and our servants, were so much better off than most of the local Indian people.

While we were in Kotagiri, a retired British Army Colonel who lived with his wife in a bungalow quite near 'Mount Pleasant', very kindly befriended us. We remember spending the afternoon of June 3rd 1953 in their home, the date when Her Majesty Queen Elizabeth II was crowned in Westminster Abbey.

In England the ceremony was taking place during the mid morning, whereas the live radio programme reached us in Kotagiri about four hours later. Our whole family was invited; including Rosemary aged four, Jennifer two and John at five weeks old. We were not sure about the wisdom of this as they were so young, but the Colonel insisted saying, 'They must come to witness such an historical occasion. Please bring them all.'

A wonderful tea had been prepared for us and we settled down to listen to this the first live broadcast from Westminster Abbey. We could hear the beautiful singing of the choir and the soaring organ accompaniment. The ceremony of course took a long time and it took quite a lot of concentration to make out what was really happening. The children were very good for the first hour or so, but they did become a little restive towards the end. They could not quite understand why we grown-ups should be so excited about this event. Of course they could not have realised that this was a momentous event being broadcast live worldwide to all Commonwealth countries.

Just after this great event we returned to Mysore. Before our holiday at 'Mount Pleasant' Rosemary had started to go to school at the Palace each weekday morning, the idea being that the Maharaja's children would have a chance to practice speaking in English while Rosemary had the chance to experience a different environment. After John was born, Jenny went with Rosemary to play in the Palace Nursery with Princess Minakshi. On nursery school mornings a charming little coach drawn by a white horse would arrive on our driveway to collect the girls. They never had any qualms about leaving their own compound.

The Palace carriage outside Sawday Lodge

All went well until November when I began to feel rather unwell. Frank and Grace Gillespie consulted together and deciding that I might be suffering from malaria they started me on a course of Camoquin. After a day or two I awoke one morning feeling really groggy. Frank went to hospital as usual about 6.45am and Rosemary came into the bedroom to visit me after eating her breakfast. She looked at me strangely for a moment or two before exclaiming, 'Mummy, are you feeling alright 'cos you are a funny colour? Your face is all black.' By this time I was beginning to feel decidedly light headed. Once again, Rosemary said, 'Mummy you really do look funny and your hands are going blue as well.' Thoroughly alarmed, I asked her to fetch my hand mirror. Imagine the shock when I looked into the mirror and saw a sickly purple and yellow face staring back at me. I quickly glanced down at my hands and realised, as Rosemary had, that they were also changing colour. In order not to alarm Rosemary I quietly called Kantaraj, as he would know what to do. After taking one look at me he quickly despatched someone to the hospital to call

Frank, there being no telephone in the house. Within half an hour Frank was back home with the hospital car and whisked me off. By this time I had become totally disorientated. The Camoquin was discontinued immediately and I became jaundiced. The final diagnosis was Infective hepatitis with metahaemoglobinaemia due to taking Camoquin. After a few days in hospital I returned home to recover quietly.

Christmas followed and was kept very low key. Because we lived a fair distance from the hospital we were able to avoid some of the more tiring events, although of course all of us were roped into taking part in the entertainment for the nurses during the afternoon of Christmas Day. On this occasion we all dressed up and enacted a doctor, visiting a village area, travelling in a bullock cart drawn by two human bullocks. During the course of the journey a wheel fell off the cart causing its contents to spill out, and the 'contents' were the Christmas presents for the nurses and other members of the hospital staff. Rosemary and Jenny helped with the distribution of the presents.

An event that caused great excitement in our house was the arrival of a black and white spaniel puppy. He was a gift from Mr and Mrs McPherson, coffee planters from Coorg. Rosemary and Jenny immediately named him 'Podgy' because he was such a roly-poly bundle of fluff. We already possessed a goose, a duck and some chickens, all living in our compound - the more pets the merrier. Dear Podgy remained with us throughout our stay in Mysore.

Rosemary and Jenny with Podgy the dog and Simon the cat

Once again when the warmer weather was beginning in 1954, it was time to think about retreating to the hills with our young family. Having become familiar with the Nilgiris we decided, this year that it would be good to spend time on our own and we were fortunate to find a small cottage, called 'Cosy Nook', for rent in Lovedale, a small village tucked into the hillside a few miles from Ootacamund. This particular holiday proved to be a great success because of its peacefulness. Miss Heath, an elderly lady and the owner of the cottage, became a great friend. She had resided in the Nilgiris for many years, at one time running a small school for local

Indian children, and now she lived in a house lower down the hillside. To reach her house we had to cross the road from 'Cosy Nook' and walk down a very steep, narrow pathway, which could be treacherously slippery during wet weather. She still taught a few young children and invited Rosemary to join them for four mornings each week.

Soon after our arrival in Lovedale we realised that twice daily the Blue Mountain Express Train stopped at Lovedale railway station during its journey from Metapalayam to Ootacamund. In a very short time Rosemary, Jenny and John in his pushchair were clamouring for a daily walk to the station to watch the train come huffing and puffing alongside the small platform and wait while passengers alighted or boarded. Then, with a blow of his whistle and wave of his flag, the signalman gave the all clear for the train to steam away.

Jenny, Rosemary and John (in pushchair) watch the mountain train

The train drivers became great friends and looked out for the children. *('The Nilgiris Mountain Railway' was one of four programmes for the BBC series 'Indian Hill Railways' shot in 1999.)* Rukmani, our ayah, and Perumal, our cook, were equally thrilled with the train. One luxury I always remember was the arrival of the baker every morning bringing a basket full of freshly baked bread. The bakery was nearby and Frank took the children to watch the bread being baked. There was a beehive shaped brick oven with very thick walls and a small door low down. A wood fire was lit on its floor and, when the oven was hot enough, the ashes were raked out and the loaves of bread placed inside to bake.

We were granted the use of the hospital car for this holiday too. Shortly beforehand, Frank had given me driving lessons, mainly driving up and down Chamundi Hill, which is quite steep, and performing 'hill starts', which was nerve racking with two little girls sitting in the back of the car crying out, 'Please Daddy you drive, we don't like Mummy driving. It's too jerky.' Not long before the holiday came the day of my driving test. The Chief Police Officer, who was taking my test, sat beside me with an inscrutable look. Imagine my dismay when only minutes into the test we came upon an elephant (one from the Maharaja's stable) being taken for exercise at an ambling pace along Ashoka Road, a wide but busy road leading to the 'circle' (roundabout) outside the Palace. I summoned as much courage as I could and passed the elephant, trying to look as if it was something I had been doing every day for years. The Police Officer nodded his head and said, 'That's alright Mrs. Tovey, just drive me back to the Police Station and drop me off.' I was quite taken aback at this quick conclusion to my test, and when he actually got out at the Police Station, I sat for a moment or two feeling almost too scared to drive away on my own. It was the first time that I had driven without Frank sitting by my side.

The outcome of all this was that Frank, having driven us up to Lovedale, returned to Mysore by bus leaving me with the children and the hospital car, which was well used and fairly ancient. It was one of those cars that everybody used and no one in particular took care to maintain. Here is a quote from a letter I sent to Frank from 'Cosy Nook' 27 April 1954 referring to the car:

'Yesterday, the man from next door looked at the car and found that the bolt connecting foot brake to rod was missing. He fixed it up temporarily then we drove into the Coronation Garage (in Ooty) and he watched them fix it up properly. Apparently he used to be a motor mechanic before coming out here, he had a brother in the trade. He cleaned up the battery for me and also says that this should be done once a month and Vaseline put on the connecting terminals. I'll have to make this one of my jobs I think, for underneath the battery was in a shocking state.'

As I write now I shudder to think what risks we ran driving around those steep and winding roads.

Not long after this holiday Frank was sent to Tumkur for three months intensive language study because, owing to pressure of hospital work, he had not yet passed his first language examination. Unfortunately, at the end of the allotted time he still did not pass but he was excused from taking it again. Just before Frank went to Tumkur we acquired a car of our own.

I am very much aware of the fact that so far in this narrative I have dwelt largely upon domestic matters because we were living too far away from the hospital for me to take an active part there whilst the children were young. Frank has written about the actual work that was taking place in the hospital, but behind all of this were the huge adjustments being made by the hospital to implement the change from Methodist Missionary Society overseas financial and personnel support to an entirely independent position within the church of South India.

Frank was working for the MMS and once a year a meeting of all Methodist missionaries working in the area was held in Bangalore. The meeting lasted for four or five days. There was a large mission compound within which stood an Ashram and a number of large bungalows, affording sufficient accommodation for folk coming from outside Bangalore. These meetings were essential because the missionary circle was made up of single ladies, teachers, nurses, doctors, as well as ministers and their wives, many of whom were stationed in fairly isolated areas. This annual gathering was a time when they, especially the single men and women, could share and discuss their problems and successes, joys and setbacks and spend some time in prayer and reflection.

The missionary Synod delegates 1955

During the early years after the formation of the CSI much time was spent planning and re-organising the appointment of new Indian Christian clergymen, doctors, nurses and teachers to replace retiring missionaries. Then came the financial arrangements to be sorted out. Previous to the formation of the CSI, all missionary personnel had been paid directly by the Methodist Church in England, and in addition to this, grants coming from England had been sent to all the Indian Church institutions, schools and hospitals individually. To start with, immediately after the formation of the CSI, the CSI was responsible for all salaries, while the Methodist Church in England continued to support the Indian church schools, churches and hospitals and village work within the diocese by sending a block contribution to be allocated by the CSI. In this way the CSI would become completely independent.

Of course this needed a huge amount of careful and sensitive handling, as such handovers do, not least because for the most part church workers, whether they be from overseas or homeland, are paid lower stipends than would be received in the commercial world. For instance, the doctors working in the Holdsworth Memorial Hospital even at the present time receive a much smaller remuneration than their counterparts working in a Government or Private Hospital, just as missionary doctors and other workers were in our time paid considerably less than those in their home country. This was all part of the 'service to others' element attached to Christian work. As you can imagine, the period of transition did cause anxiety for some and these annual meetings were a great source of strength to many.

Chapter Five
Sawday Lodge and First Furlough

In November 1954 we were asked to move across the city to Sawday Lodge, a two storey, much more modern house than Government House Road bungalow. Rev. Sawday built Sawday Lodge in the 1920s for his retirement. One sad thing about this move was that it meant we had to bid farewell to Dayakka, our cook, and Devaputra, our hardworking mali. They each lived, rent free, in their own small house on the compound, their wages being paid by the bungalow resident. When there was a change in bungalow occupancy both cook and mali remained in their respective quarters as compound caretakers until the bungalow became occupied again. They were paid a small sum by the church authority for these services.

On reaching Sawday Lodge we were greeted by our new young cook, Jayappa, and Kalappa, the mali, who was then not much more than a boy. Both were very conscientious and hard working, and were always polite and cheerful. Rukmani, the ayah from Government House Road, lived separately out in the city, and this being so she continued to serve us, although we were not too happy with her because she tended to be rather rough with the children and on occasions told them frightening stories.

The Maharaja wished his children to speak English, and, at the suggestion of a friend of ours, Phyllis Watsa, who was the palace school governess, first Rosemary, then Jenny and John started attending the palace nursery school. Rukmani continued with us for the first few months at Sawday Lodge, often accompanying Jenny and John on their visits to the Palace nursery school. One day I received a complaint regarding her behaviour when at the palace which resulted in her dismissal. The children were quite glad to be without her and we managed very well on our own, in fact, I was very pleased to be able to spend more time with the children, especially as we would quite soon be back in UK for furlough where there would be no servants.

When we first moved to Sawday Lodge I was apprehensive about taking up residence there with a young family because it was furnished throughout with beautiful, handmade, rosewood furniture, but I soon realised that I need not have worried because the children played in the garden most of the time.

However, we did have one mishap in the garden that made me think. I was upstairs one afternoon when I became aware of a commotion going on in the garden. I rushed downstairs only to find Rosemary and Jenny hauling John up the veranda steps and into the house. John had fallen into the garden pond and there he stood, dripping wet, a large puddle of water forming around his feet. John was absolutely calm. He really had no idea why the girls were so agitated. Bless them, they had managed to drag him out of the water really quickly. As the pond was fairly deep we decided to surround it with a small wire fence in order to prevent any of the children falling in again.

The children loved to play by the pond

Sawday Lodge stood in Vanivilas Road, a very busy thoroughfare in complete contrast to the quietness of Government House Road. A four-foot high brick wall enclosed the compound, and a five bar wooden gate opened straight onto the pavement. The children were not quite tall enough to unlatch the gate, which was fortunate because they loved to spend time looking through the bars. All day long pedestrians, cyclists, tongas, bullock carts, vendors selling plantains and oranges, policemen and postmen passed by our gate. Often beggars stopped to ask for alms and the children called us to give them some food. One day the palace State Elephant passed by on its daily exercise and the mahout brought it to the gate. Jenny being quite protective of her brother John, who was three years of age at the time, pulled him back from the gate, afraid that the mahout would tell the elephant to lift John up. About a year previously when I had been in town with the children this same elephant had been walking past us, when it had suddenly put down his trunk, wrapped it around John and lifted him out of his pushchair, placing him up high on his neck in front of the mahout. It all happened so rapidly that even I was slightly alarmed. Within a few moments John was gently returned to his pushchair, a bit frightened but unharmed. Some years later when visiting the elephant stables John overcame his fear and climbed onto the elephant's back with no qualms.

Usually the people passing by were friendly, but for some unknown reason, one day a group of children began throwing stones over the gate, one of which hit our beloved spaniel, Podgy. He sustained a broken leg. Frank managed to apply a plaster cast and Podgy made a full recovery after hopping around on three legs for a while. He never forgot the sympathy that was given when he bumped the plaster cast on our feet and it was always that particular back leg that would be planted

63

against our legs when he wanted an affectionate pat.

The 1950s and 60s were the years during which European and Australian young people began taking a year out to 'travel the world' on a shoestring. Many gravitated to Mysore because of its historical reputation. They would arrive with very little baggage at the bus station, and the coolies, taking note of their white skin, would direct them straight to our house for board and lodging, there being only one very expensive European-style hotel, 'The Metropole', in the city. I remember one couple in particular because they appeared quite late in the evening and after a meal went off to bed saying, 'Would it be possible for you to wash our clothes immediately? We only possess the ones we stand up in.' Startled, I answered, 'Oh yes, of course I will see what can be done.' Early the next morning Jayappa's wife very kindly washed the clothes and hung them out to dry in the sun. Meanwhile our traveller guests stayed in bed after declining to accept our offer of temporary garments. Our young family were very intrigued with the pair and nicknamed them 'Adam and Eve'. I was very touched when, on taking their leave a few days later, the young lady presented me with a small watercolour painting of an Indian dancer. This still hangs up on my study wall nearly sixty years later and the colours remain bright.

In complete contrast another such traveller, seventy years of age and going round the world on her own carrying only a small suitcase, was deposited on our doorstep by a coolie. It turned out that she had suddenly inherited a small nest egg of money and decided to take off from home for six months while she could still manage on her own.

About this time much discussion was going on amongst various missionary families in and around Mysore as to future education for their children. There were a number of families in residence and most planned to send their five to six year olds to Hebron School in the Nilgiris. Hebron catered for girls from five to sixteen years of age and boys from five to eight, with the boys automatically transferred to Lushington School in Ootacamund for the remainder of their education. The English Curriculum was taught in both schools. Hebron School was established by the Brethren Church and the fees were moderate. Some teachers were from the United Kingdom and others from Australia. All were Christian. We received an allowance from MMS towards the cost of children's education.

Frank and I felt very unhappy about sending Rosemary away to a boarding school at such a tender age, but she had outgrown the Palace Nursery School and we had tried sending her to the Catholic School in the city, where the teaching was in English and the general standard of education high. Sadly for Rosemary she was the only fair skinned child in the school and she hated the attention from the other children, who couldn't resist touching and pulling her long curly golden hair. When it came to the crunch, Rosemary herself made the decision about her schooling for us as she was absolutely determined that she must go to school with her friends Howard Pitts, Billy Nelson and Gillian Mason. So it was that we took Rosemary on the long journey up to Coonoor. I can still feel the heartbreak of leaving our little girl all on her own in a strange place with unknown people. It would be a whole term before we would see her again. This was an experience we would repeat with all of the children over the next eleven years.

With Rosemary away at school Jenny and John continued to play in the garden at Sawday Lodge. We all loved the house with its cool shady garden and goldfish pond and they particularly enjoyed playing in the fernery under the festoons of trailing greenery that hung down the trellis. It was the coolest spot in the garden.

Jenny and John spent hours in the fernery at Sawday Lodge

Often Kalappa, the mali, would join in the children's games, kicking John's ball right over the top of the house. He also took full part in a very noisy game that they would play until, desperate for some peace and quiet, I had to call a halt. They would wind up the gramophone and put the needle on a favourite record we had brought with us from England. 'Lun, labbit, lun, labbit, lun, lun, lun,' they would all yell, while Kalappa galloped around the house with John on his shoulders, Jenny and the dog in hot pursuit.

But life had its serious side as well and this kept me very busy. Recorded in our letters written during 1953 and 1954 are references to water shortages and electricity cuts, as well as the failure of monsoons and consequent shortage of food, particularly in the village areas. It was impossible to ignore the many human needs around us and I soon became involved in famine relief supplies.

In order to venture into the village area around Kastur and Hadya it was necessary to enlist the help of Sister Ethel Tomkinson. Sister Ethel worked in an Ashram (an Indian name given to a religious community) at Kastur caring for sick and needy villagers, for many, many years, ministering to their bodies as well as their souls.

Before setting up the Ashram she had worked as a nursing sister at Holdsworth Hospital between the years of 1914 and 1932. During her time at Holdsworth Ethel also cared for more than just the physical needs of her patients.

When we were in India I was unaware of a very special case where Ethel rescued a baby from an uncertain fate. Since then I have met the daughters of that special baby, who were brought up in Wales just as their mother had been before.

Susheela Lourie has permitted me to share her mother's story with you, and here it is, told in her words:-

'Manikam Sumetra's story was a mixture of tragedy and luck. In 1916, her Brahmin Hindu parents were on a pilgrimage, to a shrine. They stopped at the Holdsworth Memorial Hospital with their ailing baby girl, just a few hours old, and asked the Methodist missionary to look after her until they came back.

Sister Ethel Tomkinson duly took the baby and nursed her to health. Manikam's parents never returned. Whether the baby girl was just one mouth too many to feed, or one of unlucky twins - a common belief in India - or whether something befell them on their journey, nobody will ever know.

Out of the hundreds of orphaned children Sister Ethel nursed, this one was destined for a very different fate. As she was a Brahmin, or member of the priestly caste, the local priests came to the hospital to ask if they could take Manikam to perform Barat Natyam, the devotional South Indian temple dance.

Fearing that this life would also be one of prostitution and with war raging in Europe, Sister Ethel decided to take Manikam to her own family in Wales.

Travelling under the protection of the British Raj, with a green passport signed with her thumb-print as she was too young to write her own name, Manikam became 'Monica' and made the long journey from South India, by ship. She was never formally adopted.

The Tomkinsons of Colwyn Bay were Methodist printers. Monica flourished in an atmosphere of love and security, looked after by Ethel's younger sister Ida, after Ethel returned to South India to carry on her work. The family enjoyed respect and status in their community and little appeared to be made of their adoption of an Indian child. Monica would have been a rare sight in Colwyn Bay, in the twenties, despite her bobbed haircut and Western dress, but she was popular and happy.

My mother loved North Wales and there she remained, the seed securely planted. She had six children, some of whom have since moved away with their families, some of whom remain. None of us can venture out into a Colwyn Bay street without being recognised as Monica's offspring.

Although it is nearly a century since she came to Wales and several decades since she died, the story of the little Indian girl who found her way into the hearts of both a family and a community, lives on through us, her family, who are proud to call North Wales our home.'

Sister Ethel Tomkinson giving an inoculation circa 1916

Sister Ethel lived a very simple life in the Ashram, along with her Indian helpers, often spending a week travelling from village to village in her specially adapted bullock cart, seeking out those in distress. One day Sister Ethel undertook to introduce me to some of the villages and we travelled together in her bullock cart.

The bullock cart used for travel to villages

Bullock cart wheels are large in diameter so that they will travel over deep ruts and potholes in the ground, but they only have iron rings for tyres and there is absolutely no suspension. I found it very uncomfortable being bumped around on the hard wooden floor of the bullock cart as it negotiated the uneven tracks, so I got down and walked part of the way. Ethel took me to meet villagers in their own environment and we spent a fascinating day together. It gave me a very clear idea as to why their lives were so difficult when the rains failed. They were utterly dependent upon their crops for income and survival. I returned to Mysore fired up with enthusiasm to do something to relieve their plight.

At first, when famine relief supplies started arriving in Mysore, the Local Government, Catholic, Protestant, Muslim and Hindu groups were all receiving sacks of rice and corn, tins of milk powder and cheese from different sources. Quite unknown to one another the Local Government mainly distributed to the poor city dwellers, and so did the Muslim and Hindu communities, whereas the Catholics and Protestant Church groups concentrated mainly on the villages in the countryside where they were already working. After a while two problems arose: firstly in the countryside it was discovered that some villages were receiving supplies from two sources, whereas others received none and secondly, within the city the large 7lb tins of cheese sent by one agency were being sold within the market place. Rumour had it that I was making a lot of money from this. It was an uncomfortable position to be in, although I knew that it was not possible because the only commodities I had distributed were milk powder, corn and rice. The cheese supplies offered to us had been held back whilst we worked out the best way to use them.

In order to resolve the confusion of distribution I invited representatives from each distributing group to a meeting in Sawday Lodge. We had a lively discussion about the whole situation and worked out a programme of distribution whereby the whole region affected by drought was covered equably. Everybody felt much happier. We also looked into the difficulty with the cheese and solved this by experimenting and making 'cookie' type biscuits with a mixture of ground corn, ground peanuts, some grated cheese and a little jaggery (unrefined cane sugar). The resulting biscuits tasted quite good although they were rather hard. As the cheese was not received well the donor Agencies were requested to stop sending cheese altogether.

Our local group of 'distributors' continued to meet regularly at Sawday Lodge and we began to look for ways of providing work for the village people to do as a source of cash income that would bolster them against the effect of famine in the future. Cotton spinning, and making doormats and sandals from coconut fibre, were tried, but neither of these activities was popular and did not provide an answer to the problem.

During this time of thinking, one of my ideas was the possible introduction of silkworm rearing in the vicinity of the Kastur and Hadya area as a cottage industry to bring much needed cash into the villages. In Sawday Lodge garden there stood a mature mulberry tree, ideal, because mulberry leaves were the preferred food for silkworms. I obtained some eggs from the Mysore Silk Factory and prepared a tray for the silkworm rearing. Once the worms were hatched the children, with Kalappa's help, began the task of collecting leaves each day. The silkworms munched away happily for a week, then as they grew larger and larger, we realised what a daunting, time consuming task it was to satisfy their hunger.

It was truly amazing the amount of leaves required. When we ran out of mulberry leaves, we felt overwhelmed, thinking that we might have to abandon the project. Luckily, a worker from the Silk Factory came to our rescue and told us that lettuce leaves were a good substitute. The final outcome of our little experiment was not amazing, perhaps due to the amount of handling the caterpillars suffered from the children who could not resist sifting the cool caterpillars through their fingers, but we did achieve a few cocoons. It certainly had kept the family busy and interested for five or six weeks during the long school summer holiday that year, and over the next few years it led to a thriving industry in the villages, bringing in cash so that the villagers did not have to eat their seed grain.

During this time I also got out my typewriter and sent letters to aid organisations explaining the plight of the villagers and the projects that would rescue them out of the cycle of famine. On the one hand they needed to have a way of storing water when the monsoon rain did fall in their area, and, secondly, they needed to have a way to earn cash to pay for food in the years when the monsoons failed or when they suffered drought again simply because the clouds had dropped all their water on the ridge of hills that stood some kilometres distant from the area.

My efforts added to Sister Ethel's pleas for help and together we were able to raise the money to pay for the refurbishment of village rainwater catchment tanks.

A gathering in 1953 for the blessing by Bishop Norman Sargent of the
restored rainwater harvesting tanks in Kastur

1954 was in many ways the time when I could begin to 'spread my wings' beyond the confines of home. Our young family was thriving well and the household running smoothly with the wonderful help given by our servants. Moreover, we had been living in Mysore for three years, well beyond the probationary period when we were only to look, listen and learn. Consequently I was beginning to feel that my contribution to the church's work amongst the community lay in the village work.

The children were for the most part very happy, although the girls tended to argue about John, Rosemary adopting a special claim to him because he was born on her birthday. This often led to friction and, after much thought, Frank and I decided that maybe we would achieve a more harmonious family unit if we had a fourth child, hopefully another boy.

Our first furlough was due to begin at the end of 1956, following a five year term in India, therefore we carefully planned for our fourth baby to arrive during the early part of 1956. Imagine our surprise when Dr Gillespie unexpectedly asked Frank to take his furlough early so that he would be back in Mysore and available well before she retired in 1957. All our carefully laid plans went haywire. At the time of course Dr Gillespie did not know I was pregnant. Ultimately, we did manage to book a passage on the P & O liner 'SS Canton', leaving Bombay on 1st December 1955. Had the passage been any later I would not have been accepted so late in my pregnancy.

Preparing for furlough was no mean task. We were to be away for one year and before departure we had to list, value and pack all personal belongings being left behind in Mysore. Following this, thought had to be given to items essential for the three day and two night long train journey from Mysore to Bombay. Next, our clothing for the sea voyage and stay in England needed sorting out, listing and valuing for insurance purposes, before being packed into suitcases and trunks. This was a long and complicated operation with two adults and three children involved.

The trains in India during the 1950s and 60s were unforgettable. Huge, magnificent steam engines hauled long, long trains of carriages or goods bogeys across the vast tracts of countryside. The passenger train carriages themselves were old, large and sturdily built. Like our houses in India they had barred windows, without glass, and during the course of a journey everything inside became quite dirty from the hot, dry, dust of the countryside, and the smoke from the coal fired engine that constantly blew in through the bars.

It was possible to travel either 'soft' or 'hard' class, the difference being that 'hard' meant exactly that, for there were no bunks to sleep on, just hard unforgiving wooden benches. In 'soft class' compartments the seats were padded and the top bunks could be opened out for sleeping at night. For the journey to Bombay we reserved a six-berth compartment with adjoining toilet and washroom. The toilet was very rudimentary, being just a metal funnel with a wooden seat rim. While you were suspended on this seat the rattle of the wheels along the line was overwhelming and you could see the gravel and sleepers of the railway line whizzing by below you. The children were quite frightened that they might fall down the hole.

I was, and still am, a great list maker and this stood me in good stead when preparing for the long journeys with young children.
I still have the list for one of these journeys. It includes:-

'First Aid Kit
Brush and pan for sweeping carriage floor and toilet area
2 large pottery containers (gujahs) of drinking water.
Drinking mugs
One bedroll for each person, containing night clothes, towel
and toiletries.
Cotton sleeping bag and small pillow for each bedroll.
Clean clothes to wear on reaching our destination.
A bag of Srinivasa's sweets and some fresh fruit.
Games and books to pass the time during the long, hot journey.'

Throughout the journey each of us would wear just one set of old clothes. About an hour before arriving in Bombay we would wash our face and hands, change into clean clothes and make a bundle of our discarded clothing. This bundle, together with any leftover food, the dustpan, brush and gujahs would be given to the coolies as we left the train.

On our journey from Mysore to Bombay in December 1955, early on the day of our departure, many colleagues and friends gathered together at the station. All were there to wish us a safe voyage and a happy furlough. We were weighed down with garlands of flowers, particularly Frank. As the train trundled its way into the station and alongside the platform, its huge engine hissed out great plumes of steam. We were engulfed in terrific noise and clamour, while coolies, wearing distinctive red turbans, rushed to collect luggage on and off the train, all pushing and shouting at the same time in their eagerness to earn a few rupees. When our reserved carriage had been located, our light luggage, plus bedrolls and other paraphernalia, were quickly loaded into it. Then Frank, together with our friends, supervised the coolies in loading the heavier trunks and boxes into the luggage compartment at the rear of the train. Once the coolies had been paid it was more peaceful and we were free to chat until the very last minute. Only when the signalman blew his whistle did we scramble into the carriage, a little tearful at leaving so many good friends, but surrounded by the scent of the jasmine garlands around our necks. In 1955 this was a new experience for the children. The only contact that Rosemary, aged six and a half, Jenny, aged four and a half, and John, two and a half, had ever had with trains was watching the small steam train in Lovedale station when we were on holiday in the Nilgiris.

The train rattled along, from time to time puffing out sooty smoke, that more often than not blew in through the open windows. The train travelled carefully over the bridge that spanned the River Cauvery at Srirangapatna. We could see the old Wellesley Bridge, built after the defeat of Tipu Sultan and still at that time used as the road bridge across the river. The old fort was to our left, and to the right we could see Tipu Sultan's Summer Palace and the surrounding Temples, standing where they had been for more than two hundred and fifty years. We could just imagine the soldiers charging their way across the river to breach the walls of Tipu's fortress in bygone years.

The train travelled on through the countryside between rice fields that had been planted near to the river where irrigation was possible. Further from the river we saw sugar cane growing. Village houses backed onto the railway line and life carried on outdoors, as all over the subcontinent of India. You could see children being bathed at the village tap, bullock carts being mended, women on their doorsteps sifting the stones from shallow baskets of rice, and old men resting in their backyards under the shade of coconut leaf canopies.

The rail track from Mysore to Bangalore was narrow gauge, which meant that we had to change trains to the broader gauge track from Bangalore onwards to Poona. We made sure that the bedrolls were securely buckled and put our other travelling luggage into bags and suitcases. One or two friends would be there waiting on Bangalore station and they helped Frank transfer our luggage from one train to the other, whilst I saw to the children. I think now that the children must have found this whole procedure quite confusing although they always took things in their stride and never complained. By the time we were settled on the train bound for Poona it was dark. The sun always set between 6 and 6.30pm throughout the year. After a welcome drink of water from the gujah, we let down the bunks and spread out the bedrolls in preparation for sleep. Lighting within the carriage was poor, which made it difficult to read. During the hours of darkness we always drew down the wooden slatted shutters, partly for privacy whilst the train stood stationary in a station en route and partly to keep out the chill of the night air. It was rather fun to peep out through the gaps between the slats when the train was standing in a station.

It was not necessary to carry food on these journeys. At all the larger stations you could order a meal, then, upon reaching the next station you paid and a piping hot Indian style meal would be brought to the carriage and the bill paid. There was then plenty of time to enjoy a leisurely meal before handing the empty plates out of the carriage at the next station. Hot coffee, which was the safest thing to drink, was available at every station. We were fortunate in that the children were always content to drink coffee and, of course, we carried a good supply of drinking water in the gujah. The golden rule was never drink water unless it had been boiled.

The countryside that we passed through was all very dry and dusty. In the early morning when passing small villages we would catch a glimpse of people collecting water and taking their morning ablutions at the village well pump or stand tap. Often a light haze hung over the village and small drifts of smoke could be seen rising from the huts, a sign that 'breakfast' was being prepared. This second lap of our journey took us broad gauge from Bangalore to Hubli, and then onward to Poona, where, on the third morning, we changed trains at 6.30am for the final stretch to Bombay.

On Hubli station platform 1955

On the journey in 1955 a representative of the Methodist Church met us in Bombay and took us to spend the night in one of the church hostels. He also kindly undertook the task of transferring our luggage from the train to the dockside and thence onto the ship. The next morning, the 1st of December 1955, we boarded the SS Canton to begin our voyage back to England.

We arrived at Tilbury Docks, London on December 19th on a cold winter's day and this was the time when John piped up about the strange colour of the sun, to the astonishment of the cabby who exclaimed, 'Cor Blimey! Where on earth 'ave you come from?' On a later furlough in 1961, a year of severe drought in Mysore, we had a similar experience when arriving in England. On the train journey from London to Derby the children were amazed at the lush English countryside. They could not help remarking on how green the grass was, and how fat the cows were. The dark-suited commuters cleared their throats and shook their newspapers, peering over the top, obviously wondering where these strange children had come from.

At the time of our arrival in 1955 John was already known for his great thirst for knowledge and his habit of always asking questions. He had been given the name 'Twenty Questions' by some of our Mysore friends, and he lived up to it for the rest of his childhood.

We spent most of 1956 in a furlough house in Bristol. It was a happy year. Our next-door neighbours were most kind and friendly. Frank undertook a certain amount of deputation work in churches around the country as well as catching up-to-date with medical matters, meeting former colleagues and filling a few general practice locum posts. My time was largely spent in running the household and caring for the family.

David was born on 25th February and was treasured and fussed over by one and all. I remember the thrill of purchasing a spin dryer to help cope with wet nappies. It seemed like an absolute miracle.

The family at Belmont Road after David's christening
Also present is the children's cousin Mary

Poor Rosemary was not very happy at school in Bristol and I decided to visit the headmistress in order to discover what the problem was. 'Well,' she said, 'Rosemary keeps telling fairy stories about going to school in a palace and travelling there in a horse driven carriage with a footman standing at the back.' 'Oh dear,' I replied, 'It is all true. Would it be a good idea if I brought along some slides showing Mysore City and the palace, then her classmates could see for themselves where Rosemary had been growing up and going to school?' The Headmistress thought this an excellent idea, it was duly arranged and all ended happily. In fact Rosemary became quite a celebrity.

Chapter Six
Food Relief, Dasara and Music

On the 28th September 1956 we sailed from King Edward Docks, London, on the P&O liner SS Canton. Although we had three young children and seven month old David, this voyage was much more comfortable than previous ones. There were still restrictions regarding access to the deck space, the first class area being locked off from the tourist class, but this did not really interfere with us using the deck for fresh air and a daily constitutional walk around the deck. The deck space was marked out for games, such as deck quoits, and there were plenty of deck chairs available. The tourist class facilities included a small library, a lounge and bar. We had a six-berth cabin for our family, with an adjoining bathroom and toilet.

The P&O liner SS Canton

The ship this time had a nursery where young children could safely stay with an attendant for an hour or so. The children had a different mealtime, but to our relief, Frank and I could take our meals together knowing that all would be well. The days passed quickly, playing deck games, lazing in the warm sunshine on deck and leaning over the railings watching the flying fish and dolphins enjoying swimming alongside the ship.

After ten days at sea and the long train journey to Mysore, we took up residence once again in Sawday Lodge. We were delighted to see Kantharaj, Rukmani and Kalappa still there; after all they had become part of our family. We received a wonderful welcome from colleagues and friends. All the constraints of being newcomers were now gone, we felt much more confident and able to express our opinions on administrative matters. We experienced great joy in consolidating earlier friendships.

Rosemary and Jenny went off to school in Hebron, Jenny for the first time, and settled down happily with their fellow pupils and staff. John remained in Mysore and regularly attended the Palace Nursery School where he greatly enjoyed the company of Prince Srikanth, who was a similar age, there being only ten days between their birthdays. Srikanth possessed a large collection of mechanical toys and John's chief occupation was to take each toy to pieces in order to 'see how it worked'. The trouble was he rarely managed to put the toys back together again. Fortunately, I think Srikanth must also have taken part in this activity because John was never punished and the two boys remained good friends.

David was only eight months old and I was delighted to discover that while I had been in England, two of my friends, Sheila Irani and Caroline Parpia, had also given birth, each having a baby girl born within the same month as David.

The 1956 babies

Initially, Sheila, Caroline and I arranged a playgroup for the three babies and eventually they all attended a Nursery School with other local children. Both John and David joined Hebron School on, or just after, reaching their fifth birthday. This seems extremely young, but from remarks written in our letters at the time, it appears that they felt very aggrieved when the girls and all their friends left Mysore for school each term.

Always ongoing in the background was Frank's extremely heavy workload, due largely to a constant shortage of medical staff. Despite this he mentions in a letter, written in February 1957 to his Aunt Irene, that he was performing tendon transplants on a number of poliomyelitis cases.

This was the time when we made a really extravagant purchase for our home, a refrigerator, powered by paraffin. Although our plan was to use it to store food safely, it was a very timely purchase in another unplanned way. Poliomyelitis was very common in India and just as we acquired our refrigerator we received unexpected word from the High Commission that a supply of polio vaccine had been flown out from the UK with instructions that it was to be given to all missionaries' children immediately. We were told that it was vital that the vaccine be kept refrigerated at all times even when in transit. Had the vaccine arrived a day or two earlier a refrigerator would not have been available. We immediately emptied the precious refrigerator of its domestic contents to make room for the bulk supply of vaccine that arrived from Bangalore. We purchased a wide necked thermos flask into which we packed ice cubes and some ampoules of vaccine. In addition we obtained a goodly supply of sugar cubes. Thus armed, Frank and I set off one morning at 5am and drove to the Nilgiris.

First we visited St.Hilda's and Lushington Schools in Ootacamund, and then we went across to Hebron School in Coonoor, administering vaccine to all the children, not by injection but by drops placed on a lump of sugar. The children greatly enjoyed this unique, rather exciting experience. For us it was a very long day's work. After spending the night in Coonoor we drove back to Mysore on the following day, taking Rosemary and Jenny home for their Easter holiday.

All the time we were conscious of the increasing difficulties being experienced in the villages because of the failure of the monsoons. I wrote my very first circular letter to friends in the UK on 21st August 1957 giving a detailed account of our life as it was then.

Frank's Auntie Irene kept a copy, part of which I have transcribed below:-.

> *'I think some of you already know we have been stationed here in Mysore City since 1951 as Frank is working in the Mission Hospital. The bed capacity is officially 250, but more often than not, we have 270 to 280 patients. It is so difficult to turn patients away when they are desperately ill and have perhaps travelled 40 or 50 miles to get here. Last year, just before we went on furlough, a new Children's Block was opened. This is an entirely separate building with its own dispensary, treatment rooms, private and general wards and all other necessities.*
>
> *Two of the missionary doctors have left us this year. One returned to England and the other is having one year's furlough. This has left the senior medical staff sadly depleted, as Mission House cannot send anyone to replace them. At the moment we have two really senior doctors, my husband and one Indian lady doctor, plus three Senior Registrars and six Junior House Doctors; of these, two are men and the rest ladies. The nursing staff ratio works out as one nurse to three beds. There is an X-Ray plant with a technician and two assistants, (Frank has to do the Bariums and X-ray reporting). We also have a Pathology Department, a Dispensary and a Blood Bank. We pay Rs.5 to any donor. Without this small incentive scarcely anybody will come to give blood. Since paying the Rs.5 quite a regular number of coolies come along each Wednesday; indeed, it has proved necessary to start keeping a photographic record of the donors as some of the coolies, anxious to make easy money, try disguising themselves and come along far too often to give blood!!*
>
> *Two weeks ago we held the Nurses Dedication Service when 17 nurses, who, having passed their final examination during the year, dedicated their lives to the service of the sick. It is a lovely service in which the nurses all light their own candles from the one lamp held by the hospital Matron before processing out of the chapel singing.*
>
> *On September 7th we shall be holding our Annual Hospital Day Sale, which takes the form of a Sale of Work and Thanksgiving Service. Patients and friends of the Hospital, rich and poor alike, always come on this day and*

reckon to give what they can towards the running costs of the hospital, rather like the old Bedford County Hospital sales when it was a Voluntary Hospital. Our grants from the Government and Missionary Society are very small and the greater part of hospital expenses have to be met from fees collected and special efforts such as this sale. All the very poor patients are treated absolutely free and others pay little or much according to their circumstances. Beds and wards range from 4 annas (6d) a day to Rs.20 (£1.10s) a day. A Bible woman and a male evangelist are attached to the hospital and they conduct daily ward prayers and hold Sunday Services regularly, show filmstrips and generally help with the welfare of the patients, sometimes following them up after leaving the hospital if they know that their homes are poor and in difficulty. In addition to this, the nurses and other members of staff have morning prayers at 7am in the hospital chapel and a service at 4.30pm every Sunday.

Bible Study groups are organised amongst the nurses and a half-hour hymn singing session on Sunday evenings. (These were held in our house and often lasted for about an hour. They sang very heartily and thoroughly enjoyed themselves.)

Women's Outpatient sessions take place every morning, also Children's Outpatients. Men have to come when women are not present, so the men's outpatient sessions are held on three evenings a week at 4pm. There are four, often five, operating sessions each week, where they do almost any operation, which needs doing. Frank gets a much greater variety of experience than he could obtain in England and the Theatre here is a very up-to-date one. This makes it all sound so similar to an English hospital but there are times when we feel like running away from it all. The slightest easing off on the part of the senior members of staff would mean a slackening of the efficiency of the whole hospital. Dirty drains, insufficient care over sterilizing on the wards and a whole lot of little things. This, I think, gives a fair view of the hospital work and I will now enlarge a little on the village work.

A few months ago I took over the job of distributing free gift supplies of milk powder and other commodities, which are received from the National Christian Council of India. This has led me to a more thorough investigation of conditions in and around Mysore City than I had previously made, and when you read this short account it may make you feel rather as I did when, a few months ago, I read in the daily paper that workers in England were striking for yet more money. If only they could realise how wonderfully rich they all are compared to ¾ of the population here in India they might stop their constant cry for more and more wages! I scarcely know where to begin, but I think it is easier to enumerate the agencies to which I give the foodstuffs, and then enlarge upon the work done.

In the City itself we supply two Muslim Orphanages, both housing about 75 children, two Hindu Orphanages and two Christian Boarding Schools with approximately the same number of inmates. There is also a Boarding School for deaf and blind boys, where the boys are taught basketry and other work, with about 120 residents. At the Holdsworth Memorial Hospital, in addition to the in-patient needs, a whole crowd of dirty, ragged, underfed children attend every morning with their tin cans and are given ½ pint of milk to drink.

Outside the City we supply three or four missionaries who work amongst the villages thirty to forty miles away, and it is the plight of these villagers that is most heartrending. Most of them come from the outcaste section of the community (Dalits), amongst them some Christians, some Hindus and some Muslims. Not so many years ago each village had its so called 'Headman', who owned all the land in his area, and the outcastes worked the land for him and in return received just enough food or money to live on. Now, this practice is largely disappearing, but there are still instances where a family has become badly in debt. They go to the 'headman' to ask for a loan to pay off this debt, he agrees to lend the necessary money on condition that the man to whom he is lending the money will send one of his children to work for him without payment until such time as the original debt is paid. This means that, as the poor villager has no hope of ever being able to pay back the loan, his child will virtually become a slave. Some of our Christians still come to us and say they want help in repaying an old loan so that they can free their son or daughter. Luckily this sort of thing is dying out and we hope that soon it will be gone altogether. Now a goodly number of the villagers own their own small plot of land and rely on the harvest to keep themselves and their families. The greatest tragedy is that for the past five years the rains have failed, just a few showers and that is all. The existence of these people depends entirely upon their crops and if the rains fail . . .what then?

For the most part they live in small huts made of mud bricks and with a roof made from dried palm leaves. The whole family lives, eats and sleeps in this hut, plus any animals and chickens that they possess. At the moment they are fortunate if they have a good meal once in three days, for the rest they may eat a few peanuts or odd berries and scraps of food from the surrounding jungle. Some villages house ten families, others one hundred. Each village is divided from the other by 5 to 10 miles of scrub jungle. The people travel very little as it means a lonely walk through the jungle paths where tiger, panther, wild elephant and other animals live.

The Indian Government is doing a lot in the way of irrigation schemes and welfare work to help these people, but it will take many, many years before all are reached.

The local churches in Mysore raised a large sum of money and with this some rice and ragi seed was purchased. At the first sign of the rains beginning the villagers planted their seeds which sprang up during the first three or four weeks, then the rains failed and their crops have all but withered away - and this after five years of famine. One lady worker has started a spinning school as another means of livelihood and now a good number of the women are spinning cotton in their homes and by this means can earn one rupee per day (1s.6d.) This scheme has worked so well that they are now thinking of starting rope making for the men so that, when there is no work on the land, they at *least have a chance to earn a small amount of money.*

Last Friday I went to visit a co-operative farm 28 miles to the other side of Mysore. There they have good crops coming on, but nevertheless a sad story to tell. Two years ago the Government gave some jungle land to an Association to enable them to start a co-operative farming scheme. They collected some Tyote (farmers) who had no land and no home and gave them this land to clear and cultivate. They have built their own mud dwellings altogether on a mound in the centre of the cultivated land and looking at it last week I found it hard to realise that two years ago all the rice fields which I saw had been wild jungle. Now, they have a good crop coming on and the hardest of the work is done, indeed, they have 40 acres of land under cultivation. A few weeks ago they were informed that they have to give up this land, without compensation or payment of any kind, as it is to be given to some 'political sufferers'. This term 'political sufferers' refers to men who perhaps have lost some of their education through imprisonment during the 1947 changeover of government. Is it not heart-breaking even to think of the plight of these farmers who have put much labour, and some money, into the cultivation of the area? Now they will be left homeless and moneyless, and most likely the 'political sufferer' who is to get the land is already much better off than the farmers.

This gives you some idea of the things that are going on here. The Indian Government are doing a wonderful job with their Five Year Plans and other projects, but there are plenty of people around who are not honest or fair with their fellow men and it will be a long time before the condition of the country as a whole can be improved.

To end on a lighter note, Rosemary and Jennifer have just spent a happy ten-day holiday with us and returned to school last Tuesday. John and David are still with us at home. They provide plenty of fun. They decided the other day that Rosemary and John would both be doctors and Jenny would be a nurse when they grow up, ending the conversation with 'then there'll be three Toveys in one hospital'. I asked what David would be and they decided he might be a Ward Boy. At the moment he looks more like a rugby player.
Our greetings and best wishes to you all,
Winnie.'

Although we often felt overwhelmed with situations beyond our control, such as monsoon failure and the consequent famine, something always seemed to occur to raise our spirits again. We were living in a world of great contrasts. One day working in a desperately poor village, the next visiting a relatively rich businessman. For example, just after I had written the above circular letter that describes the hardships in the area, all the large buildings along the main streets of the City were being given a fresh coat of whitewash in preparation for the Dasara Festival held at the end of September or early October, with its ten days of lavish ceremonies in and around the Palace.

At Dasara time our house was always full to the brim with friends and colleagues from Bangalore and the surrounding area, who took leave from work and came to stay with us in order to witness some of the pageantry. Thousands of people would crowd into the city, filling every hotel, every home and spilling out on to the streets. The shops and market place bustled with trade and a huge Trade Exhibition was set up not far from the Palace, attended by merchants who brought goods from all over the country. A very fascinating day or two could be spent wandering around looking at the huge variety of wares being displayed and sold from hundreds of stalls.

Where five years earlier we had stood as strangers at the gate of the Palace, we were now part of the occasion. This year I had been invited to join the Maharani in her quarters from which we could view the ceremonies. The great day came and I dressed in the evening gown that had travelled with me from England. It was a very elegant, long, sleeveless creation in white cotton pique, with a fitted sleeveless top and a frill that swept down its length. I offset it with a gorgeous sky blue Mysore silk shawl. As the sun lowered and the parakeets racketed in the trees making their evening roost, Frank and I set off on our way to the Palace. Frank was driving in our car and after setting me down at the appropriate entrance he parked the car and joined the throng of people in the courtyard. Crowds already lined the city streets and the palace courtyard. Palace officials, priests and servants, all dressed in immaculate uniforms and colourful robes and shawls, were congregated around the front of the palace beneath the large Durbar Hall roof that overhung the entrance. In the centre of the Durbar Hall a magnificent, jewel encrusted, golden throne stood on a raised dais, and ranged on either side were rows of plush chairs on which the 'Durbarees' would sit.

Palace dignitaries in the Durbar Hall during Dasara

I was ushered up to the gallery that surrounded three sides of the Durbar Hall. Here the women of the royal house, the Maharani, the Princesses Gayathri and Minakshi, who were old enough to enjoy the atmosphere, and other female members of the

81

family, their friends and associates were gathered. There was a wooden lattice screen protecting us from the gaze of others in the Durbar Hall and we were able to watch the scene below by peeping through chinks in the latticework.

Outside in the city, the elephants and horses that belonged to the royal household were brought through the crowded streets, eventually arriving at the main entrance gate to the palace. They processed in order through the archway and straight down the main driveway, coming to rest just in front of the Durbar Hall. Their progress was accompanied by the beating drums and gongs, along with people shouting and cheering, a general mayhem. When he was ready, His Highness the Maharaja would enter the Hall and sit upon his throne. Even though he was not a tall man, dressed in his cloth of gold and wearing the gold turban upon his head (which we were told weighed 7 lbs) he was a most imposing figure.

Every evening throughout Dasara, eighty to a hundred Durbarees would pass before His Highness, each offering a token gift in homage. I was told that originally Durbarees were those who lived on the palace land and, at harvest time, they would offer part of their harvest to the Maharaja.

Our dear friend Sydney Watsa (Kamala's brother) in his Durbar clothes

Once the Durbarees' duties were finished the entertainment started on a temporary stage set up in front of the Durbar Hall. According to Hindu mythology the festival celebrates and commemorates the victory of Goddess Chamundeshwari, who slayed the demon Mahishasura, symbolizing the triumph of good over evil. The story would be enacted and then wrestlers and jugglers would perform in the courtyard below (some said to distract the evil spirits from the good people). The palace remained illuminated until about 10 o'clock after which the crowd gradually dispersed.

During the ten day festival many other special events took place at various times of the day and on the different days. On the eighth day was 'Ayuda Puja' when everyone worshipped the 'tools of their trade', which meant that the tools were not to be worked on that day.

82

The ceremonial bull on the day of Ayuda Puja

During the afternoon parade the Maharaja stood in front of the Durbar Hall and threw flowers and grains, as symbols of thanks and blessings, on his Emblems of State, his carriages, the State horse, sacred bullock and State Elephant.

The Maharaja salutes his people

His fleet of cars, dominated by the vintage Rolls Royces, were decorated with flowers and pushed by hand in front of him. The servants could work hard pushing but the 'tools of trade' had a day of rest and ceremony!

Some of the Maharaja's Rolls Royce cars on the day of Ayuda Puja

On the ninth day the Maharaja came out of the palace and made his way round the large palace courtyard, which was surrounded by temples. For the first half of this journey he was mounted on his white State Horse and surrounded by retainers acclaiming his distinctions. On the second half he was carried in the golden State Palanquin. This was a very colourful occasion when a large number of people were granted permission to stand in the courtyard and witness and take photographs of the ceremony at very close range.

Finally, on the afternoon of the tenth day, the huge Dasara procession took place. We went out to watch the parade whenever we could and never tired of the magnificent scene.

The Maharaja climbs into the golden howdah for the Dasara parade

To be particular, the Maharaja of Mysore was actually a 'Rajpramukh' from the time of the 1950 Constitution of the Indian Republic. This meant that he remained as the constitutional head of the State of Mysore and to all effect he continued to be recognised as the Maharaja. He was greatly respected and held official duties as Governor of Mysore State (now 'Karnataka') until 1964, and then as Governor of Madras State (now 'Tamil Nadu') until 1966. Although Indira Gandhi, among others, lobbied to abolish the Privy Purse in the mid 1960s, it was only once her government came into power in 1971 that this actually happened. Without the support of a Privy Purse the Maharaja of Mysore could no longer afford the Palace cavalry, the elephants, the horses, the various palace buildings in the city and certainly not the lavish Dasara celebrations. The dissolving of the royal household was very hard for the Maharaja to bear. His staff, his well-bred horses and his ceremonial elephants had to be found new employers and owners, which was not easy, for few could afford them. In 1974, aged 55, Maharaja Jayachamaraja Wodeyar Bahadur, the 25th and last Maharaja of Mysore, sadly died. However Dasara was recognised as so important to the tourism industry of Mysore that it has survived and although watered down from the old days, the grand parade is still held every year in September or October.

During our time in Mysore the Maharaja played an important role as Governor. He was greatly respected for his good judgement and his concern for the people of Mysore. He was also a musicologist and for two or three years during the time that his young family and ours were both at the palace nursery school he requested their teacher to arrange a Christmas concert. A room in the palace would be prepared and a temporary stage built and draped with richly dyed damask curtains. The princesses would perform one or two Indian dances and a short drama. This was then followed by a short nativity play and two or three Christmas carols for which I played the piano accompaniment, occasionally singing a solo by request. When the actual concert day arrived about thirty invited guests would be seated on gilded chairs before the stage. The assembled company, as would the extended family at a school concert, politely listened to our light entertainment. The Maharaja was at his most relaxed at these occasions and once when John, who was a toddler at the time, became restive he simply lifted him onto his knee for the remainder of the performance. John was a little astonished at this and stayed completely still and quiet. I only later realised that in 1949, at around the time when Rosemary was born in Yunnan in China amidst the dangers of the communist uprising, Maharaja Jayachamraja Wodeyar, as the first President of the Philharmonia Concert Society, London, was supporting the first concerts ever to be held in the Royal Albert Hall, with music conducted by Sir Adrian Boult and played by Yehudi Menuhin.

These occasional concerts only served to remind me how greatly I missed performance music during the first few years in Mysore. I had been a keen member of a musical group in my hometown of Bedford, and in China I played a portable organ for religious services and pleasure. The organ had been a wedding present, which we had transported with some difficulty all the way to Chaotung. When we evacuated in 1949 sadly we had to leave it there with nearly all our belongings.

After 1956 and during the early part of our second tour of service in India, there were a number of quite gifted singers among our missionary colleagues and we would occasionally spend a social evening together. After dinner we would gather round the piano and thoroughly enjoy ourselves singing 'On Ilkley Moor bath-at', or Negro Spirituals, hymns and carols; almost anything we could lay our hands on.

Fortunately, I had taken a good supply of music to Mysore, some books of classical piano pieces and music suitable for use as organ voluntaries, as well as some songbooks. Imagine my joy when a colleague, about to retire from the field, asked if I would be interested in purchasing his piano. He said that the strikers would require re-felting and that this work could only be carried out in Bangalore. We arranged transport for the piano to Bangalore and within a month or so it arrived back in Mysore, safe and sound, to become my most treasured possession throughout our stay in India.

To return to our singing group, 1958 we were invited to join the Bangalore YMCA Choir in singing Parts II and III of Handel's 'Messiah' to be broadcast by All India Radio. This was not recorded. It went out live and I sang the soprano solo, 'I know that my Redeemer liveth.' The programme went out over the airwaves fairly late in the evening and at that time Rosemary and Jenny were away in Coonoor at Hebron School. They were allowed to stay awake late and taken to the staff room to listen to the broadcast. We were told that Rosemary was so intrigued at hearing my voice that she searched all round the radio saying, 'Where's Mummy?'

We did possess a record player, which ran on car batteries until, one day, we returned to the house to find that burglars had stolen both the record player and the batteries. This made the piano even more important to us because as a family we spent many happy hours making our own entertainment, there being no radio in our house or television available.

When June 1958 arrived, John joined the girls at Hebron School. He had been so miserable when left behind in Mysore every time the girls went off to school that we relented and let him go too, just like the girls, starting at the tender age of five.

It was also at this time that we moved from Sawday Lodge to the 'Hospital House' (originally called the 'European Doctor's House'), which was just across the road from the hospital.

In so many ways it proved to be a wonderful move and beneficial for us all. Frank was able to join us for lunch and whenever possible he tried to get home just before the children went to bed. The only downside to this move was leaving our faithful household servants behind in Sawday Lodge. However, we found Lazarus our new cook, Marjorie, Lazarus' wife and ayah for David, and Devaputra (Putrappa) the mali, who was no longer needed at Government House Road bungalow, equally friendly and loyal. At the Hospital House Lazarus and Marjorie lived in the godowns at the back of the compound with their son Charlie and daughter Rakini.

Rakini and Marjiemma

Putrappa continued living at the Government House Road bungalow, which was within a reasonable walking distance from our compound. Rakini became a playmate for David, and Charlie and John enjoyed each other's company during the school holidays. One holiday time our beloved Siamese cat went missing and we put up a small reward for anyone who could find her. Charlie scoured the surrounding area for her and after a couple of days of diligent searching amongst the alleyways he came home triumphant, having noticed a squirming shape in a sack that someone was carrying. Charlie proudly spent his reward on some brand new flip-flops.

The Hospital House

Chapter Seven
Life in the Hospital House

By the time we moved to the Hospital House in 1958, apart from Hilda Baker, the Sister Tutor, Frank was the only missionary member of staff. The hospital now had an Indian Medical Superintendent, Dr Angeline (Angie) Stephen, and she, supported by the Board of Management, was fully in charge of the hospital.

The house stood (and still stands) on a very busy crossroad, flanked by the hospital on one side and the junior doctors' accommodation on the other. It was quite near the main city shopping area and also the railway station, which meant that a film of sooty dust fell everywhere blackening the soles of our feet. The shunting of steam engines, later joined by diesel engines, reached our ears at night. We once made a tape recording of the sounds through the night, but alas this was lost. However, I will attempt a description. The windows had no glass and the shutters were never shut because the weather was always warm, so during the night every sound could be heard.

The sun set between 6 and 6.30pm throughout the year and by 7 o'clock it was dark, there being no 'twilight' as we know it in England. When the birds had gone to roost and the cicadas had stopped their shrill burring, gradually the city noises would subside. However, we did not have much peace for through the darkest hours of the night a watchman would walk around the streets on the lookout for possible intruders and whenever he passed a house he would bang his stick loudly on the garden gate and on the nearest lamp post. During Ramadan he would bang extra vigorously at 5am to awaken the Muslim people, who lived in the streets surrounding the hospital, to break their fast before daybreak. I was never sure whether the watchman's noisy presence made me feel safer or more alarmed, because I could not see that any self-respecting burglar would be caught red-handed when he had such good warning of the night-watchman's approach from several compounds away. In the early hours the city could be very quiet but at about 4.30am the racketing of about twenty bullock carts could be heard as they hurried past our house on their way from the Octroi post at the city entrance where the Municipal Tax was collected. Following on their heels would come the tongas racing to the Railway Station to await the arrival of the early passenger train from Bangalore. As daylight broke, the evocative sound of the muezzin calling the Muslims to prayer would float across the air from the nearby mosque. Finally, at 6am the Bangalore train could be heard, hissing and puffing its way into the station. We called this particular train 'The Bangalore Flyer' because it left Bangalore in the late evening and took its time, to arrive in Mysore at six o'clock the following morning, very convenient for passengers who could spend the night sleeping. The distance between the two cities is about 100 miles.

With the passage of time we became oblivious to all these extraneous sounds and usually had a good night's sleep and we did not mind being woken early as the working day began in the cool of the morning. By the time the 'Bangalore Flyer' had pulled into the station, Frank and I would be wide awake savouring a morning cup of tea, listening to the birds singing as they perched in the neem tree which stood just outside our bedroom window. The sounds of the city waking up drifted into the house. Another day had begun.

Despite being situated in such a busy area, the garden and its surrounding trees attracted a lot of wildlife. There was a time when day after day I would discover my hairpins, combs and face powder scattered around on the floor upstairs. I scolded the children about this but they declared it was none of their doing. I was not convinced about this and It remained a mystery until one day, as Lazarus walked along by the side of the house on his return from shopping, an ink bottle flew through the air and hit him very sharply on the head. He looked up to see an impudent monkey jumping from an upstairs window into the branches of the jacaranda tree that grew beside the house. Poor Lazarus rubbed his bruised head and set about finding a solution to the antics of the mischievous monkeys. He and Devaputra came up with an ingenious plan. They purchased some firecrackers and tied them onto the end of a long bamboo pole. Then they waited by the window upstairs until the monkeys had settled themselves to sit in the tree. Very quietly they stood by our bedroom window and with the minimum of movement lit the fuses of the firecrackers, then quickly Devaputra thrust the pole right out into the middle of the branches. The explosions made the poor monkeys leap from the branches in panic. Squealing and shouting in fear, they beat a hasty retreat, never to return.

Chipmunks could also be real pests if they managed to enter the house, as they loved to chew at cushions or curtains. Outside they were a lot of fun to watch. Their stripy bodies and tails merged well with the trees until they leapt about or gave away their position with their penetrating chirping call.

At night and sometimes during the day the geckos came out. They were delightful to watch. They would emerge during the evening and spend their time on the house walls and ceilings, alternately sitting very still watching for their next meal and scuttling fast across the whitewashed surface to catch mosquitoes and other insects on their sticky tongues. It was always fascinating to watch them running upside-down across the ceiling, somehow held there on the flaky surface by their padded feet. Sometimes they would fall, and if you were superstitious you would be wise to note where they fell, because this could foretell your future.

When the sun set in the evening, large flocks of green parakeets would descend upon the neem tree. I am not sure whether it was actually the neem fruit that attracted them, but I do know that the tree is meant to have many healing properties. When the children had measles, one after the other, Marjorie picked some neem leaves and spread them under the bed sheet. The Indian people also used neem twigs to clean their teeth. The sharp end of a twig made a good toothpick and the chewed end a good brush.

Not all of the creatures in the compound were benign. We once found baby cobras in the downstairs bathroom. They must have come in through the drain hole. Cockroaches were a constant problem, although our cat kept them at bay to some extent. Once an Indian doctor who was sharing the house with us got a surprise when he drained a coffee pot and found a large cockroach in the coffee grounds.

Poor Lazarus could not explain how it had got in there. The doctor took to his bed for a couple of days. I suppose he would have not felt so bad if he had not learnt through his medical training about the many germs that cockroaches can carry.

The advantages gained by our move to the Hospital House were amazing. I became part of the hospital team and fellowship, and everyone in the family frequently visited the wards and talked to patients and staff. Sometimes the older children during their school holiday time ran urgent messages to Frank when he was in the operating theatre.

The hospital compound was not far from the centre of Mysore City and it was possible to walk from the house straight along the road and be in the midst of the busy city streets and market within ten minutes. Away from the house in the opposite direction was the maidan, an open stretch of land, ideal for ball games or walking the dog.

Usually I left the food shopping to Lazarus and, after discussing the needs of the day he would go off on his bicycle or in a tonga with the sacking 'gunny' bag rolled and tucked under his arm. It was best to let him bargain in the market because I could not get fair prices from the traders. I sometimes went to market with the children to enjoy the colour but usually I would do the shopping for items that were only available in the main shops.

Mysore had nearly all the shops you could wish for in the main shopping area along Sayajirao Road. There we found Bata's Shoe Shop, Raghulal's Pharmacy and Mr. Krishnaswami's stationery shop from which we purchased school exercise books and all our other stationery requirements. Another favourite shop was Srinivasa Stores, for they carried a good stock of European type of commodities such as bar soaps, like 'Lux' and 'Palmolive', powder, including 'Johnson's Baby Powder', as well as a lovely selection of sweets and biscuits, ideal for school tuck boxes. If I ever asked for something that they did not have they would never say that it was not in stock. Instead they would politely ask me to wait and after ten minutes the item would be there. It was never explained how this happened but I knew that a small boy would be sent out the back to run up the road, purchase the item from another shop and bring it back to be served at Srinivasa's counter.

I shall never forget the time when in 1958 India became 'metric' almost overnight. Weights, measures and currency changed all at the same time. This in itself was not too great a problem, but I do remember buying one kilo of sweets for each school tuck box instead of one lb each! None of the children objected.

Along the curbsides of the wide pavements of Sayajirao Road numerous small stalls were set up by enterprising individuals. Often a small child was left to watch over the merchandise. The little stalls sold brilliantly coloured glass bangles, hair ribbons, combs and hair slides. Some sold long lengths of braided, human hair, hung from the roof of the stall. Ladies bought these to enhance the size of their plaited hair. Others displayed knick-knacks, from coloured glass marbles, penknives, wooden spinning tops and fountain pens to leather belts for boys and tiny dolls for girls. Most of the toys were very cheap and made from brightly coloured plastic.

Sometimes we visited the Silk Emporium where customers would be seated by the counter and given a complimentary cup of coffee while they were shown bolts of fabulous material. At the Emporium you could not only buy the material, but you could also order a garment, be it choli, salwar kameez or shirt, and be measured for size. Within twenty-four hours the garment would be delivered to your home.

Another shop I must just mention was the 'Bombay Indira Bhavan' famous for its masala dosai. These crispy savoury pancakes, eaten with potato aloo and coconut chutney, were so delicious that we occasionally went there for a meal.

There were very few cars in Mysore during our first few years, so we mostly walked or cycled. Tongas, the small horse drawn carriages, were also for hire but they had their drawbacks because often the tonga wallahs, anxious to impress, would whip their poor little horses into a frenzied gallop, sending the tonga charging along the road with passengers clinging on for dear life. The alternative was riding sedately in a cycle rickshaw, gliding quietly along the road, but I did not like to see the poor cycle wallah having to work so hard. One great blessing was the fact that we always felt safe and were treated with the utmost respect and courtesy wherever we went.

When Christmas 1958 arrived, it was especially exciting for the children because it was our first Christmas spent close to the hospital. We were awakened at four o'clock on Christmas day morning by the glorious sound of the hospital nurses singing carols. They had done the rounds of the hospital staff houses and ended on our doorstep to wish us a Happy Christmas. As soon as they had gone the children dashed back upstairs to find their Christmas presents in clean pillowslips at the bottom of their beds. They spent an exciting hour before breakfast unwrapping their presents. I had to dash off to St. Bartholomew's Church to play the organ for the eight o'clock service, and Frank and the children followed a little later. When we got back home Lazarus, Marjorie and Devaputra and their family joined us for the traditional curry and rice meal together. We then gave them their presents before taking a short rest and going over to the hospital for the nurses' party.

At the end of Christmas Day 1958 we were exhausted but happy. We went to bed and slept the night through. In the morning Lazarus woke us without a cup of tea. He was in a state of shock. He had just opened up the house and discovered that during the night some burglars had wreaked havoc downstairs. We hurried down to assess the damage. Our cutlery had been stolen and Frank's office, adjacent to the dining room, had been ransacked. A huge quantity of dress and shirt material, which I had bought in Bangalore two days earlier, had all been stolen. This was awaiting a visit from the tailor, who was to start work immediately after the holiday period. Fortunately we did not keep money in the office, but every drawer and cupboard had been emptied and their contents strewn all over the floor. All our precious Christmas presents were stolen, which was especially disappointing for the children, who were looking forward to using their new torches and penknives. We felt so sorry for them. None of us had heard a sound during the night. This was our first burglary and it did leave us feeling very vulnerable. A couple of years later we were burgled again but did not suffer such a great loss.

With three of the children away at school during term time Marjorie, the ayah, was free to look after David and I was able to become more involved in the leprosy work. Three mornings a week were spent giving physiotherapy to leprosy patients and others in the hospital. I also kept an eye on Krishnappa, the shoemaker, who worked in a godown behind our house, and drove the team to the fortnightly clinic at T Narsipur. At the clinic I took notes on the patients who were being examined by the doctor in order to decide on their need for possible surgery or special shoes.

One time consuming task was keeping records for both the famine relief programme and leprosy work which entailed a good deal of correspondence appealing for financial support. Regularly playing the organ for all church services and special occasions was also very important. The children were very tolerant about my continual busyness but, always during holiday times, I endeavoured to be available for them during the daytime and made a point of reading them a bedtime story before tucking them into bed at 7pm. As they grew older bedtime remained at 7pm with no restriction about 'lights-out' time. In this way they were able to spend a quiet hour on their own which was greatly appreciated because, in such a busy household with its varied and changing adult 'visitors', they had a chance to relax together. Frequently I would stay up into the small hours of the night dealing with correspondence and accounts.

I was thankful for the early experience I had in my first job in Bedford, when aged sixteen I worked for a timber merchant, handling their orders and customers' accounts. It helped me enormously in coping with both the hospital project accounts and our personal affairs. To give an idea of our household expenditure I have the following summary, which we sent to Frank's father in 1958 after he enquired about our finances.

Wages for Cook, Ayah and Mali … … … Rs 180		Monthly stipend
Food for household … … … … … …	300	received
Electricity and charcoal … … … … …	35	Rs 700
Dhobi … … … … … … … … … … …	20	
School bills – extras … … … … … …	50	
TOTAL … Rs 585		
Balance for clothing, travel, books etc		
+ unexpected non-paying guests … Rs 115		

Missionary wives were not allowed to undertake paid employment so it was not possible to supplement income. We were, by Indian standards, comparatively rich and I willingly gave of my time and energy, but there were times when the shortage of finances could be embarrassing. On one occasion, when our monthly salary cheque was late arriving at the bank, I had to explain to Augustine and Mary that we could not pay them until the money came. I was almost in tears, but dear Mary stroked my back and said, 'Oh Ma, not to worry. I will go and say a prayer and light a candle for you this afternoon. Something will turn up.' Mary was a devout Catholic. Sure enough, later in the day, a grateful patient came to our door carrying a basketful of oranges, a gift of thanks. 'There you are Ma,' said Mary, 'I told you God will take care of us all.'

Mary and Augustine worked as our ayah and cook from 1962 to 1966

I mentioned above that we had many visitors. Among them were sometimes the relatives of patients or patients, such as planters, who had travelled a distance for diagnostic tests and check ups. The hospital's patients ranged from the poorest of the poor to the Maharaja and members of his family, from film stars, tea and coffee planters, retired army officers, missionaries and school teachers, to young people wandering around the world before settling down to work or career. Some came and went again without trace but over the years many have remained lifelong friends.

Our house became known as 'Piccadilly Circus'. Managers of Tea Estates in the Nilgiris and Coffee Estates in Coorg and their wives and families, retired Army Officers, business people and other travellers from time to time needed hospital treatment and advice. As I have mentioned earlier, there was at that time just one very grand hotel in the city catering for foreigners and this was very expensive. Relatives of patients, ladies-in-waiting (living far away from the city and awaiting the birth of a baby), travellers brought to the door by coolies and some elderly, retired gentlefolk, all were drawn to our house. This came about because we were the last missionary family living in the city in a position to offer them board and lodging. Of course, we made no charge for this but often people would make a contribution towards the household expenses. In many ways it was good for our family as they made lots of friends, of all ages, who came from differing walks of life.

I remember one old gentleman in particular. He used to attend hospital regularly every four months for blood tests and treatment and he always travelled in an ancient jeep, accompanied by his manservant, his dog and a rifle. All slept together in one room and spent the rest of the time in and around the house. John and David were particularly intrigued with the gun and loved listening to his stories about hunting for man-eating tigers in the jungle. At one time, in the not too distant past, tigers had been known to attack and kill people who lived in the villages near the jungle region. Many elderly people had spent a lifetime working in India and were without relatives in the country. They always seemed happy to come and join in with our family life and as a result we too gained many good friends.

We also received some invitations from our houseguests to go and stay with them for a break. The demands of work meant that we could rarely accept their offers, but when we did we were richly rewarded with experiences that we would never have imagined happening to us.

The kind Colonel invited us to his home in the Nilgiris. 'You two are working too hard,' he said. 'You must come and stay with me for a week. No one will be able to find you and you can have a really good rest.' After a little hesitation we accepted his invitation and made arrangements to have some time off.

His bungalow was full of hunting trophies; tiger and panther skins, elephant tusks, and deer heads mounted on wall plaques. He introduced us to the joys of fishing for trout, lending us his rods and a good selection of flies. Early in the morning he sent us off with his servant, who guided us to a mountain stream where he thought we would find trout. It was such a relief to be away from our busy work schedule, and the heat and dust of Mysore. We stood at the water's edge lazily casting our flies and occasionally we were rewarded with a catch.

One day we were caught in a heavy rainstorm and returned to the bungalow drenched and cold. 'Off you go, and have a hot bath,' said the Colonel. After changing into dry clothes we joined him in front of a blazing log fire and he served us rum punches, entertaining us with stories of big game hunting for man-eating tigers, rogue elephants and the like. We wondered what our missionary friends would have said if they had seen us, or indeed Frank's father, who was a strict teetotal Methodist of the old school!

We made other visits to the Nilgiris for Frank to attend to medical matters on some of the tea estates, where he was a voluntary advisor on the health of the tea pickers and their families. We were always made most welcome by the planters and sometimes stayed overnight before returning to the plains.

On one visit to Prospect Estate we went to see a fire walking ceremony. Fire walking is a Hindu custom and the participants, all men, had prepared for the rite by adhering to vows of abstinence, spending one month with no quarrelling, no alcohol or other indulgences. On the morning of the ceremony we followed a noisy crowd who escorted the firewalkers to the river to wash their feet. After this they walked back with bare feet to dance in a fanatic frenzy around a metre wide and ten metre long strip of red-hot charcoal. After the dance, each man in turn, walked in an almost trance-like state, right along the hot coals with bare feet. After the walk not one of them had burns, yet we, sitting about five metres away from the coals, had found the heat unbearable.

Returning to the subject of visitors to the Hospital House, for some years, because hospital staff accommodation was in short supply, any single doctors who came to work at the hospital would also live with us. Our children took this all in their stride and just included another auntie or two into the family circle. I remember when Dr Margaret Pierce was staying and I overheard her remark to a friend, 'Life is always interesting in this house. For instance, when reaching for my bedside lamp in the middle of the night, I often find a box or tin there instead. One of the children will have placed a surprise for me. The other day it was a large beetle in a tin and one day I found a cicada in a matchbox!' I think these must have been offerings from David, who loved collecting anything that moved.

In India there is a lovely custom whereby children always address their parents' friends as 'Uncle' and 'Auntie', rather than the formal 'Mr' and 'Mrs'. This being so, our family had, and still have, quite a large extended family.

Before leaving this period, I must tell of the visit of a very important person. Early in 1959 an invitation card came by post from the British High Commissioner. The envelope was marked with an embossed seal. We opened it with a tremor of excitement to find an invitation for Frank and me to attend an evening reception for His Highness the Duke of Edinburgh to be held on the 1st February 1959 in the Bangalore Club. As you can imagine we felt very honoured. It was an occasion for which I needed to wear my treasured possession - the lovely white evening gown that I bought in England for the original sea voyage to India and subsequently wore when attending a Durbar by kind invitation of the Maharani. All the men wore their dress suits. Frank's had been purchased for the sea journey and, in fact, he was wearing the same suit for special occasions until the 1990's when we really decided that the double breasted jacket was well and truly out of fashion.

We travelled to Bangalore in our own 'Standard 10' car and stayed overnight in a house on the CSI Mission Compound. Earlier in the day Frank had stood in line with others on the airstrip forming a reception party for the Duke. He tells how the 'plane landed and it seemed an age whilst waiting for the Duke to alight. As they waited, the silhouette of a man could be seen in the cockpit changing a jacket and combing his hair. It turned out to be the Duke, who had piloted the 'plane himself.

Meeting the Duke of Edinburgh at the February 1st reception in Bangalore

Frank also remembers an incident that took place during the evening reception. The Duke was being introduced to British nationals from Bangalore and further afield within the State of Mysore. He heard a planter from Coorg being introduced as 'Doctor' to the Duke. The aforesaid planter had to admit that he was not the doctor but his wife. Whereupon the Duke immediately remarked, 'Don't worry, I have the same problem.'

Two years later, Frank was once again invited to Bangalore, this time to join a group of people chosen to greet Her Majesty Queen Elizabeth II on her arrival at the airport on Monday 20th February 1961. When the day came I was outside the airport on the street with David and we were mingling with the city crowd. We met a friend who said, 'You're being presented this evening'. For some unknown reason my invitation had not arrived in the post. At first I could not take it in. (Earlier in the month we had received an invitation from the Deputy British High Commissioner to attend a reception in Madras, which was subsequently cancelled).

The Maharaja of Mysore was at that time Governor of Mysore State and we were able to find an official in Bangalore who confirmed that it was indeed true, I really was to be presented to the Queen by the Maharaja that evening at a reception to be held in his Bangalore Palace. Suddenly I had to think about my attire for this big event. Fortunately, as we had attended a friend's wedding in Bangalore on the previous day, I did have a suitable dress with me, only the dress however, no stockings, gloves or hat. Consequently the rest of my day was spent rushing around the shops in search of these articles. Gloves and stockings were found and purchased, but no hat. Finally our friend, Doris Hildebrand, who was in Bangalore for the horse racing, came to my rescue and lent me a delightfully pretty little hat decorated with tiny pink flowers. This was absolutely splendid because it blended beautifully with my dress, which was a pale turquoise colour. Thus attired I went forth in the evening to meet Her Majesty.

I felt most privileged to be one of only two non-Indian ladies to be chosen for this honour, and I was escorted into a large room where the Maharaja, as host of the reception, was seated on a chair to the right of Her Majesty. I managed my curtsey without a hitch and the Queen very graciously invited me to sit down beside her. We then spent a few moments in conversation, when she asked me about the work we were doing in Mysore City, and the famine relief and leprosy work in the village area. She also enquired about the schools that our children were attending. I was absolutely amazed that she knew so much about us, especially as the reception was being held at the end of a very hot, busy day.

At a very different end of the spectrum of famous people who touched our lives, were the movie stars and crew for the films 'Elephant Bill' and 'Harry Black', both of which were filmed in the jungle near Mysore. The film 'Harry Black' was about a British shikari and his adventures, both romantic and with a man-eating tiger. Most of the filming took place near the Bandipur Nature Reserve, with the film stars living out there in air-conditioned roomy tents. Stewart Grainger was acting the part of Harry Black and Barbara Rush was the leading lady.

The big cats were brought all the way from England, and, as it was winter back home, they carried heavy winter coats. John described the animals in a letter to his grandparents written in January 1965.

> *'Somewhere in Mysore they are shooting a film and the animals that are going to be used are staying at the Van Ingen's. There is a beautiful tigress called 'Suki', a cheetah and a leopard. Also there are some horses, and they don't smell. Every day a man has to go in and muzzle them and put them in a small cage, and then he takes them to where they are shooting the film. They are brought back again each evening to Mysore. The animals come from Chippendale's Circus.'*

The big cats were kept in temporary cages in Botha Van Ingen's compound. The children cycled over several times to see them and were amazed at how friendly they were. However, they soon learnt to be wary of their strength, after they found their wrists bruised against the cage bars by the force of the tigers pressing against their hands for a stroke.

It was during this shoot that a python attacked one of the 'grips'. The story goes that he was walking near the camp in the evening when he saw a deer being menaced by a python in a grassy glade. He stepped forward, presumably thinking that the python would take fright and slither away, and instead the python grabbed his thigh in its jaws and started to coil about his body. The young man had heard somewhere that a python relies upon the anchoring of its head to increase the squeeze of its body. He grabbed the head and wrenched it from his leg.

His leg was very badly bruised with deep haematoma and there were broken python teeth embedded in the muscle. For several weeks the young man returned to see Frank at the hospital to have the teeth that had surfaced under the skin removed and his healing wounds attended.

Our children relished this kind of tale and they were always eager to go with Hugh Warren and Kitty and Valerie Dearmun to visit Willie Tippets, a retired shikari who had a coffee estate in Coorg. After a huge lunch, Willie used to tell them about his exploits in tracking down and dispatching man-eating tigers. They were real stories and Willie was missing the middle fingers on one hand as evidence of a close encounter with a tigress. Willie had emphysema and he used to wheeze and struggle through the telling. One day after a spellbinding story, one of the children piped up, 'Uncle Willie, is that true?' They all remembered his spluttering response. 'If you don't believe me I don't know why I'm half killing myself telling you!'

The children saw all these happenings as very normal and were only too aware of the basics of life and death from the scenes they saw around them. This could be seen as a sad state of affairs, but it also created some very amusing situations.

One long Christmas holiday Frank had to visit a couple of coffee estates in Coorg and we decided to take the children to visit the seaside at a place called Tellicherry, in Kerala State. We spent time on the beach collecting shells and chasing crabs, and one day we went by boat across the sea to visit an elderly gentleman who lived on a small island. A stiff breeze was blowing and the sea was quite rough. No sooner had one of the boats been pushed into the sea than David cried out in a commanding voice, 'And now we sink!' The boatmen did not know enough English to understand why we all rolled around laughing.

Ready to go to sea in the boat at Tellicherry

Chapter Eight
Pastimes, School and Furlough in England

Time passed very quickly as the work gained momentum in the hospital and village areas, and prominence is given to this later in the book. For the moment I will concentrate on events as they unfolded within our family life during 1959 to 1961.

An entry made in my diary on May 31st 1960 reads as follows:-

'My duties are wife, mother, hospital driver, physiotherapist, stenographer, librarian, sick visitor, church organist and food aid distributor. The children joined me as much as possible in these activities and made lots of friends along the way, especially amongst the village communities.'

In this way the children acquired first hand knowledge of drought and famine conditions and its effect upon those living in the rural areas. They took it all in their stride. In fact they loved anything adventurous.

The children cross flood waters in a coracle to visit a village - 1954

On days when they were at home, they played with the servants' children and friends in the compound, flew paper aeroplanes from the upper veranda, built models from the Meccano and Baco sets that had been sent from England and took Podgy the spaniel for walks to the maidan.

Jenny with Podgy the dog (taken on her Kodak Brownie)

On Sundays they often went with Uncle Hugh for a swim. There were no other distractions such as radio, television or cinema.

Over the years we kept a few chickens and they sometimes got a sickness. The children would then take them on the back of their bicycles to the vets. Among other pets was our Siamese cat, called 'Kitty', a gift from some planter friends. She regularly had kittens and was an excellent mother, moving them from desk drawer to laundry basket, and eventually turfing them out onto the floor when they were ready to start using the sand tray and eat solid food. Later on some of our kittens went to the Tibetan Camp where they helped keep down the vermin and were well cared for in return.

David and Priscilla Strom with Kitty and kittens

At other times we were all kept busy catching grasshoppers to supplement the diet of the Slow Loris pair that I had taken pity on when a vendor produced them in the market. We discovered that putting a torch in a box proved a good way of trapping insects at night. Later on in our time in Mysore an elderly doctor friend bequeathed the children his green parakeet 'Georgie'.

Rosemary with Georgie the parakeet

Georgie could talk when he wished and at other times he would of course squawk like the wild parakeets in the trees. His favourite person was Rosemary and if she was not around then I was second best. He could be particularly talkative when guests joined us around the dinner table. We would then put a blanket around his cage and he would sulk there until it was removed.

Botha Van Ingen occasionally took the children on outings to the jungle, which they loved, especially as he was very knowledgeable about the wild animals and a good wildlife photographer as well as having been a shikari (big game hunter).

A walk in the jungle with Botha VanIngen

John was interested in outdoor pursuits and Joubert Van Ingen (Botha Van Ingen's brother) used to take him fishing on the Cauvery River.

John with a catch of fish

The children were doing well at school and seemed to be happy but we discovered that there were problems that they had to face.

Early in September 1960 we rented 'Cosy Nook' in Lovedale for the ten-day school holiday. The weather was showery and cool but the bungalow quite warm and comfortable as there was always a good supply of logs with which to make a glowing fire. We had one of the Hebron School teachers spending the holiday with us, and one Sunday afternoon, as the rain was pouring down heavily outside, we were all sitting around the fire in the living room relaxing. I was busily knitting a school pullover for one of the children and noticed that from time to time the girls were making odd little signs to me. They persisted with their gestures and began to look more and more distressed. I got up saying, 'I think it must be time for tea. Would you like to come and give me a hand Rosemary?' At this, both Rosemary and Jenny jumped up and dashed out to the kitchen with me. Once there I asked them what was the matter. 'Oh Mummy,' they cried, 'You are knitting on a Sunday!' Apparently, at school they were being taught that Sunday was time set apart for bible reading and prayer NOT under any circumstances should they attempt to do such things as knitting and sewing.

We proceeded to make and serve tea whilst I pondered as to the best way of saving the situation for the children. Eventually, after tea I sat down again, picked up my knitting and remarked to the teacher about the difficulty I experienced finding the time to knit two school pullovers per child now that three of the family were pupils. Very graciously the said teacher accepted my remark, I continued to knit, and nothing more was said.

Hebron pupils attended the Union Church, Coonoor, twice every Sunday

Although by now Rosemary and Jenny had been boarders at Hebron School for four or five years, during holiday times school was rarely mentioned. They preferred to concentrate on the joys of home life. We were aware of the fact that the living conditions in Hebron were on a par with those found in our hill station holiday bungalows, but prior to their admission to school we had only been taken on a brief tour around the premises. The girls were boarders at Hebron School, Coonoor and the boys at Lushington in Ootacamund during the 1960s and accepted the conditions as they found them. It was not until thirty years later that we discovered the real state of affairs. It came about in this fashion.

One day in June 1994 my friend Kamala sent me a paper cutting of an article that had appeared in the 'Deccan Herald' written by Phillip Ninan, entitled 'Nostalgia for a School - Hebron', in which he describes Hebron School in Ootacamund as an ideal school. To avoid confusion I should just say that the 'Hebron' School Jenny attended in Coonoor in the 1960s had been moved to Lushington in Ootacamund and the name 'Hebron School' adopted. It was from Jenny's reply to this article that Frank and I gleaned so much knowledge about our family's school life.

Jenny replied to the Deccan Herald as follows:-

'I read with interest Phillip Ninan's article of 26th June '94 in the Deccan Herald, 'Nostalgia for a School'. It was sent to my mother in England by a dear friend of hers, who has retired to Bangalore and who thought it might stir a few memories of Hebron for my sister and myself.

We do indeed share nostalgia for Hebron School with Phillip, but it is for a very different school that existed 25 years before his experience. In our time Hebron clung to a hillside about two miles distant from Coonoor - not quite as high as Ootacamund but on a site surrounded by tea plantations on three sides and to the south by dense jungle that extended onward for miles all the way to Metapalayam on the edge of the plains.

You entered the school through a red brick arch that declared 'Hebron High School', and up a tarmac drive, with rocky banks growing with 'crown of thorns', the thorny succulent with blood red flowers that remind you of the crucifixion. Symbolic and fitting this entrance was for an institution closely linked to the Plymouth Brethren teachings of its founders.

Every Sunday all 120 pupils and 25 - 30 staff traipsed down the driveway in a 'crocodile' to walk the 2 miles to church and then the 2 miles back (twice a day for seniors). In monsoon sometimes the crocodile returned in the dark, children disguised in Khaki canvas capes and Wellington boots - under every disguise a figure in Sunday uniform, clutching a Bible in sticky hand.

The Spartan way of life so enjoyed in outward-bound pursuits by Phillip was part of our everyday life. Dormitories housed rows of up to 24 beds. The wooden planked beds and horsehair mattresses needed some adjustment at the beginning of each term as you discovered the new and unique lumps and bumps of your mattress and fitted them to the shape of your body.

The toilets to most dorms were out of doors and not unknown to provide refuge for enormous rats. The water supply was collected from a stream and at certain times of year we had to rescue tadpoles from our tin basins and tooth mugs before using the water.

Rat snakes and kraits inhabited the open washing water drains and on one occasion we had a very entertaining lesson after one of the girls discovered a six foot rat snake had climbed into her desk through the empty inkwell hole!

For years I slept with my head under the covers so that the rats we imagined came into the dormitory at night would skip over my head and not into the bed!

But these slightly wild surroundings had many advantages. We had liberties that children today can hardly imagine. We had hikes; up the neighbouring mountain, along the road to the spooky, fascinating graveyard that is probably by now reclaimed by the forest, and, most notably, down the old, stone-paved foot-road all the way to Metapalayam, to return by cog railway to Coonoor Station.

We collected Nilgiri gooseberries and feasted on them, we slid down the flat slopes of tea bushes on our canvas capes (probably breaking the tender shoots that should have been harvested for tea), and we prickled with fear and whispered when sweating hill men passed us on the paths tramping uphill with slopping gourds of illegal toddy strapped to their backs.

Strangely we celebrated November the 5th in a big way, with a huge bonfire and fireworks and a guy from every dorm (except for a few years when a member of staff banned guys for fear that the local people would think it was a religious ritual!)

Sports figured highly in the school's life, much to my chagrin, as I was no good at anything to do with sport. We would tramp miles to watch a netball match with another school.

Phillip started his article with a Shakespearian quote. We had a remarkable visit from the Kendalls of 'Shakespeare Wallah' fame (Felicity Kendall's parents). I remember being very puzzled at the, to me uncalled-for, economy of Mr. Kendall's performing so many parts all at once, when I knew how keen we all would have been to help him out and share the parts. The school play, which we perfected and performed for parents' day, was one of the highlights of our year and never short of volunteers for acting.

Performing skills were developed in other areas too. We always sang lustily - mostly hymns and choruses - although a renegade music teacher taught us some 'decadent' songs like 'Funiculi, Funicula'. We had a recorder band, which I gave up because it gave me a searing headache. We did Verse Speaking, and our rendition of 'The Highwayman' by Alfred Noyes, sticks indelibly in my mind, along with our coconut shell, clip-clopping horse. But we did not dance - except for a short spell when the lovely music teacher had a country-dancing club. Dancing, along with make-up and pop music, was considered by some members of the staff to be 'summoning the devil'. They reminded us frequently of Jezebel and her fate and in our minds the scales were finely balanced between the enjoyment of dancing and the thought of rabid pye-dogs devouring us in the street.

An enlightened teacher taught us the Anglican Creed once, which caused a terrific furore. This was all very entertaining, as were the odd budding romances that just occasionally brought lonely young tea planters courting new members of staff who had freshly arrived from abroad.

It must have been a very strange life for the staff, marooned as they were, miles from anywhere with 100 odd children aged 5 to 16 and a close-knit community of teachers and matrons, all in voluntary exile from the countries of their birth. They taught the G.C.S.E. syllabus to small classes that never exceeded 12 pupils, with the very basic of tools to aid their teaching, and yet, most pupils gained more than 8 'O' levels whatever their ability. Their lives, like those of us children, were governed by the school bell that rang *sonorously over the hillside at regular intervals - rising bell, breakfast bell, assembly bell, morning break bell, back to class bell, lunch bell, - on it tolled all day, even at weekends for rising and for meals.*

For ten years my term-time life was dictated by that bell. Queuing outside the dining room for meals, we could see the bell sway, smell the pinesap from the sawpit that was located nearby and watch the whey drip from the muslin bag of curds that hung at the back of the kitchen.

We were always hungry. Nearly all of us were exceptionally lean. 'Fat' children were the ones whose ribs didn't show. We ate everything put before us, some of which was delicious and some horrible. Grace was said at every meal before the wooden floor of the dining room resounded with the chairs being pulled out and the clambering of feet. On Sunday we sang 'Holy, holy, holy, Lord God Almighty'. I can still smell the Sunday porridge. It was oat porridge, cooked slowly, delicious and gooey.

Some children were given Golden Syrup in their tuck boxes and this was very fairly doled out - a half teaspoon on each slice of bread - to the whole table until eventually all was gone.

When we were seniors we sat at the Head's table in rotation. The food was slightly better at this table and we were expected to make grown-up conversation and keep our table napkins clean for the privilege.

The staff were not stand-offish though - mostly they were very friendly. They were father and mother to us and they needed our love and friendship as mush as we needed theirs. I remember the wonderful security felt when monsoon storms raged across the tin roof of our dormitory and we all sat cross-legged on the coconut matting on the floor singing 'Rock of ages, cleft for me' and thinking of the pilgrim fathers in the bowels of a ship mid-Atlantic while a storm tossed them where it would and they prayed for a safe deliverance to the New World (our matron of the time was second generation Irish-American protestant!)

Staff came from earlier posts in Tibet, India, New Zealand - you name it, and they brought stories - stories of untamed people, untamed jungles, spiritual visitations and arduous journeys. We loved to trap them into stories in class, the dormitory or playground, and this widened our world.

So Phillip, you talk of nostalgia and so do I, for the same place and yet two very different places and times. My brothers went to school for a few years at the present Ooty site of Hebron (then Lushington School) and I expect they would be amazed to see it now. I wonder if the Toda settlement behind the school still exists and if the football pitch is still red earth and if a crocodile of pupils still winds its way twice every Sunday to church?'

To return to life in Mysore, in February 1961 there was a very heavy monsoon and in my diary I wrote: '*The monsoon rains have been very heavy with extensive flooding. The K R Saga Dam is full to the brim and the river at Scott's Bungalow has burst its banks.'*

The steps at Scott's Bungalow covered by the River Cauvery in flood

The children returned to school in early February 1961, leaving David still at home with Frank and me. We had an exciting start to the year with the Queen's visit to Bangalore, and after this we suddenly woke up to the fact that our next furlough was due to begin in June. Arrangements for our passage home and accommodation in England during the year of furlough had been put in place during the autumn of 1960. Frank planned to stay with Dr. Grace Gillespie and her brother in Liverpool as a paying guest in order to attend a course for qualification as a Master in Surgery (Ch.M.). Grace Gillespie had been Medical Superintendent of the Holdsworth Hospital from 1931 to 1956. In view of Frank's study commitment it was decided that I should stay with the children in Ockbrook, near Derby, where my mother worked as a House Mistress for a Moravian School.

The school was part of a Moravian Settlement and it took children from the age of five up to sixteen, some of whom were boarders and others local day pupils. Mother lived in a ground floor flat of a building adjacent to the school. The first floor flat above Mother's was set apart by the Moravian Church for their missionaries to use during furlough. Upon enquiry we were told that the flat would be empty throughout 1961 and '62 and we would be welcome to rent it for the whole of our stay. The children would also be able to attend the school as day scholars during that time.

With the furlough arrangements in England now settled, a crucial decision needed to be made regarding Frank's replacement in Mysore. At that time we did not have a sufficiently qualified, experienced surgeon on the staff and many months of searching and enquiring came to nought. When early June came and we were due to sail in July there was still no answer to this problem. After much prayerful consideration we began to think that we should postpone our plans, then, one morning out of the blue a young Australian doctor turned up on our doorstep. He was a surgeon, Freddie Zerfas, who was travelling around India on a motorcycle, visiting various hospitals in search of one where a surgeon was needed for a while. This seemed to be almost too good to be true. After working with Frank for a week or two, Freddie said that, if the Hospital staff agreed, he would stay and cover for Frank's furlough. What a relief this was. Surely prayers were answered the day Freddie appeared on our doorstep! We began to pack our bags in earnest, and set off for furlough early in July, leaving Freddie in our house preparing for his wife to join him.

Train journeys to Bombay became easier as the children grew older, but I well remember that on this particular journey in 1961 I created a problem where there was none. On the night before our arrival at Poona station we bedded down happily and all fell soundly asleep. Suddenly I awoke, looked at my watch, and my heart leapt! 'Wake up, wake up quickly its 6 o'clock!' I cried. Moans and groans. 'Come on,' I called again, 'We're due to change trains in Poona in half an hour's time!'

It was panic stations. We hurriedly dressed, rolled up our sleeping bags and then sat waiting and w-a-i-t-i-n-g for the train to stop at Poona. Now and then the train seemed to be slowing down, but it did not stop and there were no lights or buildings outside. Eventually one of us looked at a watch only to find that the time read 1am. Oh dear, dear, I was not very popular for a little while! In the semidarkness of the carriage I had misread 12.30am for 6am. In the end we all saw the funny side of the whole incident and all was forgiven. After a drink and biscuit we settled down to sleep once more.

On arrival in Bombay we stayed the night in a hostel, all sleeping in one huge room. Very early in the morning we were woken by a loud rumbling noise, the room seemed to rattle and Frank woke up thinking it was an earthquake, remembering a night in Chaotung when we were woken by a similar sound and it really was a minor earthquake. This time the rumbling turned out to be the sound of the Bombay Electric Trams starting up for the day. We boarded the SS 'Orontes' the next day with 1,400 passengers. It was a very interesting voyage for the family because we were calling at Athens, Pompeii and Gibraltar and they were old enough to enjoy such a wonderful opportunity to see these historic places.

We travelled straight to Derby by train and made our way to the Moravian School and Settlement in Ockbrook. We settled into the flat, Frank departed for Liverpool and the children joined their various classes in school. Ockbrook was quite a small village with a grocer's shop and butcher. There were a few short walks in and around the village and occasionally we took a bus into Derby.

Between furloughs my warm winter clothes were stored away in a trunk and brought out the next time we were home. It so happened that the winter of 1962 was extremely cold and one day, dressed in my out-of-date winter coat with a scarf over my head, I went out and walked down the hill to the village shop leaving the family at home. As I trudged back up the hill with a laden basket one of the children happened to be looking out of the window and on seeing my figure said to the others in the room, 'Look at that poor old lady coming up the hill.' Imagine their surprise when I turned in at the gate and the 'poor old lady' turned out to be me!

The flat was situated at the top of a hill overlooking the village of Ockbrook and a lovely, large sitting room was situated at the front of the flat. It had two sash windows from which it was possible to look down on the village below and there was a huge fireplace. Leading from the sitting room to the back of the flat was a small kitchen with a gas cooker, a table and four small chairs, a sink and a gas geyser for heating water. The bathroom stood just opposite the kitchen. That also had a gas geyser for hot water. Further along the passageway were three small bedrooms. Apart from the fireplace in the sitting room there was no way of heating the flat. During a normal winter I think we would have managed, but during this particular winter of 1961 to '62 the weather was particularly cold. I purchased a paraffin heater, which I placed in the kitchen. I would light it at about 6 o'clock in the morning and after half an hour we would dash out of bed, one by one, into the bathroom for a quick wash, then across the passage to get dressed in the slightly warmer kitchen. This done we would gather round the kitchen table for a quick breakfast before school began. We were fortunate to have my mother (whom the children called 'Nanna') living in the ground floor flat at this time, because we could combine our resources and take our main meals together. Mother's kitchen was big enough to seat us all, and, as it was warmer than upstairs, we sometimes had our baths in the curtained off area that served as her bathroom.

Snow fell that winter, causing great excitement because it was the first time that the children had seen snow. They dashed out into the back yard with their mouths open to catch the snowflakes. As usual they forgot to close the back door and Mother called out, 'Close that door, anyone would think you were born in a barn!'

The children's first snowman

We all enjoyed the coming of the spring flowers, and later the beautiful summer weather and freedom of the countryside near Ockbrook.

The transition to Ockbrook School went very smoothly. We managed to purchase second hand school uniform for the children since they would only need it as day scholars for one year. This was possible because quite a number of Moravian Missionary families attended the school during a furlough, leaving behind good quality unwanted garments. Our family found that their class work was up to standard, and, although they were day scholars, they felt part of the school in that it was situated within the Moravian Settlement, which comprised Church, Manse,

School, Staff accommodation and living quarters for other members of the Settlement.

We saw very little of Frank that year as he was kept busy in Liverpool, but he did spend the Christmas holiday in Ockbrook. It was during this holiday that Grace Gillespie kindly invited us all to Liverpool to see Tommy Steele play in a pantomime.

Frank's father had purchased a second-hand car for Frank to use throughout our stay in England and Frank decided to drive us to Liverpool. When the great day arrived it was freezing cold with a fair amount of snow on the ground and there was no heating system in the car. Nevertheless, he decided it was safe to drive across from Ockbrook to Liverpool. We took some biscuits and a couple of flasks of hot drink together with a couple of knee rugs and, dressed in our warmest clothes, scarves, gloves and woolly hats, set off on the journey. The road took us over the bleak Pennines where the snow had frozen solid, and the car began to slither and slide. The windows misted over and we really began to be worried because we seemed to be the only people travelling on the road. Despite the blankets it became really, really cold inside the car. Mercifully we eventually reached Grace's house safely, where we found a huge fire and a lovely hot meal awaiting our arrival. Immediately after lunch we left for the theatre. The children were spellbound at its size and the wonderful stage setting. Later in the evening we returned home. The roads were deserted but we arrived home safely, very cold and tired. Looking back on that journey, fifty years later, I am sure our guardian angel must have been watching over us, because it was very foolhardy to have set out under those conditions.

The month of May came along. Frank's thesis entitled 'Nutritional Aspects of Peptic Ulcer and its Surgery in India' had been submitted and his Master's Degree (ChM) awarded. In June Frank's parents joined me in attending Frank's Award Ceremony in Liverpool. Following this Frank returned to be with us in Ockbrook.

When August arrived we packed our bags and made our way to London, where we stayed for two days of sightseeing before boarding the SS 'Iberia' for the return voyage to India.

It was an eventful journey, with a couple of incidents taking place as we sailed through the Suez Canal and out into the Red Sea. The first was a damaged propeller, which occurred during our passage through the canal, and the second was the recovery of a sailor from the engine room, who suffering from the heat, jumped overboard in the Red Sea. The ship made a figure of eight turn and rescued him within a very short space of time. It was particularly hot at the time.

We arrived in Bombay on August 18th 1962 and were back in Mysore in time for the start of school term in Hebron and Lushington.

Shortly after August 1962 Freddie Zerfas left Holdsworth to go to another hospital for further experience, leaving his wife, Yvette, with us in Mysore. Yvette was planning to purchase Scott's Bungalow in Srirangapatna. On completion of the sale she moved out to Scott's Bungalow, sadly taking Marjorie and Lazarus with her. This left us without a cook or ayah, however, we were fortunate in securing the services of Mary and Augustine, who quickly became part of the family and helped us enormously during busy days.

We settled back into work and school, and during the Christmas school holidays the children's friends, Kitty and Valerie Dearmun, stayed with their Uncle Hugh and spent most of the daytime with us. For that particular holiday I hired some desks and chairs, which we set out on the upstairs open veranda and for a few hours each weekday we had lessons. Whilst in England I had obtained some old 11+ examination papers, which were a great help as both Jenny and Valerie were due to take their exams. The Christmas holiday period was very long, lasting through to the middle of February.

1962 was the year when I took Rosemary and Jenny with me to Bangalore to purchase Christmas presents for each of the 200 St. Bartholomew's Church Sunday School children. This had been an annual task for many years. Later we wrapped all the presents ready for the party when 'Father Christmas' (Frank disguised in costume) would distribute them. How we loved singing carols after sunset, when the stars were sparkling in the inky black sky! And so, another year passed and we were well and truly back to work.

Chapter Nine
The Leprosy Work

Having dwelt extensively on family life and my growing involvement with famine and the leprosy work as it evolved, I have asked Frank to write in more detail about leprosy and its treatment as we knew it at the time.

Below written by Frank
In the early years of my time at Holdsworth Hospital the patients who came for treatment had a wide spectrum of illnesses, but we did not see people with leprosy coming for treatment. The reasons for this were no doubt that sufferers kept away because of public fear of the disease and because at the time there was no known cure.

Winnie and I had an interest in leprosy that dated from our time in Chaotung, south west China, from 1948 to 1949, when we had been in contact with leprosy patients in the leprosy colony twenty-five miles away at Stone Gateway. The only treatment available then was Chaulmoogra oil, either applied topically (on the skin) or given by painful injections into the lesions, and it did little to help. Since then the new drug Dapsone had been introduced. Any of you who have read the book, *The Island,* by Victoria Hislop, will understand what a revolution Dapsone brought about. At long last it was possible for leprosy patients to be cured.

When walking around in the city of Mysore we had observed how leprosy affected the lives of people, leaving them with facial deformities and in some cases only stumps for hands and feet, unable to earn a living and only able to beg having been outcast as a consequence of their disease. The facial deformities resulted in wrinkling of the face, making them look prematurely old, loss of eyebrow hair and collapse of the nose due to loss of the supporting cartilage and bone, and elongated earlobes because the skin had lost its elasticity.

Boy with prematurely wrinkled face

The loss of fingers and toes was mostly due to repeated injuries or burns as a result of the loss of sensation to pain and touch.

One morning in 1957, during an X-Ray screening session at Holdsworth Hospital, I was told that there was a doctor outside waiting to see me. The door was opened and around it appeared the round, smiling face of Dr Debu Chaudhury asking if he could come in. He explained that he had been working for four years for the Gandhi Memorial Leprosy Foundation at T Narsipur, a village about thirty miles away, where he had done a leprosy survey and established a number of treatment clinics within the area. He said that he now had patients who were cured of leprosy, in that they were skin negative, but that the deformities due to the leprosy still remained and consequently they could not return to a normal life. Dr. Chaudhury was anxious that they should have reconstructive surgery, but had been unable to find anyone willing to undertake this.

I took Dr Chaudhury's request to the Hospital Committee and it was agreed that leprosy reconstructive surgery could be undertaken on three conditions:-

   1) That patients should be non-infective so that they could
      be admitted into the same wards as other patients.
   2) That other patients should not object.
   3) That it should be of no expense to the hospital.

Under these conditions the first leprosy patients were admitted. In this way we became the first hospital in India to admit leprosy patients into the General Wards with other patients. It speaks well of the reputation of the hospital and of the trust that people had in it, that the other patients without question accepted this practice. Twenty beds were allocated for the leprosy patients.

   The additional work required funding with no expense to the hospital and Winnie undertook the arduous task of raising the necessary funds. First of all there was the daily cost for patients staying in the hospital and the cost for any x-rays and surgery carried out, then there were the costs for physiotherapy equipment, the provision of shoes, that included the wages for a cobbler and the shoe materials, transport to bring some patients from outlying areas, special medicines, food for the village clinic inpatients and later the provision of a dedicated vehicle for transport of the team to and from the village clinics. The 'Leprosy Relief Fund' was set up and Winnie was successful in getting donations over the years from overseas organisations such as War on Want, OXFAM, Mission to Lepers, Lepra and Suisse Emmaus, and from Indian organisations such as the Christian Medical Association, as well as Mysore Government grants, donations from individuals, and the support of a junior school in England who specifically raised money for shoes. Many a time Winnie stayed up until the small hours in order to find the time to write the regular letters and reports that kept the supporters informed about the work that was being done.

   Winnie also gave her time free to help at the village clinics, to perform the hospital based physiotherapy and education of patients on the prevention of further injury, and she set up and administered the cobbler's work in the provision of protective footwear for the patients. The leprosy work could not have proceeded without the time and expertise that she brought to it. Once again there was a link with our time in China, when in 1948, during our orientation period in Hankow, Winnie had used her time in both language lessons and learning the principles of physiotherapy at the Union Hospital.

Before going into details about reconstructive surgery in leprosy it would be helpful to give here a more detailed account of the disease itself. In doing so I am going to use the old classification that we were using at the time. Leprosy is due to infection by the leprosy bacillus, and its effect on the body depends on the body's immune response. If the immune response is poor the infection invades the whole body. This was called Lepromatous Leprosy and in the Mysore region about fifteen per cent of cases had this type of leprosy. If the immune response is strong the infection is limited to small areas of skin producing one or more pale anaesthetic patches. This was called Tuberculoid Leprosy and we found about five per cent had this form of leprosy. In the remaining eighty per cent of cases the infection could affect the body in various ways, the spectrum ranging from towards the Tuberculoid response to towards the Lepromatous response. This was called Dimorphous Leprosy. Only the Lepromatous patients were infectious, and occasionally during a flare-up, members of the Dimorphous group who were towards the Lepromatous end of the spectrum would be infectious. In both Lepromatous and Dimorphous groups the infection tends to do most damage to the cooler parts of the body. One of the coldest organs is the nose, and infection of the nose leads to the disease being spread by nasal droplets like the common cold. Leprosy however is not highly infective. In most cases, unless the subject is unusually susceptible, it requires quite long exposure to acquire the infection.

As referred to earlier, in the Lepromatous group the exposed skin, particularly the face, becomes involved with areas of erythematous macules, papules and nodules, leading to disfiguration, with premature wrinkling and loss of the eyebrows.

In both Lepromatous, and some of the Dimorphous group, the long nerves in the arms and legs become involved and sometimes tender, leading to thickening and loss of motor function. In addition the small nerves in the hands and feet become damaged, leading to loss of sensation to touch and temperature.

In all types, particularly the Lepromatous and more active Dimorphous patients, there may be acute episodes, often during medical treatment, called lepra-reactions, in which all the lesions flare up and the subject can become severely ill. This is due to the Herzheimer Reaction to dead bacilli, which also occurs in other diseases and is a reaction to the toxins from the dead bacilli.

With the Lepromatous patients the T Narsipur clinic took regular skin smears to look for the absence of bacteria from the skin cells. Patients were also examined for the absence of sensation and for the thickening of nerves, which indicated the extent of neuropathy. Once the disease was cured, and if patients had the residual problems of neuropathy and/or problems with their hands and feet, or facial deformity, they were referred to the fortnightly clinic that we attended in T Narsipur. We assessed what was needed for each patient, which ranged from the provision of protective footwear and education to prevent injury, to reconstructive surgery for the face, hands and feet.

Such reconstructive surgery for leprosy had not been possible earlier because there was no cure for leprosy. It was therefore a new specialty, which was being pioneered by Dr Paul Brand at the Christian Medical College Hospital in Vellore. Towards the end of 1957 Winnie and I visited Vellore in order to learn more about the techniques required for the various aspects of the reconstructive surgery. Dr Norman Cockett (who by training was an anaesthetist) visited us from the Leprosy Hospital in Dichpalli, where he had been undertaking reconstructive operations, and gave us lectures and demonstrations. It was an exciting time with continuing development of new techniques.

During the fortnightly visits to Dr Chaudhury's clinic in T Narsipur to select patients and maintain postoperative care, we also held foot sessions where patients with foot ulcers were fitted with contact plasters. While in plaster these patients remained in T Narsipur accommodated temporarily on the clinic veranda. It was very important that they rested and avoided weight bearing.

The 'veranda' patients at T Narsipur

A cook, Dasappa, himself a leprosy patient, was engaged to cook their food and generally look after them. Other patients were selected either for bed rest, or for reconstructive surgery in the Holdsworth Memorial Hospital.

Once a fortnight on the night before a clinic session we would load the old station wagon with milk powder and sacks of foodstuff for the 'veranda' patients, the tools and leather for Krishnappa, the shoemaker, and bandages and tins of plaster-of-Paris powder for patients with foot ulcers, who would need contact plasters and freedom from weight bearing. On the next morning, after an early breakfast, we added the patient notes, flasks of coffee, drinking mugs and a few biscuits to the pile of goods already in the station wagon. Krishanappa, Dasappa his assistant, a junior doctor, Winnie and I crowded into the station wagon and drove the short distance to pick up Kamala, Winnie's very dear friend, who had suffered polio at thirteen years old and was consequently paraplegic. At about 8.30am we arrived at Kamala's house and made room for her in the vehicle. Luckily she benefited from the support of the many bodies that were by this time squeezed into the station wagon. Kamala was interested in the work of the clinic and subsequently gave great help with the patient notes at clinic. (Winnie has written more fully about Kamala at the end of this chapter.)

We usually arrived at T.Narsipur at about ten o'clock and by then Dr. Chaudhury had already selected a few patients needing our attention. Work began immediately and we were all kept busy for the next three or four hours.

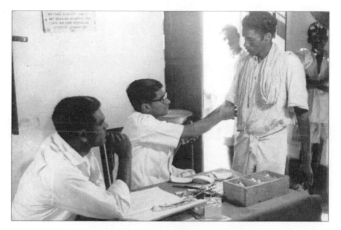

Dr Chaudhury examining a patient

Krishnappa and Dasappa worked outside on the veranda, measuring any new patients for shoes, fitting shoes made since a previous clinic and repairing shoes for others.

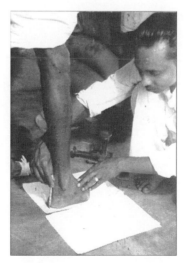

Krishnappa making a template for a patient's shoe

115

I would examine the new patients referred by Dr. Chaudhury and decide upon their future course of treatment, while Winnie took the patients' notes. Winnie then worked with the patients who had recently undergone tendon reconstruction surgery, taking them through their exercise routines.

Frank, Freddie Zerfas, Kamala and Winnie at Leprosy Clinic

It was a great hive of activity. The patients were delighted to see us and we were pleased to see them. The clinic building was quite small and became very hot when full of patients and staff, so when our work was done we took a short break for drinks, then after a chat to the 'veranda' patients we would take our leave and return home.

Now for details of leprosy reconstructive surgery: As already stated the leprosy bacillus particularly infects parts of the body with the lowest temperature. In the arm the first nerve to be involved is the superficial ulnar nerve where it runs over the elbow just under the skin (the area we refer to as the 'funny bone') and the next is the median nerve lying in the front of the wrist. Damage to these affects the nerve supply to the small flexor muscles in the hand responsible for flexing the first finger joints. The long flexor muscles in the forearm responsible for flexing the distal joints in the fingers are not affected. This results in the distal joints becoming flexed and in clawing of the fingers, damage to the ulnar nerve affecting the fourth and fifth fingers, and damage to the median nerve affecting the second and third fingers and the thumb. As the longer flexor muscles to the fingers are not affected their tendons can be transferred to restore the action of the paralysed small flexor muscles. Sometimes the deeper radial nerve lying deep in the upper arm is involved, causing wrist drop, and this would require a wrist fusion.

116

Hand tendon transplant operation – one before and one after surgery

In the leg, the lateral popliteal nerve where it lies under the skin on the outer side of the knee gets infected, resulting in a drop foot. This is corrected by transferring the posterior tibial tendon that lies behind the ankle, to the dorsum of the foot to lift it up. Damage to the posterior tibial nerve lying just above the ankle, will also cause clawing of the toes and this can be corrected by fusing of the toe joints.

A prerequisite to surgery was the need to promote physiotherapy both for preoperative correction of finger deformities due to clawing and also for later postoperative re-education. This was where the physiotherapy for conditions involving hands, arms, feet and legs, that Winnie had learnt in Hankow, was needed. Courageously Winnie agreed to undertake setting up a small physiotherapy unit in the hospital so that I could go ahead with the surgery necessary to repair hands and feet. One of the rooms built against the side wall of the hospital compound that had previously been used by patients' relatives to cook their meals, was taken over for the physiotherapy. Where patients had clawed fingers, they needed repeated stretching and plastering in order to straighten them as much as possible before surgery. Very stiff fingers were mobilised by wax baths and plaster cylinders. A zinc wax bath, set into a wooden box, was made by Mr Obed, our radiographer, and fitted with an electric immersion heater. The bath was filled with bees wax, obtained from our Vellore friends, which then had to be heated. We did not have a thermostat, therefore, before it could be used for leprosy patients with sensory loss, Winnie had to test the temperature by immersing her hands. She developed beautifully soft skin from this necessary task! Preparation for surgery could take up to three months depending upon the severity of clawing. After surgery post-operative re-education to use the transferred tendons was required until full activity was restored.

Physiotherapy after tendon transplant

Another secondary effect of leprosy is that the facial nerve gets damaged where it lies just under the skin in front of the ear resulting in facial nerve paralysis affecting the whole of one side of the face, or just the eyelids (lagophthalmos) exposing the eyes to dust and infection. These also needed muscle transfers and tendon slings, and again required re-education.

Many patients required facial plastic surgery procedures. In Lepromatous leprosy, as described above, the patients developed prematurely wrinkled faces and required facelifts. Others with loss of eyebrows needed eyebrow grafting. Also, one of the coldest parts of the body is the nose, because of its exposure to cold air, and it becomes severely infected. The lining membrane and the supporting nasal bone and cartilage get destroyed, resulting in collapse of the nose and requiring nose reconstruction. There is no skin loss and, if the skin is freed from the underlying bone of the face, the nose can be pulled out straight, but it then requires a new lining and supporting bone and cartilage. The lining is supplied by a skin graft, the bridge of the nose reformed by tiny cartilage dice taken from a costal cartilage and supported by two bone grafts taken from the iliac crest.

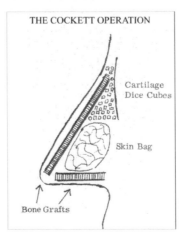

The concept of the skin graft lining was developed on the principles laid down by Sir Harold Gillies and later by Dr Noshir Antia in Poona and Bombay. The other modifications using diced cartilage to reconstruct the bridge of the nose were actually devised in Mysore by Norman Cockett, consequently it was called the Cockett operation.

The Cockett operation was very successful, especially as it left no outside scarring and because it did not introduce new skin onto the face (some procedures use skin from the upper arm as a graft) therefore it avoided any skin texture problems.

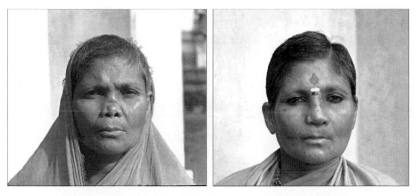

Woman before and after Cockett nose reconstruction operation

A lot of time had to be spent educating patients in the proper care of their anaesthetic hands and feet so that they avoided further trauma. Because they could not feel pain many became indifferent to injury and tended to disassociate themselves from their hands and feet. The commonest cause of loss of fingers and toes was either injury or burns and not the actual leprosy infection itself.

Many male patients required re-education in a different occupation to enable them to earn a living by following a new trade. Great help was available from the Nava Jeevana Nilayam, a voluntary Hindu organisation in Bangalore, where training was given in weaving, light carpentry, tailoring, typing and several other trades. Tools had to be adapted with especially large handles to provide adequate grip. Although I refer to male patients there were also many women needing surgery for hands and feet, also nose reconstruction. They also suffered from foot ulcers and required special shoes. The women once treated normally returned home to their domestic duties and other village work such as subsistence farming. Here education in the prevention of injury to neuropathic feet and hands was essential.

The major problem in re-education was in the care of the feet in patients with sensory loss. The patients included young and middle-aged men and women, as well as children, and many had ulcers on the soles of their feet, due to undetected injury on walking, to which they were especially vulnerable as very few possessed footwear. Patients had to be taught to inspect their feet for injury daily. If a patient had developed a plantar ulcer he would have to either be in bed avoiding weight bearing, or wear a contact plaster, until the ulcer was healed. It was far better to prevent the ulcers occurring at all, rather than having to go through the lengthy process necessary to bring about their healing.

The patients with sensory loss, as well as receiving education in foot care, were provided with special protective shoes and sandals, as were those with healed ulcers. Winnie had established a shoe workshop in one of the rooms adjacent to our house in the hospital compound and it was here that Krishnappa, the shoemaker, and Dasappa, a healed leprosy patient and his assistant, worked. The footwear required a thick cushioning insole to absorb shock and, in addition, a thick sole that could not be penetrated by thorns or other sharp objects. Old car tyres proved to be very useful for the bottom sole and Dasappa would occasionally disappear to the market to purchase one. The Bata Shoe Company was most generous in their help with free supplies of suitable cushioning material, the same type as used in flip-flops. As time went by we experimented with many types of footwear and finally devised a sandal that was acceptable because the design was not too noticeable and compared favourably with 'ordinary' footwear.

Each shoe had to be made to a pattern that fitted the particular patient's feet. Some patients had collapsed foot arches, others had clawed toes or had lost their toes altogether, or had foot ulcers, before coming to the clinic that changed the shape of their feet. Krishnappa would take a sheet of paper and place it on the floor. He would then ask the patient to stand on the paper and carefully draw around each foot to obtain the shape of the sole and the amount of toe room required in the uppers.

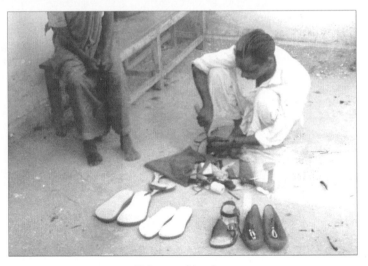

Kalappa making shoes

When back in his workshop he would first of all cut the 'hard' sole from an old car tyre and then cut the cushioning material for the insole. This done he glued them together with contact adhesive and clamped them under a weight. The next job was to sew the leather straps and for these he used waxed thread and two needles to saddle stitch the seam, his feet acting as a clamp. For some patients extra padding was required to protect vulnerable pressure points. Often the patient would pay a small sum, usually one rupee (the equivalent now to two pence) for the shoes, as this gave them a sense of responsibility to look after them. Also, when patients came to the hospital clinic for their medicines we would send them to Krishnappa's workshop, where they could polish their shoes with polish and brushes, which were to hand, free. Never having worn shoes before the patients had no idea how to look after them.

During the school holidays our children were most interested in the shoe workshop and they spent many hours watching Krishnappa at work. If a patient turned up to be measured, to their delight, he would allow them to draw around the patient's feet. He also taught them how to do saddle stitch, although I do not think they mastered the art of clamping with their feet.

Winnie undertook the organisation of this part of the project and made periodic journeys to the Bangalore leather market, usually a marathon expedition. She would set off from Mysore very early in the morning with Dasappa for company and drive to Bangalore. On arrival at the market place they found animal hides of all shapes, sizes and thickness had already been spread out in piles all over the ground. Behind each pile sat a leather merchant ready to strike a profitable bargain. Having walked around and selected a pile that she considered to be of good quality, Winnie would sit cross legged upon the ground and begin the process of inspecting each hide and negotiating the price. The bartering could be vigorous and sometimes prolonged. Once the final transactions had been completed, coolies were engaged to carry the purchases to the waiting jeep. Fortunately there were one or two good restaurants in Bangalore where it was possible to obtain a good meal before undertaking the long drive back to Mysore. After a year or two and having gained a good knowledge of the relevant price of leather, Winnie handed this job over to Krishnappa.

As a consequence of this work, when I was appointed as Consultant Surgeon in Basingstoke in 1968, I realised early on that I was seeing diabetic patients in my outpatient clinics with the same foot ulcers and clawing of the toes as I had previously seen in leprosy patients in India. This was the result of diabetic neuropathy in those patients, with the loss of sensation in the feet. At that time little was known about the care of neuropathic feet in the UK, so I started a Diabetic Foot Clinic in Basingstoke. Using the experience gained with leprosy patients, I also began writing and lecturing about the management of diabetic feet. One big problem was where to go for the provision of suitable protective footwear. The standard 'surgical' shoes available at the time were rigid and designed for patients with orthopaedic problems. What was needed was a shoe with soft uppers and soft soles, without a rigid toe box, with enough depth to accommodate clawed toes and with a cushioning inlay to protect the foot. In addition, patients with pressure points or healed ulcers required an additional semi-rigid cradle under the cushioning inlay with windows cut out under the pressure areas, and extra depth to the shoe was required to accommodate this.

It took five long years, with the help of the Vocational Surgical Shoe Training Workshop at Lord Mayor Treloar College (for children and young people with disabilities), to find suitable materials for the cushioning and cradle, before a suitable prototype was found. It then took a further year, visiting one shoe manufacturer after another, to find a company willing to take up the project. Only then, what was called the 'Diabetic Shoe' became available in the UK.

Chapter Ten
Establishing the Village Leprosy Work

Narrative by Winnie

When we returned from furlough in 1956 we moved into the house within the hospital grounds and because the girls were at boarding school and the boys so well looked after by Marjorie I was able to get more involved in Frank's work. The leprosy work started in connection with the T Narsipur clinic, but within a very short time word had got around in Mysore City that leprosy patients were being treated in the Holdsworth Memorial Hospital and, as a result, patients with active leprosy began appearing in the outpatient department.

We had not anticipated this consequence from the reconstructive surgery and rehabilitation work and we were not in a position to give long-term treatment from our base at Holdsworth Hospital when the patients came from distant rural areas. Many were coming from Chamrajanagar, a market town about thirty miles away, and its outlying villages, an area where the Church of South India had a strong following. After much thought, we decided that the best plan would be to provide treatment facilities for these patients within their own area. This would need Government grants and, in order to obtain these, it was first of all necessary to establish that leprosy was endemic in the region.

In 1956, with the help of funds from the Hind Kusht Nivaran Sangh (Indian Leprosy Association), three young men were chosen from the villages and sent to the Gandhi Memorial Leprosy Foundation training course in North India. On their return home, they were accommodated with a trained medical worker, Chinappa, in a house situated in the hospital compound at Kastur.

Although the church work at Kastur had been established since the early 1930s the nurse and doctor had by no means been able to reach every village in the area. For the purposes of our survey we needed access to every village within a ten-mile radius of Kastur. Many of these villages were quite isolated and populated by Hindus. Before undertaking the survey work in their villages it was necessary to procure permission from the Headman and elders. This could be a lengthy business entailing driving the jeep from Mysore to Kastur, where I would pick up Chinappa or one of the other boys. Under their expert guidance we would wend our way along the dusty, bumpy tracks between cultivated fields. In this dry area it was not possible to grow rice. Instead a millet, called 'ragi', was grown and used as a staple food. Other crops were maize, chillies, aubergines, ladies fingers (okra) and peppers. The villagers were desperately poor and completely dependent upon the rainfall. On our journey we were eventually forced to abandon the car and continue our journey on foot. With notebooks, pens and drinking water in hand we would walk a mile or so until we reached the village. The Headman would usually be awaiting our arrival outside his house and with introductions made we would be invited into his house for a little refreshment.

A village Headman

We always, as was the custom, removed our sandals before entering a house. The general layout of a village would be the well in the centre surrounded by the larger houses of the high caste inhabitants. The Headman, being a high caste Hindu, would live in a house made of red brick with a tiled roof, with rooms built around three sides of a square courtyard, the fourth side being set aside for the cows, goats and chickens.

The living quarters comprised a small kitchen with an open fire for cooking. Apart from a few stainless steel plates and cups very little else was needed. The fingers of the right hand were always used for eating curry and rice, therefore only a couple of large spoons were required for serving the food. Two large stones and a plank of wood served as a shelf for storing a small supply of rice, ghee and vegetables. There would be a large container for water, which would be drawn from the village well. Two or three small rooms, with tiled floors, were divided by mud brick walls and used by various members of the family. After nightfall straw mats would be spread out on the floor, together with a small pillow. The weather was never colder than an English summer day and it was possible to spend a very comfortable night with just a light sheet covering. In the morning the bedding would be rolled up and stored on a rough wooden shelf out of the way. A family latrine was available a short distance away at the back of the house. Finally, the central area of the quadrangle was open to the sky and this was the place where the family gathered to relax and tell stories at the end of the day. There was no furniture as such, because people always sat cross-legged on the floor.

Once inside the headman's home we sat down on the floor ready to partake of a drink, usually hot tea. The 'golden rule' was to always drink still hot boiled water or tea and never to accept a cold drink, as more often than not the water would be contaminated. Nothing in the countryside was done quickly, which was very wise really as to rush around in the midday sun could be quite exhausting. Frequently a lad would be dispatched to fetch firewood, a tiny packet of tealeaves, some jaggery (small lumps of brown sugar) and milk. On his return a fire would be lit and the tealeaves, jaggery, milk and a little water would be added to a small dekshie (saucepan with no handle). The ingredients were all boiled together and stewed for several minutes before the tea, Indian 'chai', was served.

This break after our trudge into the village was always welcome and it gave us an opportunity to discuss the reason for our visit. Eventually we would all make a tour of the whole village both high and low-caste sections, as, for the purposes of an accurate survey, everyone had to be examined.

In a separate part of the village were the dwellings of the lower caste people, known as the 'Dalits'. Their houses were built of unfired mud brick, sometimes with a tiled roof but usually with a grass-like thatch. These houses were often built close together in a row and each family had just one room measuring about twelve feet by ten. There would be a sunken fireplace for cooking in one corner of the room and a wooden shelf built against the wall for storing bedding and clothing.

The poorer housing in a village

The family would cook, eat, live and sleep, all in the one room. If they possessed a cow or chickens, a makeshift lean-to area alongside the house, with just enough shelter to protect the animals from the worst of the weather during the monsoon season, would be provided. The floors in these houses were often covered with a mixture of cow dung and mud that had been spread very evenly and left to dry. This dried mixture created a smooth hard surface that was easy to sweep and keep clean. Cow dung was also used for fuel. It was collected from the ground and slapped by hand onto the outside walls of the house, where it would stay, drying in the hot sunshine until such time as it was required to make a fire.

Cow dung pats drying on a wall for later use as cooking fuel

As outcastes, the dalits were not allowed to use the village well; therefore they had to fetch their water from a mud-bottomed rainwater catchment tank. Because of their social standing they also had a separate communal latrine, which was simply a large hole in the ground surrounded by a wattle fence and covered by a makeshift roof, not easy or pleasant to use, as I learnt to my cost on more than one occasion. The villagers mostly used the surrounding fields.

Larger villages had their own schools, which children attended when their parents could spare them from work in the fields. Girls would cease going to school earlier than boys, as it was not considered so necessary for them to have an education. The village schools had no books, desks or seats, the only teaching aids being a blackboard and chalk, and children's own slates and stone styluses. A lot of the teaching was done by rote, with the children copying work from the blackboard. The children sat cross-legged with wooden planks supported on stones serving as their desks.

Inside a village school

The survey team met the headman and elders first

Once the headman and elders of the villages had agreed to take part in the survey, and the preliminary planning was done, then Chinappa and his young colleagues would leave Kastur on their bicycles at dawn in order to catch the villagers at home before they went to work in the fields. They worked in pairs and visited day after day, systematically conducting the house-to-house survey until they had covered the whole survey area.

Chinappa and a colleague check a villager for signs of leprosy

In this way it was established that leprosy was endemic in the area. Only then was a Government Grant obtained and the treatment centres established in a number of locations so that no patients had to travel more than five miles to collect their medication, all treatment being free. Transport between villages was extremely limited, being either by bullock cart, bicycle, or more often than not, on foot.

127

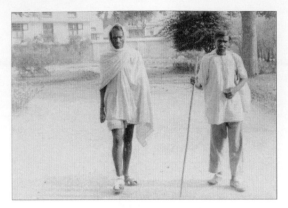
Leprosy patients walking to clinic

The team from the Holdsworth Memorial Hospital visited each treatment centre regularly to hold clinics for the diagnosis and treatment of leprosy, as well as identifying patients who needed shoes and reconstructive surgery. About fifteen per cent of the patients had the infective form of lepromatous leprosy and vigorous follow-up treatment of these patients was maintained in order to render them non-infective.

In 1976 we revisited Mysore and spent a day at Dr Singh's Home for leprosy patients, near Mysore City. There was still a need for ongoing care for those who had contracted leprosy but new cases were not as common as we had found before. This was no doubt due to two factors, one being the education of people in early recognition of the disease and the other the effectiveness of Dapsone in treating the disease.

Visiting Dr Singh's clinic in 1976

In the late 1990s, when thirty years after leaving India we returned to visit the clinics, we found virtually no remaining lepromatous leprosy cases and very little need for reconstructive surgery, this being the result of early diagnosis and the further improvements to the effectiveness of treatment brought about by the advent of multi-drug therapy.

It was in Kastur that Sister Ethel Tomkinson lived and worked, and she left the legacy of a small caring Christian community that is still there today. In 1960 I wrote 'home' to England about her work.

> *'We ourselves do not see much of her as she spends most of the time walking around villages. She is in her 70s and is amazingly active, walking ten to fifteen miles a day, visiting the sick and aged. Her ashram, where she lives with some Indian colleagues, is about thirty miles from Mysore and it includes a dispensary and nursery school. Sister Ethel cares for the women of the villages. She visits their homes and conducts Bible study, runs retreats for the women, and gives them advice and pubic health teaching. She treats illness where she can, and helps in the hospital at Kastur and another village called Hadya.*
>
> *One of her greatest triumphs just recently has been the digging of a bore well at Kastur. Water was struck and now, with the help of an electric pump, water is pouring out over the fields that before were dry and barren for most of the year. She collected the money privately and was responsible for the whole work. She has a great name in the area and is respected by everybody.'*

Sister Ethel collecting pumped water from the Kastur bore well

Before we leave this chapter I would like to tell you a little more about my friend, Kamala. As a young girl of about thirteen years of age Kamala had been struck down with poliomyelitis, which left her with paralysis of both legs and both hands. Her family struggled for many, many years to find a cure for her to no avail, consequently she was confined to the house most of the time, unable to walk or perform any tasks.

129

Kamala Watsa with her mother and sister Ruby

I first met Kamala in St. Bartholomew's Church one Sunday morning when her brother carried her in to join in the morning service. She must have been about thirty years of age then. After the service I spoke to her, and as the years went by, she became a very dear friend. We were of similar age and found so much to share. She was always smiling and never complained about her condition. One day she asked if it would be possible for her to come to the leprosy clinic with us and after one visit she was hooked, being fascinated to see what could be done for the patients and their deformities. As we carried Kamala into the clinic the leprosy patients would remark, 'There goes somebody much worse off than us, at least we can walk!'

One day, Frank made a thorough examination of Kamala's hands and thought that he might be able to help her by doing some reconstructive surgery to the tendons and, after some thought, she asked him to go ahead. First of all I worked with Kamala, using the hot wax treatment and massage, to free the tight contractures in her fingers. Frank operated on her right hand and all went well. Once the stitches were removed my services were needed again to teach her the new wrist and finger movements. I was used to treating leprosy patients, who with their loss of sensation felt no pain and usually launched into their exercises with great gusto, so much so, that I feared Frank's stitch work might break down. I was quite unprepared for the amount of pain Kamala would feel because she had not lost sensation. The pain was really severe, but we persevered slowly and gently with the exercises, until eventually she was able to hold a pencil and write. Following this Kamala asked for the left hand to be treated and later learnt to type and proof read documents for the local Wesley Press. She was then also able to help us with the patient note keeping at the leprosy clinic.

Chapter Eleven
Famine Relief

Once the leprosy clinics in the Kastur area were established it became apparent that treatment could not be confined just to the care of leprosy but that other coincidental diseases and their causes needed attention. In this way we became very involved in the welfare of villagers.

The Chamrajanagar District lies in the shadow of the Biligiri Hills. These hills often captured the monsoon rain at the expense of the area below, resulting in a failure of the monsoon in the Chamrajanagar area.

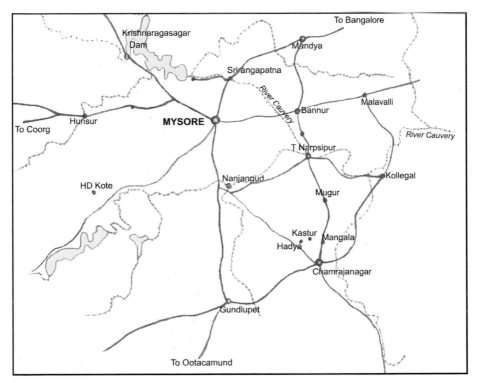

Map of Mysore area, showing the villages of Hadya and Kastur, far from a river if the monsoon failed

The villagers were all poor subsistence farmers, solely dependent upon crops from their small plots of land for a living. During really hard times the seed grain more often than not was used to feed the children. Then, in order to purchase more seed grain to plant when rains arrived, the people had to borrow money from a moneylender, usually the local landlord. Borrowers were made to sign for up to twice the sum of money taken as a loan and were frequently ordered to pay ten per cent a month interest on the 'doubled' loan, an absolutely impossible situation. Thus it came about that the poor farmer had to surrender his property, if he owned

131

any. If not the members of his family, in turn, became bonded to the moneylender. Often the whole family were virtually enslaved, providing the moneylender with free labour.

When visiting the Chamrajanagar village areas during times of famine, we discovered many families existing on just a handful of peanuts a day. In their poverty stricken state they were helpless to improve their situation in any way. I appealed to the Government officials in Mysore City for help in providing some rice, free of charge, to the area and offered to assist with distribution. Sadly, because there was plenty of rice for sale in the Mysore market, it proved to be exceedingly difficult for these officials to understand the desperate state of the penniless villagers thirty miles away. They just said, 'There's plenty of rice here in the market. Why can't the villagers come into the city by bus and buy some?' They utterly failed to grasp the devastating situation of people trying to exist entirely without purchasing power. Thus it came about that I, in addition to the physiotherapy, the fundraising, accounts and record keeping, for all aspects of the leprosy work, found myself deeply involved in famine relief work.

Grain supplies were available from the USA through the agencies of the Indian Christian Council. The sacks of grain would arrive by rail from Bombay. When notice was received of the arrival of one or two wagonloads at the Mysore railway station, I would cycle to the station and, after a certain amount of bargaining, hire a convoy of about twenty bullock carts. After supervising the transfer of grain sacks from the train on to the bullock carts I proceeded, on my bicycle, to escort them through the city streets to a large garage situated within the garden of Sawday Lodge. This procedure was necessary to ensure that no grain was stolen en route. We must have been quite a sight! The fairly strict supervision was necessary because, although often the bullock cart drivers were in need of extra food themselves, every ounce of grain received had to be accounted for, and any shortfall would be deducted from the next consignment. The rules were so strict that no exception was made for loss through holes in sacks damaged in transit. I used to feel very upset about these rules because the people's need for food was so desperate. I well remember one occasion when a coolie was happily perched cross-legged on top of his loaded bullock cart clutching a cloth bundle full of grain. He was also holding a short length of water piping which had been trimmed to a point at one end. Concealing it beneath his dhoti he had been able to use this ingenious device to pierce the sack, thus allowing some of the grain to run down the pipe into the cloth. I did not have the heart to scold him too much as he himself was in need of a good meal. This incident illustrates how far from reality some of the aid agencies were when they insisted on such meticulous accounting, especially when we heard that USA was dumping grain out at sea at the time.

After we took delivery of a consignment, arrangements had to be made for the grain to be transported to the outlying village feeding centres by bullock cart or by the jeep. Locally, the grain could only be distributed in cooked form and a register had to be kept recording every ounce given. All of this entailed a tremendous amount of paperwork. Copies of records, in triplicate, from each distribution centre had to be sent to the headquarters of the Indian Christian Council. Kitchens themselves had to be organised and supervised. The church members and village elders undertook the provision of food centres whilst I made sure that they received the necessary supplies and dealt with all the paperwork.

Food distribution in a village

I always felt sad, watching whole families queuing up for gruel at the distribution centres, and after a while it was felt that it would be more dignified, and better for the self-respect of the people, if grain could be distributed to the men and women in return for work. Consequently, during the course of really bad times, we organised some of the men into a working team.

One project was the building of a small bridge over the stream bed which, when completed, enabled our vehicle to be driven right into their village. This was a huge advantage to us because we were no longer forced to use precious time and energy walking the last mile carrying the full sacks of grain.

Another project was to improve the drainage system for wastewater in and around a number of the villages. Yet another was the encouragement of cottage industries. Some of the men and women made doormats from coconut fibre. The women and girls embroidered cotton hand towels, tablecloths and matching table napkins, these being much in demand amongst the Indian ladies in Mysore and Bangalore, and to visitors to Mysore, a city on the tourist trail. Cotton spinning was introduced although this was not popular. As the years went by, the villagers were able to earn a little cash, with which to purchase food and clothing with their own money, thus alleviating the need to beg. Unfortunately, as soon as the rains started again most people abandoned these jobs. They returned to the land only to find that, when the rains failed again a year or two later, their situation rapidly returned to subsistence level. One of the most outstanding features of this whole programme which involved feeding those in desperate need, and the development of the leprosy survey and subsequent treatment centres, was that it caused people irrespective of caste, creed or social standing to work together harmoniously for the common good.

In a final effort to solve the problem and following on from my experiment with silk worms several years earlier, I made contact once again with the Mysore Silk

Company and the National Christian Council in India. After I explained the situation, the promise of grants towards setting up a pilot scheme based in the village of Hadya was obtained. The village and church workers first of all planted out a field of mulberry bushes. A few people had some misgivings about this because the need for food was so great. However, the scheme went ahead in faith.

A field of mulberry bushes

Whilst the mulberry bushes were growing, the villagers were receiving instructions from the Silk Factory workers as to the correct way to tackle the actual feeding and care of silk worms during their growing stage. To this end large, shallow, circular trays surrounded by a raised edge were woven. A good number of the villagers were keen to take on the responsibility of rearing the worms. They were each issued with a few trays together with a rack on which to stack them.

A silkworm rearing tray

Once hatched the larvae were spread out on the trays and the task of feeding them with chopped up mulberry leaves began. The worms continued to feed non-stop for about a month. It was truly amazing to see how much food the worms consumed and the rate at which they grew. A few days before spinning they would need to eat ten times a day and this entailed the members of each household taking turns throughout the day and night replenishing the mulberry leaves. During the whole length of the feeding period it was essential to clean the feeding trays regularly. The next job was to prepare 'mats' where the worms could be placed for spinning. The spinning process takes about five or six days.

A cocoon spinning tray

Initially the Silk Factory paid for the cocoons by weight. Over 2,000 silk worms are needed to produce one pound of silk.

Weighing the silk cocoons

The silk worm rearing experiment was very popular with the villagers and we were advised that it would be more profitable to skein off the silk thread before selling. We set about devising quite primitive equipment whereby the cocoons were placed into a pot of hot water, which both killed the worms and loosened the filaments. Filaments from several cocoons were reeled off together on to a hand turned reel, making a strong thread. This was then sold in skeins to the factory at a more profitable price.

Spinning the silk

During the year 2006 a group of 'Friends of the Holdsworth Memorial Hospital' in the UK visited Kastur and Hadya area where they found the sericulture thriving. It had even extended out to the surrounding village areas. One comment made was that the villagers had risen from hard to lean times. Families were able to feed and clothe their children and all looked happy and contented.

Regarding those indebted to the moneylenders, in the early days we received some financial donations from friends in England. These gifts were used to help gain the freedom of families who were absolutely destitute and living in bondage to the moneylenders.

Endless patience was needed to cope with this part of the work; it seemed almost impossible to get anyone to understand the idea of putting money aside during the good times so that there would be some in hand for the hard times. Despite these frustrations we really enjoyed the village work and made many lifelong friendships.

Access to water was a problem in the villages. Quite a number had a well but sometimes, owing to the caste system, water from this was available to only the high caste villagers. The lower caste people had to rely on the water 'tank', which stored rainwater. These tanks were usually about the size and shape of four tennis courts and about eight feet deep with sloping sides. The base was constructed of pounded earth and clay and the sides of large stones embedded into a mixture of earth and clay. In normal times these tanks worked very efficiently, but in times of drought, when the level of water dropped, the hot sun dried out the exposed lining of the tank resulting in it cracking and loss of water through the cracks when the monsoon arrived.

During the years 1956/57, with the help of funds from OXFAM and War on Want, repairs were carried out on a number of damaged water tanks thus providing paid work for some of the villagers. Later in 1964 OXFAM arranged for two or three bore wells to be dug within the Kastur and Hadya area and this made an enormous difference. It was very evident when we visited the area in 1995 and again in 2006 that the resulting steady supply of water had led to the change from famine conditions to 'lean times'.

For about ten years my mode of transport to the villages was a very ancient, decrepit jeep. Changing gear in particular was a skilled operation of double de-clutching. I was always careful to park the jeep in the garage at the corner of the compound following the day when I came out of the house in the morning to find the vehicle propped up on piles of bricks with all four wheels missing. Two OXFAM representatives visited us in 1964 and I drove them around from village to village all day. It had been a hot, and tiring exercise, and one of them offered to drive us back to Mysore. I did warn him that the engine was rather temperamental and, sure enough, within a mile or two of coping with the uneven, tricky surface of the road, the gears refused to change. I took over again and drove us home without a word. I had no complaint to make about my dear old jeep. Imagine our joy when a year later a beautiful new Jeep Station Wagon arrived in Mysore, quite unsolicited, a gift from OXFAM, with a note to say that a group of some 160 people had walked to raise money for the purchase of the vehicle. This brand new vehicle, with its high suspension, seating for eight people and sizeable baggage space was ideal for both the leprosy work and with the distribution of food aid. On each side of the vehicle were printed the words, 'Holdsworth Memorial Hospital Mysore - Village relief - Leprosy relief - OXFAM Committee for Famine Relief'. We were so very grateful for this wonderful support.

The Jeep station Wagon donated by OXFAM

During our time in Mysore City, from 1951 to 1967, we experienced two periods of drought. The first was of three years' duration, from 1953 to 1956, and the second lasted five years, from 1961 to 1966. It was so much part of life in Mysore that I would write home to friends and family with a casual remark that 'the monsoon has failed' or 'the monsoon has broken', without any explanation of the reality that lay

137

behind the statement.

Mysore City was fortunate in that it had a very good municipal water supply piped from the Krishnaraja Sagar Dam, that contains the water of the Cauvery River just eighteen miles distant from the city. The massive dam was built over the years 1911 to 1917, another project fostered by Maharaja Krisnaraja Wodeyar, the same Maharaja who donated the land for Holdsworth Memorial Hospital. The dam water covers an area of one hundred and thirty square kilometres when full, but even so, during times of monsoon failure the people of Mysore city suffered great shortages of water, with regular cuts in the municipal supply. The hospital and some houses, including our own, had their own water storage tank on the roof, which helped, but in the surrounding area each street was depended upon its single standpipe. In times of great hardship a lorry would come round once a day. From this people could collect one bucket of water per household. In the city all the grass in the parks and gardens withered away and the mains water supply dwindled until it was just a trickle of brownish water coming through the taps.

Everywhere layers of reddish brown dust would settle. It was futile to think of sweeping. In the hospital the cleaners produced long handled mops by tying strips of old cloth to the end of a pole. Devaputra did the same at home, and, armed with the mop and a bucket of water, he would swish the wetted mop from side to side across the painted concrete floors, gathering up the dust and leaving a cool, clean, wet surface behind. It was most effective and efficient. Of course when water was desperately short mopping up the dust was a luxury that had to be forgone.

The situation was much more critical in the villages that were dotted throughout the countryside to the south of Mysore City. They were beyond the reach of canal water from the dam and were not supplied with piped water. The villages had to rely on a well for domestic purposes and on the rainwater that had been caught in the tank, as described earlier in this chapter, which collected monsoon water for irrigating the crops.

Village water tank during drought

India is a vast country and the weather pattern varies somewhat between the north and the south. In recent times rainy periods have been occurring outside of the monsoon pattern, but when we lived in Mysore the 'seasons' were quite clearly defined. During the months of November, December and January it would tend to be dry and sunny, with a clear, bright blue sky every day and an average temperature climbing from twenty-six to thirty-two degrees centigrade during the day. Through the months of February, March and April the air would become warmer and the atmosphere oppressive. May was usually the hottest month and this would hopefully bring in the time for the main monsoon of the year. Sometimes grey clouds built up and came to nothing, but when the thunder started in the distance, we would all look up and wait for the relief of rain.

When the thunder drew nearer, vivid flashes of lightning would streak across the sky. A wind would build up and bang the doors and shutters. It would be followed by another terrific crash of thunder, then, down came the rain - not just a few drops but a mighty torrent. We would rush out into the garden, just to stand and feel the blessed rain on our faces. The smell of wet earth was heavenly.

I vividly remember one year when the boys were little and the girls were home from school. We had gone with 'Uncle' Hugh in his old Morris Traveller to swim in the River Cauvery at a spot below the dam, called 'Balamori'. Here the water ran smoothly through a deepish channel past some temple steps and beside a man-made island that housed a Hindu deity and was anchored to the riverbed by the tangled roots of an old banyan tree. Hugh often took the children, along with his nieces, Kitty and Valerie Dearmun, to swim at this place where they could get into the water without the hazards of mud and thorny undergrowth.

While we were out some clouds had appeared in the sky and a cool wind began to blow. Hugh thought it would be a good idea to pack up and go home, as maybe the monsoon rains were about to begin. How right he was, for within a few minutes a terrific flash of lightning streaked across the sky, followed almost immediately by crashing thunder. The children had dressed in record time but just as we reached the car the rain came down in torrents. So heavy was the downpour that you could not see further than a couple of yards. It was impossible to drive away, so we waited in the car, with water hammering on the roof, for the deluge to die down.

Suddenly, a dazzling, crackling flash of lightning lit the area close by. It was followed by a huge bang and the car shuddered as something crashed to the ground with a bright flash only about thirty yards away. 'Was it a thunderbolt?' we wondered. Unfortunately we never did find out as the heavy rain continued for quite a time. Eventually Hugh was able to drive us home, but what a dramatic way to witness the onset of a monsoon!

During a 'normal' year there would be another, smaller, monsoon between the months of August, September and October. These days the main monsoon season has drifted to the period between June and September.

Drought still affects Mysore from time to time, with the Krisnaraja Sagar Dam waters dropping to less than half the normal level and a disastrous effect on the lives of farming families, particularly south of the city of Mysore. In 2002 the taluks of T

Narsipur, Hassan, Mandya and Chamrajanagar were badly hit by failure of rain for the second year running and crops could not be raised. In some areas the rain in 2002 was less than half the monsoon average. The village of Heggada Devana (HD) Kote faired comparatively well, with rainfall of only 583.1mm instead of 904mm, but the hardship was profound, triggering the need for loans for villagers to purchase food, income-earning alternatives and government and non-government aid to pay the farmers to plant trees and to de-silt village water tanks in readiness for hoped for rains during the forthcoming year.

In a year of good monsoon, when the rain comes in time to help break up and moisten the hard earth of the fields, the villages become alive with activity. Everyone gets busy hoeing and planting seed grain and there is at last plentiful water to enjoy a good wash beside the village water tank. In good times the villagers are happy and smiling once more in the hope that there will be a good harvest.

The experiences we had in the villages and the opportunity to be some help in famine relief would not have been possible without all the people who provided financial and prayerful support for the leprosy and village work. It also could not have happened without the hard work and loyal support we received from our wonderful servants. Only because of them was it possible for me to undertake all the multifarious jobs and duties that came my way. In fact, they entered into the spirit of the work and became part of the team. After an early morning chat to Augustine and Mary I could walk across the compound to the hospital, or go out for the day to the village clinics, knowing that they would watch over the children, prepare meals, clean the house and deal with callers until my return.

140

Chapter Twelve
The School Run and the Keddah

As mentioned in the previous chapter the pattern of our lives changed considerably at the end of 1956. Not only did we move house to live on the hospital compound but also Jenny joined and Rosemary returned to Hebron School in the Nilgiris in February 1957. To begin with it was possible to use our car for the journey to school by fitting a roof carrier, onto which their school trunks could be loaded. This arrangement worked well for a couple of years but when John, and then David, became old enough first for Hebron (primary school for the boys) and then for Lushington, (the older boys' school in Ootacamund), it became necessary to send the trunks separately to the schools by public carrier. We would then follow by car a day or two later.

The children had a large quantity of luggage to be sent to school at least once a year. They each had to take a trunk, containing their full quota of uniform (with a canvas rain cape and extra uniform for use during monsoon, when drying was extremely difficult), brown shoes for school days and black shoes for Sundays, plimsolls, Wellington boots, one set of warm 'mufti' clothes for rare special occasions, their own handkerchiefs, towels, face flannels, table napkins, bed linen, blankets and pillows, a swimsuit and swimming towel, one toy each, a Bible and a hymn book, a story book, their own sponge bag, soap and toothpaste, sweets (for the daily allowance of one sweet from the 'tuck shop') and a place setting of cutlery. Every single item had to be named clearly, the clothes and linen with tape that would resist the beating on the rocks and hanging on bushes by the dhobi wallah. I ordered Cash's nametags from England and was busy, evening after evening, sewing on the tags.

As the years went by our family grew older and larger in stature and the children from other families living in Mysore grew likewise. Even though the children travelled with only what they wore, by 1962 the small cars were not considered adequate to cope with the school journey. As several families were travelling to the same schools on the same day, arrangements were made with the hospital authorities that, providing we covered the cost of wear and tear and petrol, the hospital station wagon could be used each term for the 'school run'.

On the last day of each holiday the children would gather together early in the morning at our bungalow. It was a forlorn little group that helped load the small items of baggage, together with plenty of water, soft drinks and sandwiches into the station wagon. On one occasion the whole scene was changed when Paul Gore-Booth, then British High Commissioner to India (knighted 'Sir Paul Gore-Booth' in 1961), called unexpectedly as he journeyed through Mysore on the way to Bangalore. A snake charmer appeared at our gate almost simultaneously and Mr Gore-Booth immediately sat down on the veranda steps with the children to watch the snake charmer. All thoughts of the return to school were lost for a short time while they watched, fascinated by the wailing of the snake charmer's pipes and the control that he had over the performing cobra.

Frank or I, singly or together, would drive the party up to the hills, first dropping the older boys off at Lushington School in Ooty and then the girls and younger boys at Hebron School in Coonoor. Often we had eight children aboard including our own family, which made quite a squash.

Packing the station wagon for the journey to school

We always did our best to begin the journey really early in the morning, preferably by 6am, just as the sun was rising. At that hour there was very little traffic and we could watch the sun gradually emerging above the horizon on our left, casting long shadows from the many-rooted banyan trees that grew along the early stretch of the road. A few buses and long-distance lorries would come along but, more often than not, we drove for miles and miles without encountering another motorised vehicle.

Year by year, following our first journey to the Nilgiris in 1952, a great deal of work took place to improve the surface of the road, so that from 1956 onwards the whole journey took only about four hours. The children were always extremely good at amusing themselves, sometimes playing 'I spy' games, and at others making up eerie ghost stories or singing songs. A popular game was counting the number of milestones, or how many bullock carts we passed along the way. It was a main trunk road and scores of bullock cart 'caravans', carrying all sorts of commodities, would lumber their weary way along the road from village to village. Often the bullock cart driver would be fast asleep on the top of his loaded cart. The bullocks knew their way without his guidance, but we needed to take care because they were not always on the correct side of the road. At intervals we would come across a couple of young boys slowly driving their family's herd of goats and cows away from their village for the day in search of a few blades of grass in the surrounding countryside. During times of drought the boys carried long poles with machetes or curved blades attached to one end. With this device they would cut leaf-bearing branches down from the trees that lined the roadside. The leaves provided much needed greenery for the animals, but of course the trees suffered.

The countryside changed dramatically along the route from Mysore to

Ootacamund. The Mysore plateau stands at about two thousand feet above sea level, making the climate very pleasant for most of the year. Even in the hot season, when the temperature reaches 100+°F, there was usually a gentle, cooling breeze throughout the night. During normal climatic conditions the land was very fertile. Rice, millets, chillies, large radishes, green vegetables, plantains and mangoes all grew in abundance. Alongside some stretches of the Cauvery River sugarcane was grown extensively. Elsewhere, mulberry was cultivated as a cash crop, the leaves being sold to the local sericulture industry as food for their silkworms. When we left the country in 1966 large areas of land were being designated for growing sunflowers, a lucrative cash crop. The fields were a glorious sight when the sunflowers were in bloom. In the morning all their bright golden 'faces' would be facing towards the morning sun and, by the evening, as we drove past on our homeward journey, they would be facing the opposite way, having followed the sun from east to west.

Villages were scattered at intervals along the main Mysore to Ooty road until the point where we entered the Bandipur Forest Reserve. Here the jungle took over for about twenty miles. During the years when the monsoon rains came, both the countryside and jungle appeared beautifully green and lush, but if there had been four or five years without good rain, the scene was completely different. During our stay the rains failed, on one occasion for three years and another for five years in succession. Then we would be driving through an almost barren wasteland, with not a blade of grass in sight and the trees denuded where their leaves had been cut for cattle fodder. Fine, red dust lay on the ground like a carpet, smothering everything. The dust would billow up around the car as we drove along and at the end of our journey our hair and clothes had changed in colour and our mouths were dry and gritty. During such times the jungle region was silent, the landscape ashen grey and barren. Not a grasshopper whirred. The utter silence was quite unnerving. Everything was tinder dry and, sometimes, spontaneous fires would flare up, causing great damage. We could not imagine how the land would recover, yet, when eventually the rains came, within a couple of days the grass began to send up tiny bright green shoots. On the trees the leaf buds began to swell, the birds sang again and the insects began to stir. It was as if all nature rejoiced and was reborn. It was truly wonderful.

The Bandipur Forest Reserve covered an area of 334 square miles and contained large plantations of teak trees in various stages of maturity. Many different types of bamboo were also cultivated. Some varieties stood twenty to thirty feet high, with delicate foliage that looked very beautiful when rippling in a sunlit breeze. One year we discovered that a whole swathe of fully mature bamboo had been felled and we felt so sad about this. Later we were told that bamboo plants flower only once in 20, 30 or 50 years, according to the variety, and after flowering the plant dies. At that time the bamboo poles are cut right down for use as scaffolding, ladders and posts. Fresh planting then begins. In patches among the cultivated trees of teak, redwood and sandalwood, the brilliant red bracts of huge poinsettia bushes caught the eye. Jacaranda and laburnum trees also flowered, brilliant mauve and bright yellow, in glorious abandon within their natural setting.

During most of our journeys to school we would see a few spotted Sika deer, two or three families of various types of monkey and maybe a peacock or two. On one exciting occasion we saw a tiger crossing the road in front of us. Bandipur was a tiger reserve but the big cats were very rare. This one and only sighting in the wild happened so quickly, just a fleeting glimpse as the tiger leapt into cover on the other side of the road.

On a number of occasions we did witness the wonderful scene of a group of working elephants. Each elephant had a mahout perched just behind his or her head giving directions. The mahouts instructed mostly with their feet, pushing or kicking the leather of the elephants' great ears. The team needed hardly any instruction as they moved the logs from newly felled trees, using their trunks, tusks and feet to push, lift and position the timber. One huge elephant followed our car along the road. We felt very small as we peered upwards, not even able to see the top of his back.

Working elephants in the jungle

The elephants were mostly taken from the wild and trained. Once every ten years or so a Keddah was held in the Bandipur Nature Reserve, when scores of wild elephants were rounded up and captured. It was incredible to think that these wild creatures would be trained in a matter of a few months and most would be sold to work in the timber industry.

The Keddah was a huge undertaking. Some weeks prior to a drive a chosen area of jungle was surveyed and the wild elephant population assessed. Preparations were then made for the drive, which ideally should culminate beside the river that ran through the jungle.

Before the Keddah a large area of jungle alongside the river was cleared of trees and scrub, and a massive stockade was constructed out of tree trunks. This was then ringed by three rows of logs that were rammed deep into the ground, at an angle, leaving defence walls measuring about ten feet high above the ground. A wide funnel of logs led from the riverbank and narrowed into the stockade. Once the elephants were trapped inside the stockade a huge barrier was dropped down to cover the opening completely, thus leaving no escape for the elephants.

On the completion of the stockade, final preparations for the drive were made. Hundreds of men, mostly jungle dwellers, were hired as 'beaters', and they would be stationed at intervals to form a large semicircle surrounding the elephant herds, the pivot being the stockade.

When the signal was given for the drive to begin a great cacophony of noise would erupt. The men beat drums, shouted, blew whistles and created as much noise as possible, walking forward and slowly, gradually, decreasing the size of the semicircle surrounding the elephants. Overnight the beaters would set up camps and light fires to keep the elephants within the human trap whilst they took some rest.

Over several days the wild elephants were driven nearer and nearer to the centre of the circle, the area on the riverbank where the stockade had been erected. The beat continued daily, pulling the strings of a great noose around the herds, until the animals, trapped by the noise, had no alternative but to plunge into the river and straight into the funnel that led to the stockade. Once they were all inside, a barrier was closed behind them, making escape impossible.

It sounds simple when explained like this, but it must have been overwhelmingly frightening for the poor wild elephants, as well as for the beaters, who were mostly on foot with no more than a stout length of wood to stave off attack. It is hard to imagine the huge cacophony of noise, the terrified screaming and trumpeting of the elephants, the stampede crashing through the jungle, trees broken down in the crush, men whirling rattles, beating drums and shouting, all enveloped in billowing dust and the overwhelming heat, everywhere, culminating in the frightened elephants trying to break free from within the stockade.

We did not actually get the chance to witness the drive. This was a 'privilege' that people paid money to see, and not without risk to their personal safety. However, in January 1961, during the children's school holiday, we did visit the Keddah camp one week after the 'Drive'.

The girls and Michael Watsa (Kamala's nephew) cross the river by raft

Botha VanIngen, a retired shikari and great friend of the family, took us there. We saw the huge stockade alongside the river and were directed to a row of crudely constructed wooden benches. Once seated, we listened with rapt attention while someone explained to us all that had taken place. We then walked through the cleared area where the wild elephants were confined while they underwent training. I suppose it was a bit like breaking in wild mustang horses. The more resistant adult elephants were shackled by one fore leg and one hind leg to stout trees. It was sad to see the injuries that some had sustained by straining at the chains or during their struggle to get free from the stockade. We were somewhat reassured by the great care being given by a dedicated team of workers to those injured. One elephant that had very severe injuries from an accident in the stockade was being nursed hanging in a sling, which was suspended from a tripod constructed from strong logs. We were told that an elephant should not be left lying on the ground for periods of time.

The injured elephant was suspended between log trestle

There was one tiny elephant that had been born immediately after the drive. He looked so sweet and cuddly, standing about waist high. We made quite a fuss of him and were greatly surprised by his physical strength because he appeared to be quite tottery on his legs, rather like a newly born calf. On stroking his back, we discovered that short, very stiff and prickly, black hairs covered his skin.

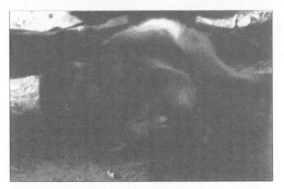

The new born elephant calf

Later in the day we watched a wild elephant, tethered between two tame elephant

146

'tutors', being led down to the river to drink and bathe.

The newly caught elephants were taken to bathe in the river as part of their training

We were told that the wild elephants quickly adapt to their new surroundings and become excellent workers. A mahout would be teamed up with each newly trained elephant, in a partnership that often lasted for the lifetime of both of them. We felt great respect for their skills and were always delighted when, driving through the jungle on the road to the Nilgiris, we would pass a group of elephants at work, deftly moving huge newly felled tree trunks into tidy stacks.

On our route to the Nilgiris there was a favourite place by a tributary river, where we often stopped for driver's rest and picnic lunch. There was always an air of excitement when we quietly brought the car to a halt. We never lost the hope that one day we might, just might, see a tiger that had come to the river to drink. To my great relief the most we ever saw at this spot were chattering monkeys and at one time otters playing in the river. Often I wonder how I would have reacted had a tiger actually appeared whilst all the children were scattered about and playing. It made me feel very nervous but I always endeavoured to appear completely calm and relaxed.

On most of our journeys we experienced hot sunny days but during the monsoon the driving was quite nerve-wracking, especially on the return journey to Mysore when darkness fell. The car headlights weakly lit the unmarked tarmac road and the rain would pour down in torrents. The old-fashioned flat windscreen wipers had to work overtime. Sometimes the rain would be accompanied by a strong wind and piercing flashes of lightning, followed by crashing thunder. I remember once driving home from school on my own with a carload of children in just such a storm after darkness had fallen. We were passing through the jungle area and to help pass the time Valerie, Hugh Warren's niece and close friend of Jenny, decided to tell a blood curdling ghost story. She described a spooky house and reached a point where, in her words, 'the blood was drip, drip, dripping, through the floorboards and through the ceiling. Drip, drip, drip!' All the time I was trying to concentrate hard on driving through the blinding rain, and we were surrounded by tall jungle trees, swaying in the wind. I could not help worrying about what we would do in this isolated spot if the car broke down. There was blackness all around and no light apart from the car headlights and the occasional blinding flash of lightning. Suddenly, the blood-dripping story was more than I could cope with and I called a halt to storytelling until we were out in the open countryside beyond the jungle. I don't think we ever heard the end of that story.

The days of tourism had not yet arrived and on our journeys throughout the countryside there were no facilities such as 'service stations'. Inevitably, after a few hours of travel we needed to answer the call of nature. On the plains often the only cover for miles around would be lantana bushes, a clump of prickly pear cacti, or perhaps one of the banyan trees. We did our best to select an isolated spot but almost always, the moment the car engine ceased to make a noise, people would appear, as if from the very ground itself, to see what was going on. We learnt to cope with this situation quite casually. Voluminous skirts did help us girls. When in the jungle there was more cover from the bushes but then there was fear that a snake or other danger might be lurking in the undergrowth.

There were two roads leading up to Ootacamund. Usually we chose the longer route via Gudalur, because the gradient was less steep, and it was therefore kinder on the engine. Also there were only seven hairpin bends to negotiate. Another advantage of this route was the welcome shade from the large trees that grew on the hillside, whereas the shorter Sighur Ghat route was fully exposed to the full strength of sunlight on the mountain slope. Along our usual longer route we would often see small groups of women squatted by the roadside beside heaps of granite stones, patiently chipping them into smaller fragments in readiness for the road menders. Otherwise the way was quite peaceful, with only a few vehicles and villages at longer intervals than on the plains.

Stones for road mending were hand broken by the roadside

The alternative route, the Sighur Ghat, was much shorter, but it was also very isolated. It also had seventeen, extremely tight, steep, hairpin bends. The children naturally were always thrilled by the challenges of this route, especially when we had almost reached the summit and it became necessary for everybody, apart from the driver, to pile out of the vehicle whilst it was turned around in order to negotiate a particularly steep portion of road in reverse gear. Nobody ever objected to trudging up that last stretch on foot. The biggest hazard, when undertaking the Sighur Ghat, was the risk of being completely stranded should the car break down, as very few people ventured this way and the chance of getting a lift to fetch help was remote. Happily, we always managed the journey unscathed and had the privilege of gazing at the spectacular views to be seen during the ascent.

Half way up the Sighur Ghat
Frank, David, Valerie Dearmun, Priscilla Strom, Rosemary, Kitty Dearmun, Jenny and Winnie (John was taking the photo) – quite a carload!

During the years when the children were at school we used to travel to the Nilgiris six to eight times a year and only twice did we experience a breakdown. The first took place in the middle of the day, just outside the Bandipur jungle area. Frank and I were travelling alone when the clutch pedal broke. We were some miles away from Gundelpet where the nearest garage was situated. In those days lorry drivers were most kind, helpful people. If they saw a stationary car at the roadside they always slowed down to ascertain that all was well. If not, they willingly changed a tyre, gave help and advice or fetched assistance from the nearest garage. On this occasion the lorry driver produced a towrope and towed us safely to the Gundelpet garage. The clutch pedal was immediately welded back into place and we safely completed our journey to Ooty. The helpful lorry driver was quite content to receive a few rupees for all his trouble in organising the rescue.

Another memorable episode occurred when the family were with us. The plan had been to take the children back to Hebron in Coonoor and, after leaving them safely at school, return as far as Ootacamund so that Frank could call on a Maharaja from one of the Princely States who was spending time in his summer residence in Ooty and needed medical attention. We were running terribly late and Frank felt that out of courtesy to the Maharaja he should call upon him before proceeding to

Coonoor. Rosemary and Jenny were thrilled with the idea of meeting the Maharaja and this offset their worry about being late for school. Shortly after our arrival at his hillside residence, the Maharaja realised their predicament and ordered tea for us all. Meanwhile, he gave instructions for his chauffeur to bring his car, a gleaming black Rolls Royce, round to the front of the house in readiness to drive the children to Hebron immediately they had finished tea. When they eventually began their journey back to school the girls realised that the 'chauffeur' was, in fact, the Maharaja's son. The girls have vivid memories of arriving at Hebron. As the Prince was unloading their luggage from the Rolls, Miss Hall, the Headmistress, was so busy scolding them for their late arrival, that she mistook the Prince for a taxi driver and scolded him as well. It was rather a mortifying end for the girls after the huge excitement of riding all the way from Ooty to Coonoor in a shiny, black Rolls Royce driven by a Prince. They just could not make Miss Hall understand. Admittedly it was dark when they reached Hebron so possibly Miss Hall can be forgiven for her mistake.

Rosemary, David and Jenny at Hebron School gate - 1962

No matter how frequently we did the journeys it never took the sadness out of parting for the children or for Frank and me. We knew we would not see one another for a whole term of three months or longer. The journey helped because we never knew what we might see on the way.

On one particularly thrilling occasion we came across a herd of wild elephants grazing quite close to the road. I told the children to keep absolutely quiet and brought the station wagon to a halt on the opposite side of the road. We sat inside quietly watching. Amongst the herd was a huge male elephant with about ten other elephants of varying age and size. After a few minutes he looked across at our vehicle, raised his trunk and waved it around. We were all spellbound by this spectacle at such close range. 'Keep very, very quiet and still,' I said. We sat looking for few more minutes then, suddenly, he raised his trunk high in the air once more, at the same time spreading his great ears and flapping them to and fro. Then he started to take a step towards us. Having read somewhere that this was a dangerous move I hastily started up the engine and took off at high speed. As we rounded the tight bends in the road our hearts beat fast as we hoped the elephant would not have taken the shorter route through the jungle and appear before us on the road.

When we reached Hebron the children were giving an excited and animated account of the incident to their friends, who were wishing that they could have been with them. However, one of the parents overheard all this chatter and he came over to me, very agitatedly. 'You should be ashamed of yourself, running such a risk with a car load of children,' he said. 'Do you not realise that the elephant was about to charge! It would have been quite capable of overturning the station wagon and trampling you all to death.' Wow, I really was reprimanded! Truth to tell I did not realise at the time how great a risk it was. Needless to say, as the road through the Bandipur Forest was the only one that took us to and from the Nilgiris, we continued to use it. However, I must confess that thereafter I was always even more on the lookout for possible trouble whenever we stopped for our picnics.

When the boys reached ten years of age they had to move from Hebron School to Lushington in Ootacamund. To start with we would take all the girls safely into Hebron first, this being the farthest point of our journey, then drive back to Ooty and leave the boys at Lushington. We made quite a few friends with Ooty residents who had come at various times to Holdsworth Hospital for treatment and we were grateful when after a long day on the move we could stay overnight with them before tackling the return journey to Mysore.

Miss Rene Guthrie, owner of Willingdon House, a rambling, single-storey guesthouse in Ootacamund, was one friend who came to Mysore for treatment on two or three occasions after falls. I shall never forget her kindness to me. I was a patient in the Holdsworth Hospital myself, when following an operation, I was given a blood transfusion and went into septicaemic shock. For a while I was very ill indeed and Miss Guthrie insisted that as soon as I could be moved I must go up to Willingdon House for convalescence. I was given a beautiful room, with adjoining dressing room and bathroom, and because I was too weak to wash and dress myself, Miss Guthrie arranged for our ayah, Marjorie, and David, who was at that time 3 years of age, to accompany me. (The other children were at school). I spent luxurious days resting and reading beside a lovely log fire. Marjorie enjoyed the change of scene and took David for walks in and around Ooty. John was boarding in nearby Lushington School and he was allowed out of school for a short time during the weekend to be with us. After a month I had recovered sufficiently to return to Mysore and I remain forever grateful to have known such a friend.

Chapter Thirteen
Holidays in Carrington

Once all our children were attending school our own holiday breaks had to coincide with school holidays. While there was nothing intrinsically wrong with this, ultimately it proved to be a drawback for Frank because the Nilgiri Hills were extremely popular and it was hard to find somewhere to stay during the school holidays. Many business companies and Missionary Societies owned holiday bungalows scattered all over the hills for use by their employees during the hot weather season on the plains. People came from far and wide, many from very remote areas of the country where they lived and worked, others from big cities, such as Madras, where the weather was not only very hot but also humid. This holiday was greatly treasured by one and all, and for those who lived in remote areas with little or no access to medical facilities it was an ideal opportunity to get medical advice and attention. When we stayed in or around Ooty Frank very quickly found that he was in great demand for medical help, advice and reassurance. Although he did not mind helping those in need, he was of course very much in need of rest himself. So it was more than welcome when, in 1964 and 1966, some kind planter friends gave us the use of a delightful bungalow, (normally used by tea estate personnel in need of a break) on a tea estate far away from Ooty. This holiday bungalow on Thiashola Estate was called 'Carrington' and it was a truly heavenly place.

Our first journey to Carrington in 1964 was a great adventure by road. It was daybreak as we left the 'Hospital House' in Mysore. We had already loaded the car with clothes, books and other items necessary for four weeks' holiday for six people, and a heavy load of bedding was lashed onto the car's roof rack. As the sun rose we started on our journey. Frank and I shared the driving and we reached Hebron by mid-morning. We enjoyed a welcome cup of coffee whilst David and the girls with their light luggage piled into the car. We then drove back to Lushington in Ooty where we found John all ready and waiting for us.

After a quick picnic lunch together we visited the Ooty market to purchase sufficient meat, fruit, vegetables, flour, powdered milk and many other grocery items to last for at least a week. We packed all of these commodities into the car boot and inside the car around our feet. At last we were ready for the final leg of our journey to Carrington, about thirty miles along an isolated road entirely unknown to us. As we drove along we chatted excitedly, delighted at being together again. To begin with the road surface was reasonably even, then the landscape changed from open, rolling grassland into woodland and the road changed from tarmac to rough earth. Frank drove with great care, mindful of the heavily laden car, but even so it was impossible to avoid all the huge potholes in the road. Imagine our surprise as we rounded a bend with Frank carefully negotiating an extra large pothole, when we saw the whole roof rack, together with its load, slide off the roof, across the windscreen, down over the bonnet, and roll to land with a crash in the undergrowth of the steep slope beside the road! To our utter amazement nothing seemed to be damaged, but we found it impossible to lift the loaded rack back onto the car roof and opted for the only alternative, to haul it to the side of the road and continue our journey. Frank planned to return later to load the luggage into the empty car and refit the empty roof rack.

Shortly after the corner where we lost the roof rack we reached the edge of the tea growing area and, although we still had to negotiate many twists and turns, the road was better maintained. About twenty minutes later, we reached Carrington where Augustine and Mary, our cook and ayah from Mysore, who had travelled up earlier by bus, were anxiously awaiting our arrival. They helped us unload the car and Frank was just about to set off back along the road to fetch the roof rack when the one and only bus of the day, an ancient vehicle, came along and stopped. The driver got down from his seat and said, 'Did you lose something a few miles back?' Wonderful! He and his passengers had yanked the whole carrier, together with its load, into the bus and brought it to us. They knew that such an article must belong to someone at Carrington because it was the only bungalow for miles around where Europeans lived.

Carrington bungalow was surrounded by tea bushes

Carrington was unique. The bungalow nestled on the side of a small hill within a huge valley. The ground fell away quite steeply from the front aspect, giving a magnificent view overlooking the tea plantation. Deep down on the opposite slope nestled the tea factory. More mountains rose and fell all around. In the far distance we could just glimpse the plain, six thousand feet below. Beyond the plains stood the Anamali range of hills. Often, on waking in the early morning, we would rush outside in our pyjamas just to witness the glorious sight of the sun rising over on our left. Below us would be a vast expanse of billowing white clouds, punctured by one or two dark blue mountain peaks.

At sunrise we were above the clouds

We watched in silence while the sky gradually changed from pale grey to blue and the clouds from white to a pearly grey, then to cream, until finally, the fiery orange-red ball of sun appeared, huge and glowing above the cloud mass. As the heat from the sun warmed the air, the clouds slowly began to rise. First we could see the bright sky above the clouds, then as the clouds levelled within our line of vision the sun was obliterated and below we had a clear view of the plains - a truly breathtaking experience never to be forgotten!

The clouds lifted to a view of the plains 5,000 feet below

Carrington Tea Estate was large, and all around the holiday bungalow were the neat, green tea fields, the bushes forming a flat surface, hand-picked to waist height, looking almost like the felt of a snooker table. At intervals shade trees were planted. The fields were interspersed with the steep winding footpaths used by the tea pickers. The tea bushes came right up to the garden border of the Carrington bungalow and we were able to pass the time of day with the tea pickers and watch them at work.

Tea pickers working beside the bungalow at Carrington

The tea picking was done by women, as was rice planting in the plains. By hand they would deftly pluck the top three tender tea leaves from each sprout of the bush and throw the pickings into a sack that was slung over the shoulder. When full, the sacks would be carried to the nearest collecting point and weighed by a Supervisor. Each day a different area would be plucked. Sometimes the pickers walked long distances from the factory to the plucking area designated for a particular day. Wages were calculated according to the weight of leaves plucked.

Just beyond the tea fields were grassy hillsides across which we could wander at will, and behind the bungalow was a small orchard containing apple, pear, plum and peach trees. Extending from this was an area of very overgrown scrubland where the children enjoyed pretending to be explorers charging through the jungle. We took long walks and discovered some wonderful locations giving fantastic views.

A spectacular Nilgiris view

It was at Carrington that we experienced our one and only real scare for the children's safety. We had planned a day trip and had prepared a picnic, but Frank and I were delayed by the queue of local people who had gathered at the door waiting for medical advice. The children asked for permission to walk along the road ahead of the car. Contrary to our usual practice of never allowing them to stray too far away from the immediate vicinity of the bungalow unaccompanied we said, 'Well, we shall be following you in the car in a few minutes, so off you go.' We did, however, make them promise not to wander off the road and into the jungle woodland that ran alongside the road on both sides. 'After all Rosemary was fifteen years of age and David, the youngest, was eight at the time, so why should they not have a little independence?' we reasoned. Augustine and Mary were anxious but could not overrule us. They urged the children to be very careful and not go too far.

We set off in the car shortly after they left and drove along the road for quite a long distance, much further than we imagined they could have walked in the time that had elapsed since their departure from the bungalow, and there was no sign of them. As we travelled along with the car windows open we caught a strong smell of big cat. We stopped the car, listened, got out of the car and called, drove on a little further, stopped and called again. We listened, sniffed the air, called again and still there was no response. Thoroughly alarmed, we turned the car around and rushed back to the bungalow for help. Augustine and the houseboy, Siddiah, came with us and we hurriedly drove back along the road. There was still no sign of any of the children and once again we could smell CATS. We got out of the car once more and were just preparing to venture into the undergrowth when to our huge relief the children appeared, walking back along the road towards us, exclaiming, 'Where on earth have you been? We waited for ages and decided to come back.'

They had been as alarmed as we were and had been waiting at a fork in the road. They also had smelt the odour of the panther or tiger but had taken comfort in numbers and the fact that they were each armed with a large, stout stick with which to beat off all manner of assailants. After a long wait they had heard the car come and go. Frank and I had badly under-estimated the rate at which they would walk when eager to explore new territory.

Frank, the children, Augustine, Siddiah and Mary outside Carrington

At Carrington the days passed happily. We had no distractions such as newspapers, or television, although we did have a tiny portable radio on which it was just possible to receive news in English once a day. We had taken a good supply of books to read and were resourceful in making our own amusements.

The weather during April, May and June, when the school holiday fell, was always very similar to a lovely summer day in England and most of our time was spent out-of-doors. Often, our friend, Colin Sausman, would take all of us out fishing for the day, the favourite venue being the reservoir below the Upper Bavani Dam. He would bring his catamaran and some of us would fish from this whilst others fished from the water's edge. On other occasions we would set off for long walks across the hills. I can still feel the thrill of sitting on the hillside and looking across the huge valley to the penstock, which snaked down the side of the opposite mountainside. The children brought their stout sticks and we used them to steady ourselves when negotiating the steep paths.

On days when we stayed put at the bungalow we would spend many hours sitting on the grassed area at the side of the bungalow, engrossed in a game of Patience or other similar card games. John practised shooting his precious Karumba bow and arrow, a gift from the jungle people who lived on Uncle Botha's Estate.

John with his Karumba bow and arrow

Jenny and David made ballet dancers from fallen fuchsia flowers and played with the guinea pigs given to them by Dr. Kurian of the Pasteur Institute. In the evening we often sat around a log fire in the lounge and made up stories.

I must not forget Mary and Augustine, our loyal cook and ayah, who, together with us, enjoyed these holidays to the full. Because we were so isolated from the main holiday area visitors rarely came and this made it possible for them to spend some extra time at leisure.

The Thiashola Estate and Carrington have an interesting history. Early in the year 1995, nearly thirty years after leaving India, Frank, Rosemary, and I were visiting Mysore with a group of the UK 'Friends of Holdsworth Memorial Hospital'. We spent just over a week in and around Mysore City before travelling on to the Nilgiris. For many members of the party this was their first visit to the Nilgiris and whilst they were looking around the Ootacamund area Frank and Rosemary and I, together with our great friend Dr. Jaiker Kumbl□ set off for a pre-arranged visit to Thiashola Tea Estate and Carrington.

We hired a taxi for the day and embarked upon our journey in a state of excited anticipation, quite early in the morning. We followed the road to Thiashola Tea Estate, a journey of around thirty miles from Ootacamund via Lovedale and Muklur Kundah. Mr. Pradeep Jadeja, Manager of Thiashola Estate, and his wife entertained us for lunch in their beautiful bungalow, after which Mr. Jadeja took us to visit the estate. He showed us around the Tea Factory and explained fully all the different processes needed to produce good tea. It was a fascinating insight and we ended the tour with some tea tasting.

Finally, we set off along the road to Carrington, which is more than 6,000 feet above sea level. It had lost none of its magical charm, being almost unchanged since our last visit in 1966. We stood in a row, silent, breathing deeply of the cool, clean air, and memories came flooding back as we gazed at the panoramic view spread before us. Slowly, we turned away and went inside the bungalow, took a few photographs and, on looking in the visitor's book, found our names entered in the years 1964 and 1966; absolute proof that we really had been there.

During the afternoon, Mr. Jadeja took us for a walk to a rather rough field situated a short distance behind the bungalow. Standing there, in the long grass, he told us that Thiashola Estate was one of the two original tea estates in the Nilgiris, both having been planted by Chinese Prisoners of War, imprisoned from 1856 to 1861, during the Opium Wars. The prisoners had actually lived in a camp on the Thiashola Estate and some were buried in the very field where we were standing. Their graves were unmarked. He also pointed out various undulations in the field, marking the remains of the foundations of the prisoners' living quarters. Previously, we had no knowledge of Carrington's background, apart from the fact that the Manager's bungalow was built in 1926. I like to think now that those Chinese prisoners found it a haven of peace and contentment in the 1850's just as we did in the 1960's. Although remote from home it must have been a contrast from the fighting and turmoil that was taking place in China at the time.

A few of the oldest tea trees on the estate have been left to grow and now stand about 20 feet tall, they are kept as genetic material and for interest.

Chapter Fourteen
Bylakuppe Tibetan Settlement

When I was working at the Bedford County Hospital in 1945 I was very interested in the possibilities of working in Tibet, and when the opportunity came up I went to a magic lantern talk at St Peter's Moravian Church by Reverend Driver and his doctor wife, who were working in Leh, in the Ladakh region of Tibet (now Jammu and Kashmir). I knew Frank then as a newly arrived houseman at Bedford County Hospital, and a colleague, Dr Adler, had pointed out that he was interested in working abroad. I invited Frank to the lecture and he came. The Drivers were anxious to take a helper back to Leh with them and I tentatively offered to go, subject to approval from Mission House and health checks. I thought this would be my great opportunity to work abroad helping those less fortunate than myself, and Tibet seemed to be so remote and challenging.

As it was, Frank, as soon as he qualified as a surgeon, was called by the Methodist Missionary Society to go to China and we married and sailed out together in the winter of 1947. So I did not go to Tibet, but to a mountainous region in China instead (described in our book 'Strangers in Chaotung'). However, it was during my time in India that, with one of the quirks of fate that seem to crop up in life, I was invited to join a committee that was being set up by the Government Authorities in Mysore City to help with a settlement for Tibetan people fleeing from the Chinese invasion of their country.

This was 1959, the year when the Dalai Lama finally had been forced to flee Tibet, along with thousands of his countrymen and women. Prior to this, negotiations had been taking place between the Dalai Lama and the Indian Government regarding the provision of possible settlements for his people. A number of offers were received, one of which was a 3,000 acre site in the Mysore region called 'Bylakuppe', that was immediately available with one acre provided per settler. Although the climate would be considerably hotter than Tibet, the offer was accepted and early in the New Year of 1960 the first batch of just over 650 settlers arrived in Bylakuppe.

Before the arrival of the Tibetan refugees, we (the Committee members) visited the Bylakuppe Camp site. We expected to see a pleasant wooded site and were appalled when we actually found the first portion of cleared forest was a barren wasteland, stripped of every living plant, grass, bush and tree. To provide clear space for the settlers everything had been cut down and burnt, leaving charred tree stumps sticking up through piles of black soot, which puffed up around every footfall. There was an eerie silence and it was hot and dry, with no shade from the midday sun - a totally inhospitable environment.

Into these conditions of tropical wasteland were introduced the first settlers, who had been chosen for their health and better ability to cope physically. For these people from the high altitude mountains of the cold north, who had no knowledge of agriculture or farming in a low altitude flat land, the cultural and physical shock was immense. A seemingly impossible task lay before them, to turn the ashes of what once had been jungle into a home and to raise crops and livestock.

The Dalai Lama, in his book 'Freedom in Exile' describes his impressions of Bylakuppe:-

'On 1 February 1960, the first settlers arrived at Bylakuppe in Mysore State. I heard later that when they saw the land, many of the refugees broke down and cried. The task before them seemed so immense. They had been supplied with tents and basic equipment, but apart from this, their only resource was such determination as they could bring to bear.

During the early part of 1961, I paid my first visit to the new settlement at Bylakuppe. On arrival, I found the settlers all to be very dark and thin. I saw immediately why they had been so pessimistic. The camp consisted of nothing but a few tents on the edge of a forest and, although the countryside was just as beautiful as I remembered it from my pilgrimage (in 1957 – author's note), the land itself did not look promising. Moreover, the heat from the burning debris, combined with the heat from the sun, was almost unbearable.

The settlers had made a special tent for me with bamboo walls and a canvas roof. But even though it was well made, it was no proof against the terrible dust thrown up by the clearing process. Every day, a thick cloud of smoke and soot hung over the whole area. At night it would settle slowly, penetrating every tiny opening, so that in the morning you woke up covered in a fine layer of powder. Because of these conditions morale was very low.'

A little later in the book, the Dalai Lama continues:-

'Not all our problems were practical, however. At times, our culture has made it difficult for us Tibetans to adapt to new conditions. On that first visit to Bylakuppe, I well remember the settlers being very concerned that the burning they were having to carry out to clear the land was causing the death of innumerable small creatures and insects. For Buddhists, this was a terrible thing to be doing, since we believe that all life, not just human life, is sacred. Several of the refugees even came up to me and suggested that the work should be stopped.'

Early settlers at Bylakuppe

In 1959 our Committee in Mysore had no official remit. We were there simply to help the settlers once they had arrived. It was pitiable to see them at first, for they were living under canvas in large communal tents. They were mostly eating together, with huge vessels of food being cooked over single-burner paraffin stoves. Likewise, Tibetan tea would be prepared in one very large pan that was stood precariously over a small paraffin stove.

When we arrived at camp tea would be ladled out and offered to us in individual cups. It was made from green tea leaves and water, mixed with a little yak fat. We found it hot and bland-tasting, with a hint of paraffin, but good to drink on a hot day when there was no alternative.

The Tibetan people were understandably very subdued at this time. They were struggling to remove the tree stumps and to plant a few seeds into the ground. The National Christian Council and OXFAM donated some cows, bullocks and chickens, and helped in many other ways.

Some of the cattle given by the NCC

The Tibetan men quickly changed from their traditional, warm clothes into cooler, cotton shirts and trousers, but the ladies did not find it easy to discard their long, heavy Tibetan dresses. The Indian ladies on our committee very soon devised a Tibetan style gown made from a hard wearing cotton fabric, called 'long cloth', which was produced in plain dark colours. They had a few such dresses made up and introduced them to the ladies in the camp. These proved to be a winner and very soon all the ladies made the change.

Within the space of a year it was truly amazing how the settlers worked to make this inhospitable place their home. To start with the men were busy doing the heavy agricultural jobs, whilst the women occupied themselves making items of jewellery from the silver dollars and turquoise stones which they had brought with them on their flight from Tibet. They sold these, and some small, exquisitely made woollen prayer mats, in the market place. I bought several items of jewellery for Rosemary and Jenny, and I still have in my possession a ring and a pair of earrings, a gift from one of the refugees.

A number of organisations were involved in helping with money and provisions to keep the people fed and housed. Gradually more and more tents were provided so that each family could live separately and cook their own food. One large tent was set aside for use as a Buddhist Temple and prayer flags were erected all around the camp. Thus, the people took heart and began to feel more at home.

Fortunately the burning of vegetation had not penetrated deep into the earth and after the first rains, as after a period of drought, the green shoots of grass sprang up almost overnight and the crops that they had so laboriously planted began to grow.

Within three or four years the whole camp became a much happier place and full of life. In the fields the crops were growing well, the cows were producing plenty of milk and the chickens were providing eggs. True to their religious beliefs, the Tibetans would not eat meat or eggs, so the cows were used for milk, the oxen for ploughing and other work, and the eggs were sold on, bringing in much needed income.

The National Christian Council donated money to set up a crèche, a much needed facility for the families with young children.

The crèche at Bylakuppe

Back home in Mysore we had the pleasure of giving hospitality to the Dalai Lama's sister and her Interpreter when they stayed for a three-day visit to the camp.

The Dalai Lama's sister on her visit to Bylakuppe in 1963

During their visit we had great fun making conversation. I drove them out to the camp each day and we were able to gather first hand knowledge about the requirements of the settlers. Many of the Tibetans had no immunity to some of the common diseases and this was the cause of great concern to the Dalai Lama and his sister. Tibet had previously been very cut off from the rest of the world so natural immunity to many diseases had never been acquired.

A woman and child from Bylakuppe visit Holdsworth Hospital

A local medical clinic had been set up in Bylakuppe and this provided a vaccination programme. When any of the refugees fell ill and needed surgery or hospital treatment they would be brought to the Holdsworth Memorial Hospital.

As a token of gratitude a group of Tibetan boys came to Mysore to demonstrate Tibetan dancing at our annual fundraising 'Hospital Sale'. This usually took the form of lots of stalls set up in the hospital compound and selling a mixture of goods, rather like a hospital Sale of Work in England. There would also be entertainment of some sort. One year a small elephant from the Maharaja's stables was brought by his mahout to give rides to all the children.

On the particular year when the Tibetans came to dance, a group of eight young boys arrived from the Tibetan Camp, all dressed in traditional clothes with long sleeves that they unrolled and used like flags for the dance. Our youngest son, David, was at home and halfway through the afternoon of the hospital sale, he, along with the Tibetan boys, 'went missing'. After hunting around the hospital compound I walked across the road to our house, there to find David entertaining the Tibetan lads. It seems that the boys had needed the toilet and David took them over to the house where we had flush toilets. The boys had never before seen such a wonder. They were having the whale of a time, half of them pulling the chain in the upstairs bathroom then rushing down to see what had happened downstairs, whilst the other half reversed the proceedings. Little did they realise how precious that water was, because frequently the water pressure was so low that it could not fill the upstairs cisterns, and then our poor mali had to carry water upstairs to fill the roof tank. This was before we installed a hand pump in the garden.

Sometime during 1965 the Dalai Lama visited Bylakuppe again and we, the members of the Committee, were privileged to meet with him for a short time. He always showed a great interest in the welfare of his people and was most appreciative of the help being given to them. We, in turn, were able to learn from him more about the needs of his people. During this visit the Dalai Lama kindly presented each member of the Committee with a small white scarf, a token of blessing.

Also involved in the Tibetan settlement was Mrs Kay Webb, formerly a planter's wife. Her husband had passed away and her children were grown up and settled in Australia. Having stayed so long in India, Kay felt most at home there and she became involved in aid work. Later, after I returned to England with the children in 1966, Kay carried on the leprosy control work in the Chamrajanagar district.

A strong connection with the Holdsworth Hospital in Mysore was soon established through the referral of patients from Bylakuppe clinic when they needed more complex treatment. This connection has continued and as I write in 2011, several Tibetan girls from the settlement join as students of the Holdsworth Memorial Hospital Nursing School each year. It is common to see Tibetan people, including groups of young monks in their burnt-orange robes, walking around freely in the City of Mysore, where once they were looked upon with apprehension.

More information about the thriving present-day township of Bylakuppe can be obtained by going online to a section in Wikipedia. You will see that Bylakuppe has grown into a population of about 22,000. It has a police station, commercial banks, a telephone exchange, a post office and several lodges and hotels. There are some small agricultural settlements and a number of Buddhist monasteries and schools that give quality education for up to 5,000 Buddhist monks.

The Golden Temple of Bylakuppe is described as 'walking into another world, the noisy streets of South India suddenly so very far away'. What a far cry this is from the small tent that was originally set up in the first camp in 1959!

I count myself very privileged to have lived long enough to learn about the growth of this camp brought about by the sheer pluck and determination of the first settlers, who, when they found themselves living in a few tents surrounded by the burnt, sooty remains of a jungle, did not sit down and weep for long, but set about with a will, to cultivate the land and make a home for themselves.

Chapter Fifteen
Family Journey Home

From time to time between 1964-5 Frank and I discussed the subject of the future for our family. Frank's appointment with the Methodist Missionary Society would come to an end late in 1967 and should he wish to return to Mysore it would be for a further five years.

The year 1965 arrived; Rosemary was by then fifteen and planning to take Senior Cambridge Examination in the September. She strongly adhered to her original choice of career to become a doctor and we were faced with a huge decision. Rosemary would not be able to take her 'A' levels without moving to Madras or returning to the UK on her own and neither of us wanted to split our family unit. Over the years we had witnessed a number of very sad and lonely children (whose parents were missionaries abroad) left behind in England to attend boarding school and spend school holidays with elderly relatives.

For a while Frank and I just talked things over without coming to a conclusion. There seemed to be such a huge need for workers in the Christian Hospitals and so few able to give their services for a lower than average salary, and yet, when considering the situation prayerfully, was anybody irreplaceable?

Thus it was that in September 1965 Frank and I wrote to our parents saying:-

'During the last few days we have finally come to the decision that Winnie will come home with all the children next July/August (if we can get passages) and Frank will follow in July 1967 when his present tour ends. We feel the children must get home soon to settle down to life in England and have now written to Mission House asking their views. We have also asked whether they can arrange any accommodation in the Bristol area. We have also written to Edgehill, Kingswood and Prior's Court schools regarding admission of the children next September. Finally we have asked for provisional sea passages to be booked, but wonder whether this will be possible as some ships have been taken off this run. Now that we have finally made up our minds what is right we feel much happier. We have not told the children and shall not do so until everything is cut and dried. Who knows, we may be home before then if the war business develops.' (Refering to the problems on the Pakistan border.)

Again I wrote on April 18th 1966:-

'You will be pleased to know that today we have heard that our passages have definitely been booked on the 'Galileo', a Lloyd Triestino ship, leaving Bombay on July 29th and reaching Genoa on August 10th. We hear that the rail journey onwards from Genoa takes about 15 hours, but shall no doubt receive more details about this nearer the time. The heavy baggage will be bonded through to England and cleared customs by Cook's and we shall only have to bring a couple of suitcases with us from Genoa. The children will get a chance to use their French!'

The letter continues:-

'On Wednesday we are expecting four of the staff members from OXFAM Oxford office. They are to stay with us for four days. I shall have to take them to Kastur and to the Tibetan Camp. It should be interesting to meet and talk with them; I hope they will be satisfied with what we are trying to do here. Certainly the famine conditions at Kastur and around are terrible - and we still have had no rain. Going through the jungle area to and from school we were amazed to see the utter desolation. The only greenery to be seen was on a few scattered trees. We were told that holes were being dug in the riverbed, which runs through the jungle to enable the wild animals to find a little water to drink. The hot weather is very tiring, especially as we put in a fourteen-hour working day, including Saturdays and Sunday.

'You will, of course, have heard about the famine conditions prevailing all over India. We are, as you know, especially concerned with the Chamrajanagar area and the district where the Leprosy Control Work is situated. In some ways this famine is a difficult thing to describe for there is food in the shops but the prices are rising almost daily. I think, for the most part, people living in the towns and cities are managing fairly well, even the coolies now get more money for the work they do. It is in the rural areas where the conditions are so very bad. Many villages have scarcely any water, the fields stand dry and empty, and this means there is no coolie work for the villagers on the land. Even if they wished they couldn't earn any money with which to buy food. Many village folk are coming into the towns in search of work. Those who stay on in their villages have eaten every bit of grain, (including their seed for the next crop). Wheat is coming in large quantities from America but it does not reach the more remote places unless someone with a bit of influence takes an interest.

Many Indian people say there is no famine in the land as there is really plenty for everybody in the towns, but certain people are making enormous profits on the sale of rice and other grain in what is called the 'open market'; this open market business is allowed but it is actually a black market. Food grains are rationed in that a certain quantity is allotted to each person at controlled rate but, at the same time, one can buy any amount at a much higher price in the open market! So much for this. I shall probably say too much one day! At the same time there is the huge problem of how to help the villagers in their present plight. I do not know what will be the outcome of the Oxfam staff's visit this week. They will see plenty of poverty and malnutrition but whether there is any long-term project that can be started in order to lift the whole of economic level of the villagers remains to be seen.

The leprosy work continues as before but we have not yet received the promised Government Grants for the Control Work. This recurring grant was due last June and we have been running, paying salaries etc, all these months on money donated from friends in England. Now that money is almost finished

166

(we have enough to continue running the units for about four more months) if the Government Grant does not come we shall have to close down the Control Unit. The Relief Work and hospital operative work continues and the support for this is all donated from agencies in England. People are interested in this work and we feel sure that support will continue to arrive for as long as we need it.

The hospital remains as busy as ever, if anything busier than before, but our greatest worry is finance. It is unfortunate that finance always seems to be rearing its head. Our position at the moment is that, on the general income and expenditure account we are running at a heavy loss and are unable to pay our staff as well as we should, especially the servants who unfortunately, just before an increment was being implemented for them, decided to join a Union. As a result of this they put forward some terrific claims, which the hospital could not possibly meet and now, because negotiations have been going on for the last 18 months and are still not settled, the servants have had no increase in pay. It is terribly worrying to see them now looking so thin and haggard and knowing that they are not receiving even the barest minimum of pay. We have enhanced the fees paid by patients but this does not seem to keep pace with the ever-increasing cost of drugs, linen and so on.

We are always up against shortage of medical and senior nursing staff but this is a difficulty one almost expects. Our hospital is by no means the only institution with these difficulties; indeed, I think by and large, all mission institutions whether colleges, hospitals or schools seem to be in the same position. We wonder sometimes where things have gone wrong. Is it that in the past the Missionary Societies gave too much and therefore have brought into existence a church that has not yet realised its responsibilities and commitments? Is it that the Missionary Societies withdrew their support too quickly? Looking back over the last ten years in our own Institution it is surprising the huge amounts of money that have been donated by outside organizations, as well as from Government Grants. Admittedly these grants have all been made for specific items of equipment or building. Nobody seems to want to give money towards maintenance and so we go round and round in a circle; we need more and better-paid staff, but where is the money coming from? Being so intimately involved in the work perhaps tends to make it much more difficult to see one's way through clearly. What is needed is for one or two interested 'outsiders' to come and make sweeping alterations and suggestions in order to set things on the right footing.

I would not like you to quote from this letter too widely, but thought you should know a little of the problems that confront us daily. It will also help you to understand why it is that we are all (not just Frank and I, but all of the senior staff), always so fully occupied that everything apart from the hospital gets crowded out of our lives. This is good up to a point because we are here to serve but when one is so tired that the joy disappears from the service then something should be done about it for we can neither do our work properly, nor show forth true Christian love, when we are very overtired. All this makes it the more difficult for us to completely make up our minds about leaving for good, but now I think we both feel sure that for some years we must put the children first and give them a little more of our time and energy before they grow up and go away from us. These next few years are very important for all of them and they will need us (I hope) during the process of growing up.

Now that the date of our sailing is confirmed we can begin to make definite plans. Frank may decide to come home a little before July 1967, if it proves possible, but he would have to wait before making up his mind finally until the new doctors have come and settled into the work. In any case he wants to stay long enough to teach them the operative techniques for leprosy surgery. He has written to a few friends asking them to let him know of any suitable openings in England and we have had to send a long account of all the work he had done - quite a lengthy epistle. In India he has such wonderful opportunities and variety in his work that it will not be easy to confine himself to one field when he returns to England, but we feel sure that all things will work together for good.
We send our love etc.'

This just goes to shows how, despite all my misgivings in April 1966, the hospital continued to grow from strength to strength, albeit with considerable financial and prayerful encouragement from the Mysore and UK Friends of the Hospital, the members of the South India Association and our loyal group of friends and well-wishers who work tirelessly year after year raising funds to support the work both in Mysore City and Kastur/Hadya rural area.

As soon as I departed to England with the children it had been decided by the Hospital Committee that Frank should move to share house with a colleague. This would leave the Hospital House free in readiness for his successor. This being so, I set about the task of packing up all our personal belongings ready for shipment to UK. For insurance purposes it was necessary to list and value, item by item, all our personal belongings which included not only books and clothing, but pictures, ivory inlay coffee tables, clothing and other household items.

We also had to think about our pets. Podgy, the dog, having reached the good age of thirteen and having recovered over the years from mange and other infestations that were common in India, fell very ill with hookworm. Veterinary treatment in Mysore was very hit-and-miss, so we did all we could for him to combat the effects of the hookworm and keep him hydrated. This was not enough though, and he died while the children were in Mysore just after our return from the Carrington holiday. Devaputra dug a grave for him under the hedge and the children sadly said their goodbyes. The cat, 'Kitty', was as self-sufficient as all cats are, so we decided to leave her with the household. Augustine and Mary would look after her. The parakeet, 'Georgie', was to go with Frank to the house in Government House Road.

Rosemary had taken her O levels before the 1965 Christmas holidays and because the schools did not teach A levels she returned to Hebron School in February 1966 as a 'Junior Helper'. She started studying for her A level work in Physics, Chemistry and Biology, while doing more work towards retaking her O level French exam. At the same time she was teaching Geometry, Arithmetic and Science to the nine girls who made up the class of 'Standard 6a' (eleven to twelve year olds), as well as looking after the little children in 'Nest' dormitory during their after-lunch nap and 'putting a dorm to bed' one evening a week.

During the term that followed the May holiday, Frank and I decided that we would fetch Rosemary home early after she had done her French exam.

She was such a help to me with the sorting out and packing ready for our departure to England. Once the trunks and boxes were packed and labelled they were collected by lorry to be driven directly to the docks ready for shipment onwards to Genoa and thence overland by lorry to Western-super-Mare. After this was accomplished, all we had to do was prepare our luggage for the sea voyage and bedrolls in readiness for the train journey from Mysore to Bombay.

It was at this time, in fact on the 11th June 1966, that we heard that Frank had been appointed O.B.E. The honour was both for his contribution to surgery and for the leprosy work, work that we had only been able to do with the support of all the organisations that had provided funding, and the dedicated team who laboured every week to run the clinics, make shoes and provide medical and surgical treatment. We were absolutely thrilled about the O.B.E. I wrote to the boys, who were at school in Lushington, and to Jenny in Hebron. We sent the boys a cutting from the paper and Rosemary added a note to my letter asking them to keep the cutting and bring it home.

Jenny wrote from school to her grandparents, '*Isn't it marvellous – Daddy getting the OBE. He wrote and said he got 21 garlands at one celebration!!*'

Queen Honours Peter Sellers, Sir John Hunt

LONDON, June 11: Sir John Hunt, who led the successful British expedition to Mount Everest in 1953, was one of the five people made barons by Queen Elizabeth in the Queen's Birthday Honours list announced yesterday.

The international affairs expert, Richie Calder, was also made a baron. Peter Sellers, renowned British actor, was made a Commander of the Order of the British Empire.

Sir Norman Kipping author of Kipping Loans received the G.C.M.O.

Among the recipients of honours in India are: Knight Bachelor: Harvey Kincaid Stewart Lindsay, Managing Director, Metal Box Company of India Ltd. Order of the British Empire: Bernard Maurice Lott, Director of Studies, Central Institute of English, Hyderabad, and Frank Ivor Tovery, Medical Missionary, Holdsworth Memorial Hospital, Mysore.

Rosemary and Winnie with some of the garlands

There were times when we felt uncertain about our move back to England. I came across an old letter to Frank's parents where I wrote:-

'There is a leprosy patient at the door, come to collect his shoes. What a tragic disease leprosy is! The other day, a woman came – she must have been about my age – she had had leprosy for twenty years or so. Now arrested, but not before she had lost all her toes and all her fingers and thumbs. Both her hands are just stumps. Fortunately, her family are kind enough to feed and clothe her, but many are sent out to spend the rest of their lives begging, becoming more and more hopeless and helpless. Seeing their need makes it so difficult to decide that we must come away, and it also makes us realise how grateful we should be for our health and strength and daily food.'

In a way Frank receiving the O.B.E. helped, because it underlined the achievement that our team had made and encouraged us that the work would continue.

At home, preparing for our departure, the days seemed to fly past. We fetched Jenny, John and David from school and during our last couple of weeks in Mysore many friends invited us to share a meal with them. We virtually ate our way out of Mysore as we found ourselves going out for breakfast, lunch and dinner day after day. The children took this in their stride and thrived on an Indian diet. They thoroughly enjoyed the opportunity of sitting cross-legged on the floor with a beautiful bright green, freshly washed, 'banana leaf plate' spread on the floor in front of them. I'm sure their mouths were watering in anticipation of the meal to come long before it was actually served. They were well versed in the skill of eating with the right hand. Within the hospital the nurses prepared an evening entertainment of song and dance followed by a celebratory dinner.

A family portrait taken on the veranda steps of Hospital House in 1966

Finally the day of our departure arrived, Frank was to travel with us to Bombay. Coolies arrived at the house to collect our baggage and bedrolls, a few nurses and

170

servants came to wave us off. Within ten minutes we were at the railway station there to find a huge throng of hospital staff and friends assembled to wish us well. We were showered with lovely sweet scented jasmine flower garlands and some sweetmeats all of which were piled into our carriage. After many fond embraces we boarded the train at the very last minute just as the guard blew his whistle. Off went the train hissing out steam and lumbering chuff, chuff, chuff as the engine gathered up speed. I remember us all sinking down onto the carriage seats without a word and sitting very quietly for a few minutes holding back the tears, each lost in our own thoughts. It was not long however before we were roused from our reverie for the 1966 monsoon had broken with a vengeance a week before our departure causing widespread flooding along the course of the River Cauvery. Srirangapatna especially had been greatly affected. As our train passed over the railway bridge water was lapping just four or five inches from the rail track. We could see the Wellesley Bridge, built in 1802/4 by Colonel Wellesley, (later to become Duke of Wellington) almost submerged beneath the fast flowing water. It was an awe-inspiring sight.

The Wellesley Bridge in flood (above) and normal conditions (below)

As darkness fell we reached Bangalore there to be met by yet more friends who willingly helped Frank transfer our baggage over to the broad gauge line train. More farewells said and we were off on the long haul to Bombay via Poona. Being seasoned travellers we opened our bedrolls and settled down for the first night on the train. We arrived in Bombay very early in the morning of the third day to find our great friend, Beth Cooper, waiting on the station platform. She had very kindly offered us overnight accommodation and took us straight to her apartment where we shed our luggage and were able to wash off some of the dust and soot gathered on our clothes during the long train journey. The greater part of the day was spent looking around Bombay after which we returned to Beth's apartment feeling quite tired and ready for the early evening meal that she had prepared. During the meal Beth told us that the film, 'The Sound of Music', was showing in one of the cinemas and, if we left immediately after supper we could be at the cinema in time for the next showing. In Mysore there had been no opportunity to see English speaking films and this would be a huge treat and make for a happy ending to our last day in India. I still have a very vivid memory of walking through the deserted streets of Bombay as we left the cinema at midnight. We walked six abreast singing at the tops of our voices, 'The hills are alive with the sound of music', flinging out our arms to the sky as we walked. The night air was cool and the dark sky lit by millions of brightly shining stars. The noisy Bombay traffic was hushed for just a short time. It was a truly wonderful moment which took away some of the sadness of our impending parting from Frank and our beloved India.

On the following morning, July 29th 1966, we boarded the Lloyd Triestino ship 'Galileo', Frank was able to come on board with us to look around and he wrote a letter the next day to his parents saying:-

'Winnie and the children sailed yesterday evening. The ship is a very beautiful Italian one, and they have a very comfortable six-berth cabin (leaving one empty bunk) on D Deck near the front of the ship. The food is a bit strange but I think they will enjoy it too. The ship looked a beautiful sight as it steamed away, it was so brilliantly illuminated.'

We had all stood along the railing waving a white handkerchief hoping that Frank could see us, although we found it impossible to see whether or not he was still on the quayside.

The Lloyd Triestino ship 'Galileo Galilei'

As we sailed away the wind began to blow, the rain slashed down and within a few hours the ship was tossing and turning - the monsoon had arrived with a vengeance. For the very first time I succumbed to seasickness, and Jenny and David were also afflicted. Rosemary and John thoroughly enjoyed themselves as they were free to wander all over the half empty ship and savour the wonderful food being served up in the half empty dining room whilst the rest of us, and other passengers, along with quite a number of the crew, lay prone on our bunks for two or three days! Apparently it was the strongest storm this ship had ever encountered. If I had not been laid low with sea sickness I would have been very worried that Rosemary and John were out on deck in such seas.

The ship made a stormy passage across the Arabian Sea

Eventually we entered calmer waters and thoroughly enjoyed the remainder of the voyage. Because it was to be our last we decided, despite the cost, to be extravagant and take all the sight seeing opportunities offered. There was just one downside with this arrangement, we should be leaving the ship at Port Suez to travel across the desert to Cairo and from thence pick up the ship again in Port Said, the downside being that our ship was going to be one of the last passenger liners to travel through the Suez Canal before its closure. However as we had sailed through the canal during previous journeys the overland trip to Cairo proved to be the greater attraction.

We sailed through the Gulf of Suez until we reached Port Suez, which is situated at the entrance to the Canal. Here, along with other fellow passengers, we joined a coach that transported us across many, many miles of desert to Cairo. Upon entering the coach we were greeted by our Tour Guide who said, 'I shall be looking after you during this whole trip across the desert to Cairo and onward to meet the ship again at Port Said. Call me Moses, my name is Moses.' This was a delightful moment for the children because, dare I say it of my own brood, this Moses had a beard and was dressed in a flowing white robe, and they were highly amused at the thought of being taken across the desert by Moses. Visions of Sunday school story times about the tribes of Israel must have passed through their minds.

It was a wonderful trip; we were taken to the museum in Cairo and saw all the amazing artefacts discovered in Tutankhamen's burial chamber. We visited the mosque at a time when the white alabaster still covered its walls. Finally, we were driven to the outskirts of Cairo where we saw the pyramids. We were offered camel rides but the children preferred to take the more exciting opportunity of climbing the steps that led into the very centre of the pyramid. Of course, Mum had to go also, so off I went with the four of them. To begin with there was adequate headroom but as the steps advanced deeper in towards the centre of the pyramid they became steeper and headroom became lower for an adult at least. I managed the ascent fairly well but remember that climbing out again was most uncomfortable. The children, being shorter, experienced no difficulty but I had to descend doubled up, head first with just a wobbly rope to hold onto. Moses was an excellent guide and we all reached Port Said tired after a long hot day but exhilarated by all that we had seen.

We sailed onwards calling at Messina, Piraeus, Naples and Pompeii until finally landing in Genoa on August 10th 1966. We had asked for bookings to be made by coach to Lausanne including an overnight stay there prior to us taking an overnight train onward to Paris. All went well and with tickets in hand we boarded the train for Paris safely and took our seats.

The train commenced its journey and we made ourselves comfortable for the night. After travelling for a while the train pulled up at a station and took on more passengers. Off we went again then, suddenly we heard a very noisy exchange of words going on just outside our compartment, then our door was pulled open and a flustered guard started shouting in high speed French. To begin with neither Rosemary nor I could make out what he was trying to tell us. The newly arrived passengers began to join in the conversation at the same time waving their tickets in the air. Gradually it dawned upon us that there was a problem with double booking of the sleeping compartment. The newly arrived passengers harangued the guard and in the end we were overridden and he was most insistent that we moved, even to the point of threatening to turn us off the train, lock stock and barrel, at the next station. It was a frantic moment, trying to make ourselves understood, let alone the thought of my being dumped alone in the middle of nowhere with four children in tow. To add to our misery and despair poor Rosemary was feeling quite ill and developing a very high temperature. Because of this I felt we must press on home as quickly as possible. Great and swift calculations were needed. I already possessed the tickets for the onward train journey from Paris to Calais and ferry to Dover/London. Other than that I had Travellers Cheques with which to purchase train tickets from London to Derby, taxi to Ockbrook and our first week's provision of food. Having done my sums I reckoned that after paying extra for the overnight train to Paris I would be left with a few pounds sterling and just enough Travellers Cheques to cover the journey from London to Ockbrook. Eventually, after paying for a fresh set of tickets, we were allotted another sleeping compartment and were able to settle down for the night. The family slept but I spent rather a sleepless night. What a nightmare!

On arrival in Paris, because Rosemary's condition was worsening, we decided to continue our journey home rather than spend a day sightseeing. The railway station platform in Paris seemed to be the longest I had ever seen. We made a rather sorry sight, each tired and dispirited, clutching a small suitcase, struggling to board the train that was to take us to Calais where we hoped to catch a ferry to England. The train journey went without incident but when we reached the ferry terminal we found long queues waiting to go on board. This was early in the afternoon of 12/13th August, and the temperature quite high. We eventually managed to get on board and find seats. By this time we were all rather thirsty and there was just enough cash with which to buy a cup of coffee each and send a wireless cable to my mother, saying that we would be arriving that same evening.

After disembarking from the ferry we took a train for London, which ended at Victoria Station. In order to reach Derby we needed to get to St. Pancras station. By this time Rosemary was really poorly with a very high temperature. With tired children in tow I made my way to the end of a very long queue for taxis. I think we must have looked a sorry sight for as we waited a taxi driver stopped his cab beside us and called out, 'Come on, get in quickly, where do you want to go?' I looked around fearful that someone in the queue might object. 'Don't worry,' he said, 'You've got the four kids. Where do you want to go?' 'St. Pancras.' I replied and climbed in after the children as fast as I could. He whisked us away and in no time we were at St. Pancras.

Once again we found ourselves standing in the middle of a vast crowd and I was wondering where to go in order to change Travellers Cheques when a cheerful porter came up and asked if he could help. When I explained my predicament he immediately took charge, saying to the children, 'Now, look, you stay together here with your luggage and don't move. I'll take your Mum to get some money and tickets then we'll be back for you and I will see you safely on to your train.' This kindly porter was so helpful and understanding and refused to accept a tip for all his trouble. We heaved a sigh of relief and boarded our train.

It was late that Saturday evening, long after the shops had closed, that we eventually arrived in Ockbrook, only to find that my cable had not reached Mother. Understandably she was rather upset to find us on her doorstep, unexpectedly early and with a taxi fare to pay. The shops would be closed until Monday morning. It must have been such a shock having a family of five descending on her doorstep at such an inconvenient time. Once she had recovered, she called on her kindly neighbours, who rallied around and helped with offers of food to tide us over until Monday morning.

The other vital need was for medical attention for Rosemary who had Tonsillitis and was running a temperature of 104°F. Eventually Mother's GP came to the rescue and ordered some medicine for her and after a few days' treatment and rest she made a good recovery.

I contacted Mission House and within a few days received a cheque. Then we made our way to the furlough house in Weston-super-Mare, where we found our Mysore luggage awaiting us. This house would be our temporary home for the next year or two until such time as Frank had obtained a permanent hospital appointment in England. It was for this reason that we had decided that it would be better for the children to go to boarding school rather than risk changing schools whilst we had no fixed abode.

School terms were due to commence during the first week of September, which meant we had two weeks in which to purchase, label and dispatch all four sets of school uniform. We hastily arranged to go and stay with Frank's Aunt Irene in Bath, where there was a shop that carried a stock of Kingswood School uniforms. Through the agencies of this shop's tailor, all the children (girls and boys) were measured. The boys' uniforms were available immediately from the shop. Uniform for the girls had to be sent, as soon as possible, to our address in Weston-Super-Mare. What a job we had with four sets of uniform and mufti clothes to name tag! Armed with special marking pens, needles and thread, between us we named every item of clothing before packing it into the respective trunks ready for sending to the schools.

As I had no form of transport it was fortunate that each of the school terms began on a different day. This made it possible for me to take Rosemary and Jenny by train to Edgehill in Bideford one day, leaving the boys with Aunty Irene in Bath. Then, on the following day it was John's turn to go to Kingswood in Bath. He was 13 years of age, a far from easy transition for him at that age (in the middle of the 1960's) to join an English boys' school after spending all his previous years in a school abroad. Finally, on the very next day it was time for me to take David to Prior's Court in Chieveley, near Newbury (Kingswood Prep School). I still recall the feeling of desolation that I experienced during the taxi journey from Newbury station to Chieveley. All those years ago there was no motorway nearby and it seemed so far away. During the drive we kept up a cheerful conversation and then turned into the school drive. The red brick building surrounded by stately trees and green lawns looked very attractive but very quiet. A master came to the door to greet us but the taxi was waiting and I was worried about the additional cost of the waiting time. After a quick word with the master I bid David a hasty farewell on the doorstep and sped away. That was a very sad hour for me. I shed a few tears and prayed that our family would be able to face the future with confidence.

One day during the voyage home I sat on deck with the children and talked to them about the different situations they might encounter between their lives in India and the day-to-day life of their contemporaries in England. Only later did I discover how little I knew about the changes that had taken place during the early 1960s. English newspapers and radio were almost nonexistent in Mysore. I knew nothing of the Beatles, Rolling Stones, the Flower People and so on, nothing about the surge of interest in football and rugby, or people's attitude towards missionaries, Christianity and religion as a whole. It was so far removed from anything the children had encountered before, and to add to their difficulties, they (and I) were quite unprepared for the then unkind attitude to people remotely closely associated with missionaries. This was because it was not widely known that missionaries' work then was quite different from that undertaken by the early workers. One saving grace was the fact that their academic standard was as good as, if not better than, that of their contemporaries in England.

At long last, after many adventures along the way, we were settled in England and prepared to wait until Frank could join us in twelve months' time.

Chapter Sixteen
Frank's last year in Mysore

Below written by Frank

After seeing Winnie and the family off on the ship to England I returned from Bombay to Mysore by train to take over straight away as Acting Medical Superintendent of the Hospital, following the retirement of Dr Angeline Stephens. My immediate task was to move out of the Hospital House to Government House Road bungalow in the town, where we as a family had lived from 1951 to 1954 during our first years in Mysore. This was to provide accommodation in the Hospital House for Geoffrey Bird, his wife, Beris, and their children. Geoffrey was an Australian Surgeon and had been sent by the Methodist Missionary Society to cover the changeover period resulting from my departure the following year and the appointment of John Iswariah as Medical Superintendent. John Iswariah had previously worked with me in the Holdsworth Memorial Hospital, as the equivalent of a Senior Registrar in the U.K., and had then gone to work in England, where he passed both the English and Edinburgh FRCS Examinations. He had subsequently gone to the USA to fill a Surgical Research Post, and was due to return to India in July 1967. The Holdsworth Hospital was by now entirely handed over to the Church of South India so John Iswariah's appointment was direct from the C.S.I.

It was now possible for me to share the surgical work with Geoffrey, and, as he was living on the compound, he was able to take care of the emergencies. This released me to spend the time that was needed for the administrative and other responsibilities of the Acting Medical Superintendent. The hospital's financial situation was still a big concern. We were helped by the arrival of a pharmacist, Alan Cranmer, who took over the running of the Pharmacy and the increasing legal work that this involved. He was able to introduce cost accountancy and establish more realistic costs for medicines and treatments.

Alan lived in the other half of the Government House Road bungalow and we travelled together to the Hospital by car each morning at 7.00am to arrive in time for the morning prayers in the Chapel. The C.S.I. bungalows were large, as you will realise from Winnie's earlier descriptions, and it was very common for the accommodation to be shared. We had six or seven single doctors or nurses living in our household at different times during our time in the Hospital House, and at other times we shared the house with other families. Freddie and Yvette Zerfas family, with their little son Jamie, stayed for some time before our 1961 furlough in England, and on other occasions the parents of sick children from Hebron or Lushington stayed, while their children were receiving inpatient treatment at the hospital.

Although not as big as the Hospital House, there was plenty of room in my part of the Government House Road bungalow, and Mrs Kay Webb stayed there with me whenever she was in Mysore.

From 1961 to 1966, supported by the Church of South India Diocese, Kay had been living in a large tent in the Tibetan Settlement at Bylakuppe, where she looked after the health care of the Tibetan community. In late 1966, with a Diocesan grant for salary, she took over the Leprosy Control Work that Winnie had started in the Chamrajanagar District and moved her main living place to the clinic building at Mangala. She opened two small wards in outbuildings at the Clinic, one for men and one for women. The beds were elevated concrete slabs, which made it easier to nurse patients, who had in the past been sleeping on the floor, just as they would be doing if they were at home. Kay had an ancient Jeep, which she used for her village work, and sometimes I would join her on her visits. Geoff Bird took over the medical and surgical work of the village clinics, and Krishnappa, the shoemaker, continued to make the shoes that were needed by leprosy patients.

As well as the Holdsworth Hospital work, I continued to make regular visits to the tea and coffee estates, and to Ooty as a Governor of St Hilda's School, an Anglican school for girls, linked with St Stephen's, the Anglican church in Ooty. The pupils were mostly Indian nationals and they were taught the Indian Matriculation syllabus. I also continued as Chairman of the South Indian Examining Board for Nurses and made several visits to Madras to help set exam standards. At that time we were having a struggle to prevent the Nurse Training from becoming too academic with less hands-on training on the wards.

I also had the great honour of visiting Bangalore to receive the O.B.E. medal from the High Commissioner. I very much wished that Winnie were there to share the credit for the O.B.E. that owed so much to her time and dedication.

With the financial situation of Holdsworth Hospital in mind I was anxious to get the local community more involved in the running of the Hospital, and, with the help of the Diocesan Treasurer, I redrafted the Hospital Constitution, involving the formation of a Management Committee, which included a number of local people of standing in the community.

John Iswariah was due to return from America early in July 1967. It was therefore arranged that I would have two weeks in which to hand over to him, after which I would leave to rejoin the family in England. By now it had become cheaper to fly to the UK than to travel by ship, and a flight from Bombay to Heathrow, London, was booked for me in mid July. Towards the end of June I began packing up items that needed to be sent by sea, so that I would be free for the handover to John Iswariah when he arrived.

The handover went very smoothly. Part of the time was spent introducing him to local Government Officers and other friends of the Hospital. John did most of the driving as he wanted to get used to the Indian roads. He needed reminding a few times that he was not in the USA and should now be driving on the left hand side of the road!

We spent a long day in Bangalore introducing him to the State Government Officers. I remember it well because, in the same way as Winnie and the family had to eat their way out of Mysore, I found that I had to do the same! After an exhausting morning visiting Government Offices, John and I retreated to a Chinese Restaurant for a hearty lunch, only for the Manager to approach us at the end of the meal to say that we had a telephone call. We had completely forgotten that Dr Subramaniam, a physician who had worked in the Holdsworth Hospital in the early 1960s and had moved to a private practice in Bangalore, was expecting us for lunch. So, full as we were, we had a second lunch!

Before leaving Bangalore, I paid a visit to the Navajeevanna Nilayam rehabilitation centre for leprosy patients, and to the Government Leprosarium in Bangalore, from which a number of our leprosy patients had come. Several of our post-operative patients were still in training for various work skills in the Navajeevanna Nilayam and they gave me an envelope containing 500 rupees, in notes, which they had collected from the sale of items that they had made in the workshops. This was to be used for the care of leprosy patients in the Holdsworth Memorial Hospital. It was very moving, but almost more so was the heavy paper bag of one anna and one rupee coins for the same purpose, that was given to me by the patients in the Leprosarium, the outcome of money collected by their begging on the streets.

The time came in mid-July for me to prepare to leave. The Hospital organised a surprise farewell meeting, held in a large shamiana (marquee). All the hospital staff and many old friends were invited. It was a very moving occasion. On the day of departure, I left on the morning train to Bangalore. When I arrived at the Mysore Station platform I was almost overwhelmed to find the whole platform packed with friends and ex-patients, who had all come to bid me farewell. I climbed into the railway carriage nearly buried in the many garlands that they had given to me.

Frank wearing just some of the garlands presented on his departure from Mysore

There was a similar smaller gathering at the Bangalore station, which included some patients from the Navajeevanna Nilayam, who had brought a guitar that they had made in the workshops to take for the family in England. And so it was that I journeyed on to Bombay and the airport and flight home.

Narrative resumed by Winnie

The return to the U.K. proved to be a time of adjustment for Frank. In India he had no choice but to be what was known in the past as a 'General Surgeon'. His work in India had involved the whole range of surgery, including orthopaedic and plastic surgery. He arrived in England at the age of forty-six, ten years older than the average age for the appointment of a Consultant Surgeon. When he left England in 1947, it was during the days of Voluntary Hospitals and prior to the formation of the NHS in 1948. By the time of his return, in 1967, great changes had taken place. While he had been abroad a programme of surgical training had been introduced and most candidates for Consultant posts had undergone a period of structured surgical training, whereas in the 1940s, when we left for work overseas, surgical trainees had learnt partly by apprenticeship, partly from surgical books and journals, and partly by experience.

Shortly after arriving in Weston-Super-Mare, an old surgical friend, who was a Consultant Surgeon in Frenchay Hospital, Bristol, suffered a stroke and Frank was invited to act as his temporary locum. While acting as a locum he applied unsuccessfully for several vacant posts, including one in Frenchay.

At times the situation gave rise to a crisis of confidence. However, on returning home from the unsuccessful interview for the Frenchay post, he received a phone call from the College of Surgeons representative, who had been at the interview. He was a Consultant Surgeon in Winchester and a visiting surgeon to the Cottage Hospital in Basingstoke. He phoned to say that a new hospital was going to be built in Basingstoke and they would be looking for an older candidate with administrative experience to join the Commissioning Team as the hospital opened up. He suggested that Frank should apply for the appointment as a temporary locum, and then, in due course, apply for the permanent appointment.

Fortunately, in 1968 Frank was successful in obtaining the appointment, and he had the challenging time of seeing Basingstoke District Hospital being built and sharing in its commissioning at different stages of its growth.

At first, being the only surgeon in Basingstoke, he had to continue to work as a General Surgeon, except for orthopaedics, but as more colleagues were appointed he was able to pursue his main interest in gastroenterology. One interesting development was that he noticed that a number of diabetic patients coming to his Outpatient Clinic suffered from the same type of foot lesions, due to sensory loss, as the leprosy patients that he had been treating in India.

The care of neuropathic feet was at that time a new field in the U.K. and Frank set up one of the first Diabetic Foot Services. Diabetic patients with anaesthetic feet required shoes made with soft uppers, with plenty of toe room and enough depth for suitable cushioning insoles, and some required underlying cradles to relieve pressure

180

from vulnerable high-pressure areas in the sole of the foot. One of the initial problems was the absence of suitable footwear for patients with anaesthetic feet. Only rigid orthopaedic shoes were available. Fortunately, at that time there was a vocational Surgical Shoe Training Workshop at the nearby Lord Mayor Treloar Training College for Disabled Children, and they were able to assist in developing suitable shoes.

From 1971 to 1976 Frank and the shoe workshop experimented with different materials for cushioning and for weight-relieving cradles, until the problems were solved. Then Frank and I toured the country with the prototype, searching for a shoe manufacturer, who would undertake the commercial manufacture of the shoes. Eventually a cooperative manufacturer in Kettering was found, and in this way the 'Diabetic Shoe' became established.

Frank retired from surgery in 1986, but continued with the Diabetic Foot Clinic until 1992.

Just as Frank found he had much adapting to do on his return to England, so also the children and I went through a similar period. We arrived back to live in Weston-Super-Mare in an unheated house, on the very modest allowance that could be spared from Frank's stipend. We were propelled into the time of mini skirts and high material expectations. The children had never caught a bus (except the girls who had travelled on the Ooty bus to Mysore on a couple of their return journeys from school). They had never used a public phone box, nor had they really handled money. Their only experience of shopping and cooking was accompanying me to Srinivasa Stores to buy sweets and groceries, and the occasional afternoon cooking Victoria sponge cakes in our Mysore kitchen, using a charcoal fire with a square biscuit tin perched on top, which served as an oven. (Incidentally, this method produced excellent sponges.) Most important of all, the children had absolutely no experience of teenage British culture in the mid-sixties and I am sure at times they must have found that they had very little in common with their schoolmates.

My greatest difficulty during the year was finance. School fees were not a great problem because the Methodist Missionary Society gave an allowance towards these, and the U.K. Government Education Authority also gave a small grant during the first year. I found the train fares to and from school ate up most of our money and consequently I used very little heating when in the house on my own. Dear Joan Dove, who lived next door, would occasionally invite me into her home for an evening so that I could warm up before going to bed. Rosemary and Andrew (Joan's son), both shared an interest in stamp collecting and planned to study medicine. They formed a strong friendship and married in 1973. Since then they have continued in their careers in medicine.

When, shortly after his arrival home, Frank was asked to take a locum Consultant post, imagine our surprise and joy when we received his first pay cheque as a locum and found that his 'earnings' had jumped from £700 per annum to £6,000. This made so much difference to our comfort and well-being and on this happy note I will end our story. A new dawn had arrived for us all. We moved to Basingstoke and settled down to watch another quite different type of hospital being built and commissioned.

We think that moving 'back home' at that time was the right thing to do. Although we had a huge amount of adapting to do and there were times when it was not easy, it would no doubt have been even more difficult had we left it any later. However, a part of us still belongs to India and if anyone asked us today, 'Where on earth 'ave you come from?' we might still answer 'Mysore City, South India.'

Continued by Frank

Subsequent years have shown many changes at the Holdsworth Memorial Hospital. It is now entirely staffed by Indian personnel, and within the Church of South India has had to become financially independent and at the same time cope with the increasing costs of providing medical care and adequate staffing.

Over the years the hospital has become departmentalised to meet the requirements of a modern health practice, and the number of full-time specialists has grown. New buildings for the Laboratory, Pharmacy and Midwifery have been added. Special units such as Intensive Care, High Dependency, Neonatal, Special Care Baby and Dialysis Units have been opened.

Fifty years ago (as in 1906) the only other hospital in the city was still the Government Hospital. Over the past three decades more and more private hospitals have opened, and now there are over twenty, providing a wide range of medical services. In addition there are now three Medical Schools in Mysore.

The future of the Holdsworth Memorial Hospital has to be seen in the light of this background. It is still unique in providing medical care at an affordable cost to a large number of poorer people and has a high reputation in the community. The Nursing School has become a College, with a continuing yearly admission of around twenty students, and courses for the BSc nursing qualification, as well as basic nursing. There is post-graduate training for doctors, who take the examination of the National Board (Delhi). Holdsworth Hospital's School of Nursing is known throughout the south of India for its high standard of training, and its nurses are sought throughout the country. The Hospital is also unique in being the only one in Mysore with village extension work, and in its link with the twenty-bed daughter hospital situated in the village of Mangala, thirty-five miles away.

Having reached its Centenary Year in 2006, there were many problems attached to the continuing work of the Hospital. The major one being, as in this country, the huge challenge of adapting one-hundred-year-old buildings to meet the needs of modern medicine. In addition, progress in the type of investigations and the medical and surgical treatments arising from modern medicine, has brought about enormous increases in costs.

Financially the Hospital depends largely upon local income from charges made to patients, with the fees graded as far as possible to the patients' financial circumstances. But there remains the difficulty of meeting the needs of the desperately poor people who are not able to pay. This applies particularly to the work in the villages, which brings in very little income to the Hospital. After much discussion and prayer the Hospital Management Committee launched a 'Centenary Project' to facilitate improvements in stages.

As you will realise after reading this book, for many years after our return to England in 1967, we were receiving donations for Holdsworth Hospital from friends who were interested in the hospital's work. Organisations such as OXFAM and War on Want also continued for a while to support some of the village and leprosy work. Later on, in the 1980s, we were offered items of decommissioned NHS hospital equipment. This was wonderful, but the cost of transporting the items had to be met. Many friends helped us raise the necessary funds for this purpose and this led to the needs of the hospital becoming more widely known. After 1995 it was no longer practical to send decommissioned items because they were getting held up for long periods at the Indian docks and impossibly high customs charges were levied. It was decided that in order to continue supporting the work in Mysore into the future we should form an association called (the UK) 'Friends of the Holdsworth Hospital'.

Winnie and I cannot adequately express our thanks to all who have so generously given of their time and money to the Hospital. We know how much their help and encouragement means to the doctors, staff and patients of Holdsworth. The improvements that have taken place to date, and those still to come, will make sure that Holdsworth Memorial Hospital enters its second century equipped to continue providing health care for the poor, and in the spirit of its original name – 'Karuna Shala' (Home of Compassion).

Interesting Cases and Surgical Problems

Written by Frank

This section is intended for those with an interest in surgery and in some of the unusual problems that presented during our time in Mysore. I am therefore using some medical terminology, trusting that it will be understood.

In the first half of the twentieth century most surgeons in the United Kingdom were General Surgeons and their training encompassed almost the whole range of surgery. Orthopaedics had become separated early on, but knowledge of orthopaedics was still required for the FRCS Examination. This training proved invaluable when I worked in Mysore. When we arrived in 1951 I was the only trained surgeon in the hospital, and there was only one other hospital, the Government Hospital, in the whole City. It meant that all types of problems had to be tackled, because otherwise there was nobody else to tackle them. Now only a specialist would undertake some of the treatments that we had to give, but then the choice was to treat or just leave events to take their course. We had some good successes and learnt a lot in the process. The following is an account of some of these cases and problems. Patient's names are omitted or pseudonyms have been adopted.

Mr Iyengar was in his sixties and had held a senior position on a Coffee Estate. He had been a patient in the Hospital four years previously with tuberculous ascites and a pleural effusion, both of which had been treated. His wife had died from tuberculosis and his son had been treated for pulmonary tuberculosis. On this occasion Mr Iyengar had been suffering from attacks of abdominal pain and vomiting and episodes of bleeding into the intestine. X-ray investigations were negative and it was decided to do an exploratory operation. At operation grossly dilated veins were found over the anterior surface of the duodenum, which burst spontaneously with torrential bleeding. The only thing that could be done was to apply large clamps, pack tightly to stop the bleeding, and close the abdomen around the clamps. He lost six pints of blood, which were replaced. Two days later he was re-opened and the vein ruptures were controlled by sutures. Although the liver looked normal a small biopsy was taken. The post-operative progress was delayed by a temporary fistula that was discharging pancreatic juice and by a breakdown of part of the wound, but eventually he made a complete recovery. The liver biopsy showed multiple tuberculous tubercles, and he was given a further course of anti-tuberculous treatment. Such varices are reported as a very rare complication of tuberculosis of the liver.

An unusual occurrence in the area around Mysore was a spontaneous blocking (thrombosis) of the main splenic vein. This resulted in the spleen becoming very large and all the blood from the spleen draining through the normally small veins that drain from the spleen into the greater curvature of the stomach. As a result they become greatly dilated and may bleed into the stomach. The only treatment is to remove the spleen and tie off the dilated veins. Two such patients came into the hospital on different occasions, early at night. They were completely bled out and a normal anaesthetic would have killed them. Mr Obed, our radiographer, was sent out in the hospital car to the ice factory and brought back buckets of ice. The patient was lightly sedated and cooled with the ice cubes wrapped around them until the rectal temperature fell to 92 degrees Fahrenheit. The patient was then operated on, and the spleen removed. After this the patient was warmed up. Both patients made good recoveries.

A young Anglo-Indian lad, Anthony, just twenty years old, became depressed and tried to commit suicide by lying in front of a train. As a result he lost both hands just above the wrists. We operated on him and did what is called a Krukenberg operation. In this operation the two bones of the forearm, the radius and the ulna, are separated and covered with skin, part of which is done by embedding the forearm in the abdominal wall. This results in crablike claw 'hands', which can grasp and rotate and have normal sensation. Following this surgery he was able to button up his coat and to hold a pen. He subsequently learnt to type, to ride a bicycle and eventually to drive a car. He was greatly motivated by the successes that he achieved and, wanting to share these with others, he established and ran a rehabilitation and sheltered workshop for disabled people in Bangalore., as well as getting married and bringing up a family.

Another young man attempted suicide by drinking caustic. He developed a stricture of the oesophagus and could not swallow. We were able to replace the oesophagus by bringing up a loop of small intestine through the front of the chest and anastomosing it to the pharynx above the stricture.

A different problem involving the oesophagus was an eight-day-old baby, weighing three and a half pounds, who could not swallow. The baby had a divided oesophagus with a one inch gap, the lower end of which opened into the trachea. We were able to close the opening into the trachea and to join up the two halves of the oesophagus.

Another unusual patient complained of food collecting in his throat while swallowing and then having to spit it out. A barium swallow showed that he had a pouch or diverticulum opening into the left side of his pharynx (pharyngeal pouch), and this was removed through an incision in the side of his neck.

Syphilis was not common at that time, but there was one patient, Perumal, who had a syphilitic stricture of the larynx and was breathing through a tracheotomy tube. We were able to dilate the stricture and insert a skin graft lining over a stent. Eventually we were able to close the tracheotomy and he recovered normal breathing and speech.

A middle-aged man in his thirties came in with dangerously high blood pressure and heart failure. We suspected that it was due to narrowing of a renal artery to the kidney on one side which leads to an over secretion of a hormone called renin, but the question was 'which side?' We prepared to do an aortogram with our rather limited X ray machine. This had to be done by lying the patient down flat on his abdomen, inserting a long needle alongside a lumbar vertebra into his aorta and injecting an opaque medium to outline the renal arteries. This necessitated taking a quick series of five X rays in a matter of seconds. We achieved this by quickly passing cassettes holding the X ray films manually through a tunnel under the X-ray table and taking exposures. We had several practice runs first of all to get up speed and then we were ready to go. We were able to show which kidney had the stenotic artery and were able to operate to remove it, with the result of his blood pressure falling to normal.

Another patient requiring an aortogram had severe pain in his legs on walking (intermittent claudication) and no palpable pulses in the legs. The aortogram showed a blockage at the bifurcation of the aorta and at the upper end of both common iliac arteries supplying the legs. Exploration showed that the blockage was due to atheromatous plaques and these were removed through an incision into the arteries (endarterectomy).

Hydatid cysts were not uncommon, especially in the Tibetans who arrived in the refugee camp at Bylakuppe in 1961. They were mostly in the liver, but could occur in most unusual sites. One such was in the lower lobe of the right lung in a six year old boy and required removal by a lobectomy. One enormous one appeared as a tumour completely filling the pelvis. Amoebic abscesses also occurred in the liver and required localisation and treatment by aspiration with a needle and anti-amoebic drugs to control the infection.

I have already mentioned that duodenal ulceration was a frequent problem, especially in male patients. The most frequent complications were not bleeding or perforation, as found in Western Countries, but pyloric stenosis, where the duodenal scarring and inflammation is such that the stomach cannot empty and the patient has very large vomits of whole meals. In some of these patients the stomach became so dilated that it filled the pelvis and could be mistaken for a distended bladder, except that on palpation a splash could be obtained from the stomach contents. These patients required appropriate surgery for the causative duodenal ulceration. Three other patients were also admitted with a history of abdominal pain and vomiting, and in whom the obstruction was at the upper end of the small intestine just below the duodenum. One of these patients had a stricture due to tuberculous ulceration, and two had small round polyps attached to the bowel lining which had caused an intussusception in which part of the bowel led off by the polyp had telescoped within itself.

In the U.K. surgery for enlargement of the prostate and for bladder tumours forms a considerable part of the work of an urological surgeon, but in Mysore the main problem was with urethral strictures due to gonorrhoea, or with kidney or bladder stones. Bladder stones often occurred in children, and this was thought to be possibly due to diet.

Osteomyelitis, both acute and chronic, was a frequent problem. In cases of acute osteomyelitis, drilling holes in the cortex attained drainage of the affected bone. Cases of chronic osteomyelitis required opening into the bone and the removal of any dead bone (sequestrum) followed by open drainage. The availability of antibiotics made an enormous difference, particularly after it became possible to make a culture of the infecting organism and to test it for sensitivity to a selection of antibiotics.

We had also to operate on babies who elsewhere would have been under the care of specialist paediatric surgeons. Sometimes babies were born with pyloric stenosis, a condition in which the pylorus at the lower end of the stomach has a very thick wall and very narrow lumen so that the baby has projectile vomiting after feeding because the stomach will not empty. This requires a longitudinal incision through the thick layer of pyloric muscle, and with practice the operation can be done under sedation and local anaesthesia. Occasionally we would have babies requiring emergency surgery admitted with abdominal pain and vomiting, caused by an intussusception of the lower end of the small intestine into the caecum, which is situated at the beginning of the large bowel.

There was a small venture into cardiac surgery. We had two patients who had a constrictive pericarditis, a result of tuberculosis. The pericardium surrounding the heart had become thickened and fibrotic and was constricting the heart so that it could not pump adequately. The thickened layer in front of the heart was removed. Another patient was a boy with a patent ductus arteriosus (i.e. a communication between the aorta and the pulmonary artery), which meant that blood was being diverted from the aorta into the lungs. The communication was successfully ligated. Another boy had a mitral stenosis, the result of earlier rheumatic fever, where the valve between the left auricle and the left ventricle was constricted. This was dilated through a small incision into the left auricle.

In conclusion, when in India at that time in history, one had to be truly a general surgeon and often anaesthetist and radiologist too. It was quite different to the work of a surgeon in the changing situation of the NHS in the U.K. when I joined it in 1968 as a Consultant Surgeon, and which I found needed considerable personal adjustment.

Cor Blimey!
Where 'ave you come from?

Glossary

aloo - potato

anna – an old money coin, worth one sixteenth of a rupee

ashram – a religious community, often providing refuge and charitable care

ayah – a children's nanny and housekeeping help

bandicoot – a medium-sized mammal of the rat species

bedroll – a canvas sheet rolled up and buckled around a thin mattress, sheets, blanket and pillow, made up as a. bed, for use when travelling

chai – tea, made the Indian way by boiling tea leaves with water, milk and jaggery or sugar

chipmunk – a small, burrowing, ground squirrel, with grey fur and distinctive black stripes along its length

choli – a bodice worn with a sari

cicada – a type of grasshopper that makes a shrill noise, usually through the first hours of darkness

coolie – an unskilled labourer

dalit – member of the lowest Hindu caste

dasara – a Hindu festival

DDT – an insecticide, now banned in many countries

dekshie – a deep, cylindrical or rounded cooking vessel (saucepan)

dhobi wallah – a laundry man

dormitory – a communal bedroom

durbar – a public reception held by an Indian prince or important person

durbarees – the official attendees of a durbar

flit gun – a small, hand-pumped spray gun

furlough – leave of absence (for soldiers or missionaries), usually a year-long break after four or five years of service

gecko – a nocturnal lizard with gripping foot pads that make it able to climb walls and ceilings

ghat – a Hindi word for the mountain chains to the east ad west of South India

godown – East Asian word for utility buildings or warehouses, in S India the buildings behind a main house, sometimes servants' quarters

gujah – an earthenware drinking water container, that cools the water by allowing evaporation through the porous surface

gunny bag – a bag made from sack cloth (jute)

howdah – a seat with a canopy, carried on an elephant's back

jaggery – unrefined (brown) palm-sap or cane sugar

keddah – a drive to capture wild elephants

machete – a large cutting blade, usually used for cutting branches and undergrowth

maharaja – a title for an Indian ruling prince

mahout – a man who cares for, trains and drives a working elephant

maidan – an open space for recreational, parade and festival use

mali – a gardener and household help for heavy tasks, such as water carrying

masala dosai (or dosa) – a pancake made with rice and gram flour with a curried vegetarian filling

memsahib – the respectful term of address for a married European woman

mufti – non-uniform (casual) clothing

neem tree – a tropical tree with medicinal properties

pye-dog – a stray mongrel dog

peon – a porter and/or errand boy or man

plains – flat countryside

plantain – a small, sweet-tasting, type of banana

puja – Hindu ceremonial worship

rajpramukh – the term given to the Indian princes permitted to remain in local governmental positions within their princely states during the early years of India's independence from British rule

rupee – the Indian currency unit

salwar kameez – a tunic and trousers, originally the dress of Muslim women and now widely worn in India by women in urban areas

sari – a long piece of cloth worn as the traditional dress of Hindu women, now mostly worn as everyday dress by women in the countryside and special occasion dress by urban women

sericulture – the raising of silkworms and production of raw silk

shamiana – a marquee-type of cover, used for weddings and large gatherings

shikari – a big game hunter and/or hunter's guide

silver fish – a small wingless insect covered in silver scales, noted for liking to eat paper, particularly the glued spines of books

taluk – an Indian rural village area (the equivalent to a 'parish')

toddy – a strong alcoholic drink, often made from palm sap

tonga – a small, two wheeled pony-drawn carriage (see photo on opposite page)

tiffin – a light meal or snack

tuck box – an individual box for a child's belongings at boarding school (often used in boarding school as the term for a child's supply of sweets)

tyote – the Indian word for farmers, sometimes applied to a farmed area

wallah - an Indian suffix used for a man when describing his role/activity (e.g. dhobi wallah, tonga wallah, ticket wallah)